TABLE OF CONTENTS

2005 SUPPLEMENT

CASES AND COMMENTS

CRIMINAL PROCEDURE

SIXTH EDITION

by

JAMES B. HADDAD
Late Professor of Law,
Northwestern University

ELIZABETH P. MARSH
Professor of Law
Quinnipiac College of Law

JAMES B. ZAGEL
Judge, United States District Court for the
Northern District of Illinois

LINDA R. MEYER
Professor of Law
Quinnipiac College of Law

GARY L. STARKMAN
Attorney-at-Law, Chicago, Illinois;
Former Assistant United States Attorney,
Northern District of Illinois

WILLIAM J. BAUER
Judge, United States Court of Appeals
for the Seventh Circuit

FOUNDATION PRESS

NEW YORK, NEW YORK

2005

© 2004 FOUNDATION PRESS
© 2005 By FOUNDATION PRESS
          395 Hudson Street
          New York, NY 10014
          Phone Toll Free 1–877–888–1330
          Fax (212) 367–6799
          fdpress.com
Printed in the United States of America

ISBN 1–58778–867–5

 TEXT IS PRINTED ON 10% POST CONSUMER RECYCLED PAPER

*

TABLE OF CASES

2005 SUPPLEMENT

CASES AND COMMENTS

CRIMINAL PROCEDURE

*

CHAPTER 2

CONFESSIONS AND INTERROGATIONS

A. VOLUNTARINESS OF CONFESSIONS

Page 48   Add new note:

Consider the en banc decision in United States v. LeBrun, 363 F.3d 715 (8th Cir. 2004), *cert. denied* ___ U.S. ___, 125 S.Ct. 1292 (2005).

■ HANSEN, CIRCUIT JUDGE

After thirty-three minutes of questioning, Michael LeBrun confessed to naval investigators that in 1968, while he was enlisted in the United States Navy, he strangled to death his superior officer, Ensign Andrew Muns, on board the U.S.S. Cacapon after Ensign Muns caught LeBrun robbing the safe in the ship's disbursing office. . . .

Muns and LeBrun served as shipmates during the Vietnam War aboard the U.S.S. Cacapon. Ensign Muns served as the disbursing officer, and LeBrun served as the disbursing clerk. On January 16 or 17, 1968, while the U.S.S. Cacapon was moored in the Subic Bay, Muns disappeared. After conducting an investigation into Muns' disappearance, the Navy concluded that Muns had stolen $8600 from the disbursing office and had deserted. Thirty years later, still unconvinced of her brother's wrong-doing, Muns' sister convinced Special Agent Peter Hughes of the Naval Criminal Investigative Service ("NCIS") Cold Case Homicide Unit to reopen the investigation.

In the fall of 1999, NCIS agents conducted four interviews with LeBrun. On each of these four occasions, LeBrun cooperated with the investigators and voluntarily answered questions regarding Muns' disappearance. On three of these occasions, he was given his *Miranda* warnings by the interviewers. During an interview conducted on November 20, 1999, LeBrun told NCIS agents that he realized that he may have been involved in the death and disappearance of Ensign Muns. LeBrun also told the agents that he felt that he had repressed memories, and he asked Agent Hughes if he knew of a therapist who could help LeBrun recover those memories. After completing the first round of interviews, the NCIS agents did not have any further significant contact with LeBrun for approximately ten months as they continued to investigate other leads. By September of 2000, however, the NCIS had focused on LeBrun as the lead suspect in the case. At that time, NCIS agents decided to interview LeBrun again.

On September 21, 2000, NCIS Special Agent Early and Corporal Hunter of the Missouri Highway Patrol arrived unexpectedly at LeBrun's place of employment. Hunter told LeBrun that he and Early were conducting an investigation and requested that LeBrun accompany them to the Missouri Highway Patrol office to participate in an interview. Although the officers did not tell LeBrun the subject of their investigation, LeBrun agreed to accompany the officers because he thought that the officers might be investigating certain criminal allegations concerning LeBrun's employer. At the officers' suggestion, LeBrun rode in the front seat of an unmarked patrol car to the station house. The door was unlocked during the trip, and LeBrun was not restrained in any manner.

After they arrived at the patrol office, but before they went inside, Agent Early told LeBrun that he was not under arrest, that he was free to terminate the impending interview at any time, and that he was free to leave at any time. He was also told that he was subject to audio and visual recording anywhere inside the building. The officers then took LeBrun inside the office to a windowless interview room. The authorities had prepared the room prior to LeBrun's arrival, adorning the interview room walls with enlarged photographs of scenes from LeBrun's life. After LeBrun took a seat, NCIS Agents Early and Grebas identified themselves and initiated the interview. At no point immediately prior to or during the September 21, 2000, interview did the agents recite to LeBrun the *Miranda* warnings. The district court found that the decision not to warn was a conscious one made by the interviewers. Special Agent Early testified that no warning was thought necessary because it was not an under arrest custodial situation.

Despite the agents' failure to recite the *Miranda* warnings, LeBrun testified at the suppression hearing that at the time of the interview he understood what his *Miranda* rights were. LeBrun also testified that at the time the interview commenced he believed that he was not in custody and that he was free to leave at any time. The government concedes that the officers used psychological ploys during the course of the interview to facilitate a confession. For example, the agents told LeBrun that he was the prime suspect in Muns' death and that they had significant evidence establishing that LeBrun was the killer. The agents also told LeBrun that a protracted trial in a distant district would drain his financial resources and would ruin his family's reputation. At no point, however, did the agents shout at LeBrun or use physical force against him. After approximately thirty-three minutes of questioning, LeBrun confessed to the crime. LeBrun explained that while he was robbing the safe, Ensign Muns walked into the disbursing office. He confessed that he rushed Muns and killed him by strangling him and then smashing his head against the deck of the disbursing office. At the agents' urging, LeBrun then physically reenacted the robbery and attack. He also explained how he had dumped Muns' body and the missing money into a tank of caustic fuel oil to dispose of the evidence.

After LeBrun confessed to the killing, Agents Early and Grebas asked whether he wanted to apologize to Muns' sister, Mary Lou Taylor, who had flown in from Milwaukee to assist in the interrogation if it became necessary. He indicated that he did. Dr. Taylor, accompanied by Agent Billington, who was posing as Muns' brother and whom the agents had told LeBrun was stricken with cancer, then entered the interview room. LeBrun acknowledged to Taylor and Billington that he was responsible for Muns' death, and he apologized. After the agents had completed their questioning, LeBrun consented to having his house searched. LeBrun then withdrew a cellular telephone from his pocket and called his spouse. The agents drove LeBrun to his house and searched it. After conducting their search, the officers left LeBrun at home. They did not arrest him that day.

LeBrun was arrested at a later date and charged with felony murder in violation of 18 U.S.C. § 1111. . . .

* * *

The facts surrounding the confession are straightforward. LeBrun confessed to strangling Ensign Muns after only thirty-three minutes of questioning. Neither Agent Grebas nor Agent Early was armed during the interview. The agents never shouted at LeBrun or physically threatened him. The government concedes that it used psychological pressure to facilitate a confession. The district court correctly recognized that the type of psychological pressure Agents Grebas and Early exerted on LeBrun here did not alone render his confession involuntary. *See Astello,* 241 F.3d at 967–68 (holding that tactics such as subjecting a suspect to psychological pressure, making false promises, playing on a suspect's emotions, and using his family against him did not render a confession involuntary). The district court concluded, however, that these tactics, when coupled with certain statements that Agents Early and Grebas made concerning nonprosecution, rendered LeBrun's confession involuntary. The critical exchange occurred as follows:

LEBRUN: So, am I hearing that I won't be prosecuted?

GREBAS: That's what you are hearing.

LEBRUN: Is that what I am hearing?

GREBAS: That's what you are hearing.

EARLY: If it's [the killing of Ensign Muns] spontaneous and that's the truth, you will not be prosecuted.

GREBAS: That's absolutely right.

LEBRUN: I am here to tell you there was no premeditation.

EARLY: All right.

LEBRUN: It was spontaneous.

EARLY: Okay.

GREBAS: So it was, let me get this clear. It was spontaneous?

LEBRUN: Correct.

GREBAS: If this is true, then you killed him and it was over, it was over the money; is that right?

LEBRUN: I don't know what it was over.

(R. at 65–66.) The district court noted that the agents qualified their representations by stating to LeBrun that it was only "possible" that LeBrun would not be prosecuted. The district court explicitly did not "make any findings as to what-if any-promise was actually made, or what the legal effect of any promise [was]." (R. at 83–84.) Instead, the district court found only that "LeBrun *believed* he would not be prosecuted if he confessed to a 'spontaneous' murder." (R. at 83.)

Applying the facts as found by the district court to the controlling legal standard, we conclude that LeBrun's confession was not compelled because a defendant's mistaken *belief* that he could not be prosecuted does not render a confession involuntary. *See United States v. Kilgore,* 58 F.3d 350, 353 (8th Cir.1995) (stating that defendant's mistaken belief that he had been promised leniency would not render confession involuntary); *Winfrey v. Wyrick,* 836 F.2d 406, 411–12 (8th Cir.1987) (concluding that defendant's murder confession was voluntary even though defendant was encouraged to talk because of erroneous *belief* that if the shooting was accidental it would negate an element of the offense), *cert. denied,* 488 U.S. 833, 109 S.Ct. 91, 102 L.Ed.2d 67 (1988).

Even assuming that a reasonable person would view the Agents' statements as a promise, a promise made by law enforcement "does not render a confession involuntary per se." *Simmons,* 235 F.3d at 1133; *see also Tippitt v. Lockhart,* 859 F.2d 595, 598 (8th Cir.1988) (concluding that defendant's confession was voluntary despite officers' promise), *cert. denied,* 490 U.S. 1100, 109 S.Ct. 2452, 104 L.Ed.2d 1007 (1989). A promise is merely one factor in the totality of the circumstances. *See Simmons,* 235 F.3d at 1133 (stating that a promise made by law enforcement is only one relevant consideration). Whatever the facts of an individual case, our polestar always must be to determine whether or not the authorities overbore the defendant's will and critically impaired his capacity for self-determination. Thus, it is not enough to show that the authorities' representations were the but-for cause of a confession. *See Schneckloth v. Bustamonte,* 412 U.S. 218, 224, 93 S.Ct. 2041, 36

L.Ed.2d 854 (1973) (concluding that a but-for type analysis is inadequate because "[u]nder such a test, virtually no statement would be voluntary because very few people give incriminating statements in the absence of official action of some kind"). Therefore, even assuming that the agents' statements could be construed as a promise and that the statements induced LeBrun's confession, our inquiry remains the same: whether the facts surrounding this interview demonstrate that the authorities overbore LeBrun's will and capacity for self-determination. This is a very demanding standard, and we are of the view that the facts of this case do not rise to that level.

We have previously concluded that a promise not to seek execution or a promise not to prosecute failed to render the confessions of similarly situated defendants involuntary. For example, in *Tippitt*, we held that the government's promise to a defendant not to prosecute him for capital murder in exchange for a confession did not render the confession involuntary in light of other facts showing that the interrogation was brief and that the defendant possessed an eleventh grade education. *See* 859 F.2d at 598. We do not think it unreasonable to assume that the psychological pressure exerted on the defendant in *Tippitt* to render a confession and thereby avoid execution would be at least as great as the psychological forces presented in this case. In *United States v. Larry*, 126 F.3d 1077 (8th Cir.1997), we held that the defendant's statement implicating himself as being a felon in possession of ammunition was voluntary even though it was induced by a promise that the defendant would not be prosecuted for a separate offense involving a drive-by shooting. *See* 126 F.3d at 1079. The facts of this case are no more compelling than those in *Tippitt* or *Larry*.

We place substantial weight on the fact that LeBrun confessed after a mere thirty-three minutes. Thus, this is not a situation where the officers wore down a defendant's will with persistent questioning over a considerable length of time. We also place significant weight on the fact that LeBrun testified that he had a subjective understanding of his *Miranda* rights at the time of the interview. *See Simmons*, 235 F.3d at 1133–34 (stating that a particularly compelling fact militating in favor of finding a voluntary confession was that defendant understood his rights). We also place substantial weight on the fact that LeBrun was a sophisticated individual with legal training. LeBrun was fifty years old at the time of the interview. He has served in the military, attended five years of college and one year of law school, and worked as a manager in a real estate office. As we have noted, "one of the key concerns in judging whether confessions were involuntary, or the product of coercion, [is] the intelligence, mental state, or any other factors possessed by the defendant that might make him particularly suggestible, and susceptible to having his will overborne." *Wilson*, 260 F.3d at 952. Generally, we have concluded that where the defendant possessed at least average intelligence, then his inculpatory statements were not compelled. *See, e.g., United States v. Gallardo–Marquez*, 253 F.3d 1121, 1123–24 (8th Cir.) (concluding confession was voluntary where defendant was of average intelligence and had prior contact with law enforcement), *cert. denied*, 534 U.S. 1031, 122 S.Ct. 570, 151 L.Ed.2d 443 (2001); *Astello*, 241 F.3d at 968 (concluding that confession of an eighteen-year-old was voluntary where he had completed eleventh grade and possessed a capacity to understand what was being said during the interview); *Simmons*, 235 F.3d at 1134 (concluding that confession was voluntary where defendant had full scale I.Q. of 88); *cf. Wilson*, 260 F.3d at 949 n. 4 & 952–53 (finding involuntary confession where defendant was mentally retarded, his overall mental abilities were in the bottom two percent of the population, and testimony revealed that he could be "talked into anything").

In addition to possessing average intelligence, LeBrun did not display any unique sensitivity that would indicate that the agents might overbear his will. LeBrun had met with NCIS investigators on four prior occasions. The videotape of the interview demonstrates that LeBrun was composed and aware of his surroundings and the circumstances confronting him. In fact, as LeBrun and the Agents discussed the potential statute of limitations problems, LeBrun became more animated and much more interested in the interview. After watching the videotape, it is apparent that LeBrun is an intelligent, calculating person who erroneously perceived a potential loophole in the prosecution's case and tried to take advantage of it by confessing to "spontaneous" murder. Whatever his motivation, it is clear to us that LeBrun's capacity for self-determination was not impaired. Thus, the district court erred in concluding that LeBrun's confession was involuntary.

* * *

■ Morris Sheppard Arnold, Circuit Judge, with whom McMillian, Bye, and Smith, Circuit Judges, join, dissenting.

   ... Our panel opinion in this case, *see United States v. LeBrun,* 306 F.3d 545, 548–50, 552–56 (8th Cir.2002), very effectively rehearsed the tactics used to bring Mr. LeBrun to the point of confessing, which included threatening to ruin him financially, preying on fears related to his cancer, and vividly limning the effects that protracted civil and criminal litigation in a faraway place would have on his family, on its reputation, and in particular on his pregnant wife. I will therefore content myself with some observations on the court's opinion. . . .

   While, as the court notes, the agents never shouted at Mr. LeBrun or threatened him physically, the district court found on ample evidence that the atmosphere at the interrogation was police-dominated and that the agents frequently raised their voices and changed their tone when doing so. They also interrupted Mr. LeBrun in a bullying manner and demonstrated a threatening kind of impatience with him. . . .

   The court ... adverts to the fact that the district court made no findings as to what promises the interrogators actually made, but instead found only that Mr. LeBrun reasonably believed that he was promised that he would not be prosecuted if he would say that he had killed Mr. Muns "spontaneously." The court then looks for support in cases that hold that a mistaken belief as to what the law is will not render a confession involuntary. But in at least one of those, *Winfrey v. Wyrick,* 836 F.2d 406, 411–12 (8th Cir.1987), it was crucial to the holding that the defendant's mistaken belief that he would not be prosecuted was not induced by anything that his interviewers told him; it was based entirely on his own ideas about what the law was. I agree that that kind of mistake cannot possibly render a confession inadmissible. But the clear purport of what the agents said in this case was that Mr. LeBrun would not be prosecuted if he said what the agents wanted him to say, and they even assured Mr. LeBrun that Mr. Muns's family approved of the deal. Indeed, they said that the family would not pursue civil remedies if he confessed and apologized. What the family wanted, the interrogators said, was simply to clear Mr. Muns's name.

   In addition to the part of the interview that the court quotes in its opinion, the record reveals that, both before and after the exchange that the court isolates, the interviewers made reference to an alleged statute of limitations difficulty that would prevent prosecution for a "spontaneous" murder; and the officers intimated, moreover, that if Mr. LeBrun would simply admit to a spontaneous killing, they would call the United States Attorney in charge of the prosecution and tell him that there was no case against Mr. LeBrun. In addition, I respectfully suggest that the district court did not, as the court maintains, note that the agents qualified their representations by telling Mr. LeBrun that it was "only 'possible' "that he would not be prosecuted. In relevant part, the transcript of the interview reveals only that one of the agents said at one point that "it was possible, beyond possible" that no prosecution would take place if Mr. LeBrun would cooperate, which is significantly different from what the court asserts was said. Taken in their entirety, the agents' assurances, which operated both as representations of what the law was and as promises, were categorical.

The district court shrank from holding that an absolute promise not to prosecute was made, not because of this part of the exchange between Mr. LeBrun and his interrogators, but because the promise not to prosecute was fleetingly qualified at one point, by one agent, by the condition that Mr. LeBrun must be telling the truth that the killing was spontaneous before the government would refrain from prosecution. This transitory allusion to truth-telling does nothing to undermine the district court's factual finding that Mr. LeBrun believed that he would not be prosecuted. My own examination of the transcript and the video tape leaves little room for doubt that the agents were in fact making such a representation about the law and a promise that Mr. LeBrun would not be prosecuted, and indeed it appears that the entire interview was deliberately structured around this stratagem. But nothing in particular really turns on this point: The coercive effect, if any, of a reasonably perceived promise is exactly the same as that of an actual promise.

In addition to the coercive tactics that the court briefly rehearses, among the enlarged pictures displayed prominently on the wall of the small interrogation room was a picture of Mr. Muns's family at his gravesite. The agents, moreover, did not merely invent generic phantom witnesses to the killing; they contrived a bizarre tale of a suicide note implicating Mr. LeBrun, and even claimed that there were other witnesses to the killing who were so haunted that their lives had been ruined by what they had seen. These were all knowing falsehoods. None of this finds a place in the court's opinion. Finally, and perhaps most importantly, the court fails altogether to mention the district court's finding that, despite the agents' assurances, Mr. LeBrun did not feel free to leave as the interview progressed. This is a finding of fact that is supported by Mr. LeBrun's testimony and cannot be reasonably rejected as clearly erroneous. It is also a finding that weighs heavily in favor of the district court's conclusion that Mr. LeBrun's confession was involuntary.

This is probably the right juncture to observe that it is not immediately apparent why statements by interrogators that are untrue, and known to be false, are more "coercive" than statements that are true. Such techniques may be reprehensible, but that fact would not seem to contribute to their propensity to overwhelm the will. Perhaps it is enough simply to note that the Supreme Court has said that "[t]he fact that the police misrepresented the statements that [a witness] had made is . . . relevant," *Frazier v. Cupp,* 394 U.S. 731, 739, 89 S.Ct. 1420, 22 L.Ed.2d 684 (1969), in circumstances like the present ones. But we need also to consider the possibility that what lies at the bottom of these kinds of cases is not merely an aversion to something called coercion, but a general uneasiness about the fairness of admitting confessions that were induced by knowing, lurid falsehoods and unfulfilled promises, whether "coercive" or not. In fact, the Supreme Court has specifically said that "the admissibility of a confession turns as much on whether the techniques for extracting the statements . . . are compatible with a system that presumes innocence and assures that a conviction will not be secured by inquisitorial means as on whether the defendant's will was in fact overborne." *Miller v. Fenton,* 474 U.S. 104, 116, 106 S.Ct. 445, 88 L.Ed.2d 405 (1985).

In sum, a consideration of the evidence in this case, including the kinds of pressure that were brought to bear on Mr. LeBrun, the assurances of leniency that went unfulfilled, and the deceit that the interrogators practiced, leads me to the conclusion that his confession was illegally obtained and should have been suppressed. At the very least, it seems to me relatively plain that the government has not carried its burden, *see Lego v. Twomey,* 404 U.S. 477, 489, 92 S.Ct. 619, 30 L.Ed.2d 618 (1972), of showing that the relevant statements were voluntary.

I therefore respectfully dissent and would affirm the judgment of the district court. . . .

B. MIRANDA V. ARIZONA AND THE INTERPRETATION OF ITS REQUIREMENTS

2. INTERPRETATION OF MIRANDA REQUIREMENTS

(a) THE MEANING OF "CUSTODY" AND "DEPRIVATION OF FREEDOM OF ACTION IN ANY SIGNIFICANT WAY"

Page 105. Add to end of note (d) Indicia of Arrest of the textbook.

In the context of a habeas proceeding, the Court addressed the test for what constitutes custody for purposes of *Miranda*:

Yarborough v. Alvarado

United States Supreme Court
541 U.S. 652, 124 S.Ct. 2140 (2004).

■ OPINION: JUSTICE KENNEDY delivered the opinion of the Court.

. . . The United States Court of Appeals for the Ninth Circuit ruled that a state court unreasonably applied clearly established law when it held that the respondent was not in custody for *Miranda* purposes. *Alvarado* v. *Hickman*, 316 F.3d 841 (2002). We disagree and reverse.

I

Paul Soto and respondent Michael Alvarado attempted to steal a truck in the parking lot of a shopping mall in Santa Fe Springs, California. Soto and Alvarado were part of a larger group of teenagers at the mall that night. Soto decided to steal the truck, and Alvarado agreed to help. Soto pulled out a .357 Magnum and approached the driver, Francisco Castaneda, who was standing near the truck emptying trash into a dumpster. Soto demanded money and the ignition keys from Castaneda. Alvarado, then five months short of his 18th birthday, approached the passenger side door of the truck and crouched down. When Castaneda refused to comply with Soto's demands, Soto shot Castaneda, killing him. Alvarado then helped hide Soto's gun.

Los Angeles County Sheriff's detective Cheryl Comstock led the investigation into the circumstances of Castaneda's death. About a month after the shooting, Comstock left word at Alvarado's house and also contacted Alvarado's mother at work with the message that she wished to speak with Alvarado. Alvarado's parents brought him to the Pico Rivera Sheriff's Station to be interviewed around lunchtime. They waited in the lobby while Alvarado went with Comstock to be interviewed. Alvarado contends that his parents asked to be present during the interview but were rebuffed.

Comstock brought Alvarado to a small interview room and began interviewing him at about 12:30 pm. The interview lasted about two hours, and was recorded by Comstock with Alvarado's knowledge. Only Comstock and Alvarado were present. Alvarado was not given a warning under *Miranda* v. *Arizona*, 384 U.S. 436 (1965). Comstock began the interview by asking Alvarado to recount the events on the night of the shooting. On that night, Alvarado explained, he had been drinking alcohol at a friend's house with some other friends and acquaintances. After a few hours, part of the group went home and the rest walked to a nearby mall to use its public telephones. In Alvarado's initial telling, that was the end of it. The group went back to the friend's home and "just went to bed." App. 101.

Unpersuaded, Comstock pressed on:

"Q. Okay. We did real good up until this point and everything you've said it's pretty accurate till this point, except for you left out the shooting.

"A. The shooting?

"Q. Uh huh, the shooting.

"A. Well I had never seen no shooting.

"Q. Well I'm afraid you did.

"A. I had never seen no shooting.

"Q. Well I beg to differ with you. I've been told quite the opposite and we have witnesses that are saying quite the opposite.

"A. That I had seen the shooting?

"Q. So why don't you take a deep breath, like I told you before, the very best thing is to be honest.... You can't have that many people get involved in a murder and expect that some of them aren't going to tell the truth, okay? Now granted if it was maybe one person, you might be able to keep your fingers crossed and say, god I hope he doesn't tell the truth, but the problem is is that they have to tell the truth, okay? Now all I'm simply doing is giving you the opportunity to tell the truth and when we got that many people telling a story and all of a sudden you tell something way far fetched different." *Id.*, at 101–102 (punctuation added).

At this point, Alvarado slowly began to change his story. First he acknowledged being present when the carjacking occurred but claimed that he did not know what happened or who had a gun. When he hesitated to say more, Comstock tried to encourage Alvarado to discuss what happened by appealing to his sense of honesty and the need to bring the man who shot Castaneda to justice. ("[W]hat I'm looking for is to see if you'll tell the truth"); ("I know it's very difficult when it comes time to 'drop the dime' on somebody[,] ... [but] if that had been your parent, your mother, or your brother, or your sister, you would darn well want [the killer] to go to jail 'cause no one has the right to take someone's life like that ..."). Alvarado then admitted he had helped the other man try to steal the truck by standing near the passenger side door. Next he admitted that the other man was Paul Soto, that he knew Soto was armed, and that he had helped hide the gun after the murder. Alvarado explained that he had expected

Soto to scare the driver with the gun, but that he did not expect Soto to kill anyone. Toward the end of the interview, Comstock twice asked Alvarado if he needed to take a break. Alvarado declined. When the interview was over, Comstock returned with Alvarado to the lobby of the sheriff's station where his parents were waiting. Alvarado's father drove him home. (Cites omitted)

In few months later, the State of California charged Soto and Alvarado with first-degree murder and attempted robbery. Citing *Miranda, supra*, Alvarado moved to suppress his statements from the Comstock interview. The trial court denied the motion on the ground that the interview was noncustodial. App. 196. Alvarado and Soto were tried together, and Alvarado testified in his own defense. He offered an innocent explanation for his conduct, testifying that he happened to be standing in the parking lot of the mall when a gun went off nearby. The government's cross-examination relied on Alvarado's statement to Comstock. Alvarado admitted having made some of the statements but denied others. When Alvarado denied particular statements, the prosecution countered by playing excerpts from the audio recording of the interview.

During cross-examination, Alvarado agreed that the interview with Comstock "was a pretty friendly conversation," that there was "sort of a free flow between [Alvarado] and Detective Comstock," and that Alvarado did not "feel coerced or threatened in any way" during the interview, (cites omitted). The jury convicted Soto and Alvarado of first-degree murder and attempted robbery. The trial judge later reduced Alvarado's conviction to second-degree murder for his comparatively minor role in the offense. The judge sentenced Soto to life in prison and Alvarado to 15–years-to-life.

On direct appeal, the Second Appellate District Court of Appeal (hereinafter state court) affirmed. The state court rejected Alvarado's contention that his statements to Comstock should have been excluded at trial because no *Miranda* warnings were given. The court ruled Alvarado had not been in custody during the interview, so no warning was required. The state court relied upon the custody test articulated in *Thompson* v. *Keohane*, 516 U.S. 99 (1995), which requires a court to consider the circumstances surrounding the interrogation and then determine whether a reasonable person would have felt at liberty to leave. The state court reviewed the facts of the Comstock interview and concluded Alvarado was not in custody. The court emphasized the absence of any intense or aggressive tactics and noted that Comstock had not told Alvarado that he could not leave. The California Supreme Court denied discretionary review.

Alvarado filed a petition for a writ of habeas corpus in the United States District Court for the Central District of California. The District Court agreed with the state court that Alvarado was not in custody for *Miranda* purposes during the interview. "At a minimum," the District Court added, the deferential standard of review provided by 28 U.S.C. § 2254(d) foreclosed relief. [*Cites omitted*].

The Court of Appeals for the Ninth Circuit reversed. *Alvarado* v. *Hickman*, 316 F.3d 841 (2002). First, the Court of Appeals held that the state court erred in failing to account for Alvarado's youth and inexperience when evaluating whether a reasonable person in his position would have felt free to leave. It noted that this Court has considered a suspect's juvenile status when evaluating the voluntariness of confessions and the waiver of the privilege against self-incrimination. See *id.*, at 843 (citing, *inter alia, Haley* v. *Ohio,* 332 U.S. 596, 599–601 (1948), and *In re Gault,* 387 U.S. 1, 45 (1967)). The Court of Appeals held that in light of these authorities, Alvarado's age and experience must be a factor in the *Miranda* custody inquiry. 316 F.3d at 843. A minor with no criminal record would be more likely to feel coerced by police tactics and conclude he is under arrest than would an experienced adult, the Court of Appeals reasoned. This required extra "safeguards . . . commensurate with the age and circumstances of a juvenile defendant." See *id.*, at 850. According to the Court of Appeals, the effect of Alvarado's age and inexperience was so substantial that it turned the interview into a custodial interrogation.

The Court of Appeals next considered whether Alvarado could obtain relief in light of the deference a federal court must give to a state-court determination on habeas review. The deference required by AEDPA did not bar relief, the Court of Appeals held, because the relevance of juvenile status in Supreme Court case law as a whole compelled the "extension of the principle that juvenile status is relevant" to the context of *Miranda* custody determinations. 316 F.3d at 853. In light of the clearly established law considering juvenile status, it was "simply unreasonable to conclude that a reasonable 17–year-old, with no prior history of arrest or police interviews, would have felt that he was at liberty to terminate the interrogation and leave." *Id.*, at 854–855 (internal quotation marks omitted).

We granted certiorari.

II

    .   .   .

Miranda itself held that preinterrogation warnings are required in the context of custodial interrogations given "the compulsion inherent in custodial surroundings." 384 U.S., at 458, The Court explained that "custodial interrogation" meant "questioning initiated by law enforcement officers after a person has been taken into custody or otherwise deprived of his freedom of action in any significant way." Id., at 444. The *Miranda* decision did not provide the Court with an opportunity to apply that test to a set of facts.

After *Miranda*, the Court first applied the custody test in *Oregon* v. *Mathiason,* 429 U.S. 492 (1977) *(per curiam).* In *Mathiason,* a police officer contacted the suspect after a burglary victim identified him. The officer arranged to meet the suspect at a nearby police station. At the outset of the questioning, the officer stated his belief that the suspect was involved in the burglary but that he was not under arrest. During the 30–minute interview, the suspect admitted his guilt. He was then allowed to leave. The Court held that the questioning was not custodial because there was "no indication that the questioning took place in a context where [the suspect's] freedom to depart was restricted in any way." *Id.*, at 495. The Court noted that the suspect had come voluntarily to the police station, that he was informed that he was not under arrest, and that he was allowed to leave at the end of the interview. *Ibid.*

In *California* v. *Beheler,* 463 U.S. 1121 (1983) *(per curiam),* the Court reached the same result in a case with facts similar to those in *Mathiason.* In *Beheler,* the state court had distinguished *Mathiason* based on what it described as differences in the totality of the circumstances. The police interviewed Beheler shortly after the crime occurred; Beheler had been drinking earlier in the day; he was emotionally distraught; he was well known to the police; and he was a parolee who knew it was necessary for him to cooperate with the police. 463 U.S., at 1124–1125. The Court agreed that "the circumstances of each case must certainly influence" the custody determination, but reemphasized that "the ultimate inquiry is simply whether there is a formal arrest or restraint on freedom of movement of the degree associated with a formal arrest." *Id.,* at 1125 (internal quotation marks omitted). The Court found the case indistinguishable from *Mathiason.* It noted that how much the police knew about the suspect and how much time had elapsed after the crime occurred were irrelevant to the custody inquiry. 463 U.S. at 1125.

Our more recent cases instruct that custody must be determined based on how a reasonable person in the suspect's situation would perceive his circumstances. In *Berkemer* v. *McCarty,* 468 U.S. 420 (1984), a police officer stopped a suspected drunk driver and asked him some questions. Although the officer reached the decision to arrest the driver at the beginning of the traffic stop, he did not do so until the driver failed a sobriety test and acknowledged that he had been drinking beer and smoking marijuana. The Court held the traffic stop noncustodial despite the officer's intent to arrest because he had not communicated that intent to the driver. "A policeman's unarticulated plan has no bearing on the question whether a suspect was 'in custody' at a particular time," the Court explained. *Id.,* at 442. "[T]he only relevant inquiry is how a reasonable man in the suspect's position would have understood his situation." *Ibid.* In a footnote, the Court cited a New York state case for the view that an objective test was preferable to a subjective test in part because it does not " 'place upon the police the burden of anticipating the frailties or idiosyncrasies of every person whom they question.' " *Id.,* at 442, n. 35 (quoting *People* v. *P.,* 21 N.Y. 2d 1, 9–10 (1967)).

Stansbury v. *California,* 511 U.S. 318 (1994) *(per curiam),* confirmed this analytical framework. *Stansbury* explained that "the initial determination of custody depends on the objective circumstances of the interrogation, not on the subjective views harbored by either the interrogating officers or the person being questioned." *Id.,* at 323. Courts must examine "all of the circumstances surrounding the interrogation" and determine "how a reasonable person in the position of the individual being questioned would gauge the breadth of his or her freedom of action." *Id.,* at 322, 325 (internal quotation marks and alteration omitted).

Finally, in *Thompson* v. *Keohane,* 516 U.S. 99 (1995), the Court offered the following description of the *Miranda* custody test:

"Two discrete inquiries are essential to the determination: first, what were the circumstances surrounding the interrogation; and second, given those circumstances, would a reasonable person have felt he or she was not at liberty to terminate the interrogation and leave. Once the scene is set and the players' lines and actions are reconstructed, the court must apply an objective test to resolve the ultimate inquiry: was there a formal arrest or restraint on freedom of movement of the degree associated with a formal arrest." 516 U.S., at 112. (internal quotation marks omitted).

We turn now to the case before us and ask if the state-court adjudication of the claim "involved an unreasonable application" of clearly established law when it concluded that Alvarado was not in custody.... we conclude that the state court's application of our clearly established law was reasonable. Ignoring the deferential standard of § 2254(d)(1) for the moment, it can be said that fair-minded jurists could disagree over whether Alvarado was in custody. On one hand, certain facts weigh against a finding that Alvarado was in custody. The police did not transport Alvarado to the station or require him to appear at a particular time. Cf. *Mathiason*, 429 U.S., at 495. They did not threaten him or suggest he would be placed under arrest. *Ibid*. Alvarado's parents remained in the lobby during the interview, suggesting that the interview would be brief. See *Berkemer*, 468 U.S., at 441–442. In fact, according to trial counsel for Alvarado, he and his parents were told that the interview was " 'not going to be long.' " App. 186. During the interview, Comstock focused on Soto's crimes rather than Alvarado's. Instead of pressuring Alvarado with the threat of arrest and prosecution, she appealed to his interest in telling the truth and being helpful to a police officer. Cf. *Mathiason*, 429 U.S., at 495. In addition, Comstock twice asked Alvarado if he wanted to take a break. At the end of the interview, Alvarado went home. *Ibid*. All of these objective facts are consistent with an interrogation environment in which a reasonable person would have felt free to terminate the interview and leave. Indeed, a number of the facts echo those of *Mathiason*, a *per curiam* summary reversal in which we found it "clear from these facts" that the suspect was not in custody. *Ibid*.

Other facts point in the opposite direction. Comstock interviewed Alvarado at the police station. The interview lasted two hours, four times longer than the 30–minute interview in *Mathiason*. Unlike the officer in *Mathiason*, Comstock did not tell Alvarado that he was free to leave. Alvarado was brought to the police station by his legal guardians rather than arriving on his own accord, making the extent of his control over his presence unclear. Counsel for Alvarado alleges that Alvarado's parents asked to be present at the interview but were rebuffed, a fact that—if known to Alvarado–might reasonably have led someone in Alvarado's position to feel more restricted than otherwise. These facts weigh in favor of the view that Alvarado was in custody.

These differing indications lead us to hold that the state court's application of our custody standard was reasonable. The Court of Appeals was nowhere close to the mark when it concluded otherwise. Although the question of what is an "unreasonable application" of law might be difficult in some cases, it is not difficult here. The custody test is general, and the state court's application of our law fits within the matrix of our prior decisions. We cannot grant relief under AEDPA by conducting our own independent inquiry into whether the state court was correct as a *de novo* matter. "[A] federal habeas court may not issue the writ simply because that court concludes in its independent judgment that the state-court decision applied [the law] incorrectly." *Woodford* v. *Visciotti,* 537 U.S. 19, 24–25 (2002) *(per curiam)*. Relief is available under § 2254(d)(1) only if the state court's decision is objectively unreasonable. See *Williams, supra,* at 410; *Andrade,* 538 U.S. at 75. Under that standard, relief cannot be granted.

III

The Court of Appeals reached the opposite result by placing considerable reliance on Alvarado's age and inexperience with law enforcement. Our Court has not stated that a suspect's age or experience is relevant to the *Miranda* custody analysis, and counsel for Alvarado did not press the importance of either factor on direct appeal or in habeas proceedings. According to the Court of Appeals, however, our Court's emphasis on juvenile status in other contexts demanded consideration of Alvarado's age and inexperience here. The Court of Appeals viewed the state court's failure to "extend a clearly established legal principle [of the relevance of juvenile status] to a new context" as objectively unreasonable in this case, requiring issuance of the writ. 316 F.3d at 853 (quoting *Anthony* v. *Cambra,* 236 F.3d 568, 578 (CA9 2000)).

. . .

There is an important conceptual difference between the *Miranda* custody test and the line of cases from other contexts considering age and experience. The *Miranda* custody inquiry is an objective test. As we stated in *Keohane,* "[o]nce the scene is set and the players' lines and actions are reconstructed, the court must apply an objective test to resolve the ultimate inquiry." 516 U.S., at 112. The objective test furthers "the clarity of [*Miranda*'s] rule," *Berkemer,* 468 U.S., at 430, ensuring that the police do not need "to make guesses as to [the circumstances] at issue before deciding how they may interrogate the suspect." *Id.,* at 431. To be sure, the line between permissible objective facts and impermissible subjective experiences can be indistinct in some cases. It is possible to subsume a subjective factor into an objective test by making the latter more specific in its formulation. Thus the Court of Appeals styled its inquiry as an objective test by considering what a "reasonable 17–year-old, with no prior history of arrest or police interviews' would perceive."

At the same time, the objective *Miranda* custody inquiry could reasonably be viewed as different from doctrinal tests that depend on the actual mindset of a particular suspect, where we do consider a suspect's age and experience. For example, the voluntariness of a statement is often said to depend on whether "the defendant's will was overborne," *Lynumn* v. *Illinois,* 372 U.S. 528, 534 (1963), a question that logically can depend on "the characteristics of the accused." *Schneckloth* v. *Bustamonte,* 412 U.S. 218, 226 (1973). The characteristics of the accused can include the suspect's age, education, and intelligence, see *ibid.,* as well as a suspect's prior experience with law enforcement, see *Lynumn, supra,* at 534, 9 L. Ed. 2d

922. In concluding that there was "no principled reason" why such factors should not also apply to the *Miranda* custody inquiry ... the Court of Appeals ignored the argument that the custody inquiry states an objective rule designed to give clear guidance to the police, while consideration of a suspect's individual characteristics—including his age—could be viewed as creating a subjective inquiry. Cf. *Mathiason*, 429 U.S., at 495–496 (noting that facts arguably relevant to whether an environment is coercive may have "nothing to do with whether respondent was in custody for purposes of the *Miranda* rule"). For these reasons, the state court's failure to consider Alvarado's age does not provide a proper basis for finding that the state court's decision was an unreasonable application of clearly established law.

Indeed, reliance on Alvarado's prior history with law enforcement was improper not only under the deferential standard of 28 U.S.C. § 2254(d)(1), but also as a *de novo* matter. In most cases, police officers will not know a suspect's interrogation history. See *Berkemer*, *supra*, at 430–431. Even if they do, the relationship between a suspect's past experiences and the likelihood a reasonable person with that experience would feel free to leave often will be speculative. True, suspects with prior law enforcement experience may understand police procedures and reasonably feel free to leave unless told otherwise. On the other hand, they may view past as prologue and expect another in a string of arrests. We do not ask police officers to consider these contingent psychological factors when deciding when suspects should be advised of their *Miranda* rights. See *Berkemer*, *supra*, at 431–432. The inquiry turns too much on the suspect's subjective state of mind and not enough on the "obective circumstances of the interrogation." *Stansbury*, 511 U.S., at 323.

The state court considered the proper factors and reached a reasonable conclusion. The judgment of the Court of Appeals is reversed.

■ CONCUR: JUSTICE O'CONNOR, concurring.

I join the opinion of the Court, but write separately to express an additional reason for reversal. There may be cases in which a suspect's age will be relevant to the *Miranda* "custody" inquiry. In this case, however, Alvarado was almost 18 years old at the time of his interview. It is difficult to expect police to recognize that a suspect is a juvenile when he is so close to the age of majority. Even when police do know a suspect's age, it may be difficult for them to ascertain what bearing it has on the likelihood that the suspect would feel free to leave. That is especially true here; 17 1/2–year-olds vary widely in their reactions to police questioning, and many can be expected to behave as adults. Given these difficulties, I agree that the state court's decision in this case cannot be called an unreasonable application of federal law simply because it failed explicitly to mention Alvarado's age.

■ DISSENT: JUSTICE BREYER, with whom JUSTICE STEVENS, JUSTICE SOUTER, and JUSTICE GINSBURG join, dissenting.

In my view, Michael Alvarado clearly was "in custody" when the police questioned him (without *Miranda* warnings) about the murder of Francisco Castaneda. To put the question in terms of federal law's well-established legal standards: Would a "reasonable person" in Alvarado's "position" have felt he was "at liberty to terminate the interrogation and leave"? *Thompson* v. *Keohane*, 516 U.S. 99, 112 (1995); *Stansbury* v. *California* 511 U.S. 318, 325 (1994) *(per curiam)*. A court must answer this question in light of "all of the circumstances surrounding the interrogation." *Id.*, at 322, And the obvious answer here is "no."

I

A

The law in this case asks judges to apply, not arcane or complex legal directives, but ordinary common sense. Would a reasonable person in Alvarado's position have felt free simply to get up and walk out of the small room in the station house at will during his 2–hour police interrogation? I ask the reader to put himself, or herself, in Alvarado's circumstances and then answer that question: Alvarado hears from his parents that he is needed for police questioning. His parents take him to the station. On arrival, a police officer separates him from his parents. His parents ask to come along, but the officer says they may not. App. 185–186. Another officer says, " 'What do we have here; we are going to question a suspect.' " *Id.*, at 189.

The police take Alvarado to a small interrogation room, away from the station's public area. A single officer begins to question him, making clear in the process that the police have evidence that he participated in an attempted carjacking connected with a murder. When he says that he never saw any shooting, the officer suggests that he is lying, while adding that she is "giving [him] the opportunity to tell the truth" and "tak[e] care of [him]self." *Id.*, at 102, 105. Toward the end of the questioning, the officer gives him permission to take a bathroom or water break. After two hours, by which time he has admitted he was involved in the attempted theft, knew about the gun, and helped to hide it, the questioning ends.

What reasonable person in the circumstances—brought to a police station by his parents at police request, put in a small interrogation room, questioned for a solid two hours, and confronted with claims that there is strong evidence that he participated in a serious crime, could have thought to himself, "Well, anytime I want to leave I can just get up and walk out"? If the person harbored any doubts, would he still think he might be free to leave once he recalls that the police officer has just refused to let his parents remain with him during questioning? Would he still think that he, rather than the officer, controls the situation?

There is only one possible answer to these questions. A reasonable person would *not* have thought he was free simply to pick up and leave in the middle of the interrogation. I believe the California courts were clearly wrong to hold the contrary, and the Ninth Circuit was right in concluding that those state courts unreasonably applied clearly established federal law.

B

What about the majority's view that "fair-minded jurists could disagree over whether Alvarado was in custody"? *Ante*. Consider each of the facts it says "weigh against a finding" of custody:

(1) *"The police did not transport Alvarado to the station or require him to appear at a particular time." Ibid.* True. His parents brought him to the station at police request. But why does that matter? The relevant question is whether Alvarado came to the station of his own free will or submitted to questioning voluntarily. Cf. *Oregon* v. *Mathiason*, 429 U.S. 492, 493–495 (1977) *(per curiam); California* v. *Beheler*, 463 U.S. 1121, 1122–1123 (1983) *(per curiam); Thompson, supra*, at 118 (Thomas, J., dissenting). And the involvement of Alvarado's parents suggests *in*voluntary, not voluntary, behavior on Alvarado's part.

(2) *"Alvarado's parents remained in the lobby during the interview, suggesting that the interview would be brief. In fact, [Alvarado] and his parents were told that the interview 'was not going to be long.'"* Whatever was communicated to Alvarado *before* the questioning began, the fact is that the interview was not brief, nor, after the first half hour or so, would Alvarado have expected it to be brief. And those are the relevant considerations.

(3) *"At the end of the interview, Alvarado went home."* As the majority acknowledges, our recent case law makes clear that the relevant question is how a reasonable person would have gauged his freedom to leave *during*, not *after*, the interview.

(4) *"During the interview, [Officer] Comstock focused on Soto's crimes rather than Alvarado's."* In fact, the police officer characterized Soto as the ringleader, while making clear that she knew Alvarado had participated in the attempted carjacking during which Castaneda was killed. Her questioning would have reinforced, not diminished, Alvarado's fear that he was not simply a witness, but also suspected of having been involved in a serious crime.

(5) *"[The officer did not] pressur[e] Alvarado with the threat of arrest and prosecution . . . [but instead] appealed to his interest in telling the truth and being helpful to a police officer."* This factor might be highly significant were the question one of "coercion." But it is not. The question is whether Alvarado would have felt free to terminate the interrogation and leave. In respect to that question, police politeness, while commendable, does not significantly help the majority.

(6) *"Comstock twice asked Alvarado if he wanted to take a break."* This circumstance, emphasizing the officer's control of Alvarado's movements, makes it *less* likely, not *more* likely, that Alvarado would have thought he was free to leave at will.

The facts to which the majority points make clear what the police did *not* do, for example, come to Alvarado's house, tell him he was under arrest, handcuff him, place him in a locked cell, threaten him, or tell him explicitly that he was not free to leave. But what is important here is what the police *did* do—namely, have Alvarado's parents bring him to the station, put him with a single officer in a small room, keep his parents out, let him know that he was a suspect, and question him for two hours. These latter facts compel a single conclusion: A reasonable person in Alvarado's circumstances would *not* have felt free to terminate the interrogation and leave.

C

What about Alvarado's youth? The fact that Alvarado was 17 helps to show that he was unlikely to have felt free to ignore his parents' request to come to the station. See *Schall* v. *Martin,* 467 U.S. 253, 265 (1984) (juveniles assumed "to be subject to the control of their parents"). And a 17–year-old is more likely than, say, a 35–year-old, to take a police officer's assertion of authority to keep parents outside the room as an assertion of authority to keep their child inside as well.

The majority suggests that the law might *prevent* a judge from taking account of the fact that Alvarado was 17. I can find nothing in the law that supports that conclusion. Our cases do instruct lower courts to apply a "reasonable person" standard. But the "reasonable person" standard does not require a court to pretend that Alvarado was a 35–year-old with aging parents whose middle-aged children do what their parents ask only out of respect. Nor does it say that a court should pretend that Alvarado was the statistically determined "average person"—a working, married, 35–year-old white female with a high school degree. See U. S. Dept. of Commerce, Bureau of Census, Statistical Abstract of the United States: 2003 (123d ed.).

Rather, the precise legal definition of "reasonable person" may, depending on legal context, appropriately account for certain personal characteristics. In negligence suits, for example, the question is what would a "reasonable person" do " 'under the same or similar circumstances.' " In answering that question, courts enjoy "latitude" and may make "allowance not only for external facts, but sometimes for certain characteristics of the actor himself," including physical disability, youth, or advanced age. W. Keeton, D. Dobbs, R. Keeton, & D. Owen, Prosser and Keeton on Law of Torts § 32, pp 174–179 (5th ed. 1984); see *id.,* at 179–181; see also Restatement (Third) of Torts § 10, Comment b, pp 128–130 (Tent. Draft No. 1, Mar. 28, 2001) (all American jurisdictions count a person's childhood as a "relevant circumstance" in negligence determinations). This allowance makes sense in light of the tort standard's recognized purpose: deterrence. Given that purpose, why pretend that a child is an adult or that a blind man can see? See O. Holmes, The Common Law 85–89 (M. Howe ed. 1963).

In the present context, that of *Miranda*'s "in custody" inquiry, the law has introduced the concept of a "reasonable person" to avoid judicial inquiry into subjective states of mind, and to focus the inquiry instead upon objective circumstances that are known to both the officer and the suspect and that are likely relevant to the way a person would understand his situation.... This focus helps to keep *Miranda* a workable rule....

In this case, Alvarado's youth is an objective circumstance that was known to the police. It is not a special quality, but rather a widely shared characteristic that generates commonsense conclusions about behavior and perception. To focus on the circumstance of age in a case like this does not complicate the "in custody" inquiry. And to say that courts should ignore widely shared, objective characteristics, like age, on the ground that only a (large) *minority* of the population possesses them would produce absurd results, the present instance being a case in point. I am not surprised that the majority points to no case suggesting any such limitation. Cf. *Alvarado*

v. *Hickman*, 316 F.3d 841, 848, 851, n. 5 (CA9 2002) (case below) (listing 12 cases from 12 different jurisdictions suggesting the contrary).

Nor am I surprised that the majority makes no real argument at all explaining *why* any court would believe that the objective fact of a suspect's age could *never* be relevant. But see *ante* (O'Connor, J., concurring) ("There may be cases in which a suspect's age will be relevant to the *Miranda* 'custody' inquiry"). The majority does discuss a suspect's "history with law enforcement," *ante*—a bright red herring in the present context where Alvarado's youth (an objective fact) simply helps to show (with the help of a legal presumption) that his appearance at the police station was not voluntary.

II

As I have said, the law in this case is clear. This Court's cases establish that, even if the police do not tell a suspect he is under arrest, do not handcuff him, do not lock him in a cell, and do not threaten him, he may nonetheless reasonably believe he is not free to leave the place of questioning—and thus be in custody for *Miranda* purposes. [cites omitted]

Our cases also make clear that to determine how a suspect would have "gaug[ed]" his "freedom of movement," a court must carefully examine all of the circumstances surrounding the interrogation, including, for example, how long the interrogation lasted (brief and routine or protracted?), how the suspect came to be questioned (voluntarily or against his will?); where the questioning took place (at a police station or in public?); and what the officer communicated to the individual during the interrogation (that he was a suspect? that he was under arrest? that he was free to leave at will?). In the present case, every one of these factors argues—and argues strongly—that Alvarado was in custody for *Miranda* purposes when the police questioned him. [*cites omitted*]

Common sense, and an understanding of the law's basic purpose in this area, are enough to make clear that Alvarado's age–an objective, widely shared characteristic about which the police plainly knew—is also relevant to the inquiry. Cf. *Kaupp* v. *Texas*, 538 U.S. 626, 629–631 (2003) *(per curiam)*. Unless one is prepared to pretend that Alvarado is someone he is not, a middle-aged gentleman, well-versed in police practices, it seems to me clear that the California courts made a serious mistake. I agree with the Ninth Circuit's similar conclusions. Consequently, I dissent.

C.   INTERROGATION OF SUSPECTS AFTER INITIATION OF FORMAL PROCEEDINGS: THE SIXTH AMENDMENT RIGHT

Page 209. Add as a new note 1 on page 209 following *Texas v. Cobb* and renumber the subsequent notes accordingly:

After *Texas v. Cobb* established that the Sixth Amendment is offense specific, the Second Circuit faced the issue of how to apply the Cobb principles to cases involving charges that have the same essential elements but that are brought by different jurisdictions?

In *United States v. Mills*, the defendant was charged with a state offence of being a felon in possession of a firearm. Officers interrogated him without his counsel present and he made statements that linked him to the firearm believed to the weapon used to murder a police officer. Federal prosecutors charged the defendant with a federal crime of possessing a firearm after being adjudicated a felon.

The federal prosecutors conceded that the interrogation of the defendant after he had been formally charged, but relying on a Fifth Circuit precedent, *United States v. Avants*, 278 F.3d 510 (5th Cir. 2002), urged that the "dual sovereignty exception to double jeopardy" prevented the attachment of the defendant's Sixth Amendment Rights.

The Second Circuit did not follow *Avants* and refused to recognize a dual sovereignty exception.

This seeming split among the Circuits may now require Supreme Court intervention.

CHAPTER 4

WIRETAPPING AND ELECTRONIC SURVEILLANCE

B. NON-CONSENSUAL WIRETAPPING AND ELECTRONIC SURVEILLANCE

Page 331. Add to note 3:

Congress later prohibited the installation of a pen register without a court order. 18 U.S.C. § 3121(a). Evidence obtained through the illegal installation of a pen register is still admissible in a criminal trial, however, since the seized evidence is seized in violation of a statute and not in violation of the Fourth Amendment constitutional provisions. United States v. Thompson, 936 F.2d 1249 (11th Cir. 1991), *cert. denied*, 502 U.S. 1075, 112 S.Ct. 975 (1992).

In the past this statute authorized a judge in a court with jurisdiction over the crime to enter an order to permit a pen register or a trap and trace device that could be used only in that jurisdiction. 18 U.S.C. § 1323 (2000 ed.). Now, the Patriot Act permits the government to apply to a court with jurisdiction over the crime for an order that may be used anywhere in the United States 18 U.S.C. §§ 3123 (B)(1)(c), 3127(2).

page 331. Add to note 4:

Professor Orin Kerr has written about the survival of the property paradigm after *Katz*. Orin G. Kerr, "The Fourth Amendment in New Technologies: Constitutional Myths and the Case for Restraint," 102 Michigan L. Rev. 801 (2004). See also Swire, Peter P. "*Katz* is Dead, Long Live *Katz*," 102 Mich. L. Rev. 904 (2004).

Page 347. Add to note 9:

In 2004, courts issued 1,710 authorizations for intercept orders as a result of 730 federal applications and 980 state applications. This represents an increase of 19% over the number issued in 2004. The number of applications for orders by federal authorities jumped a full 26% over the preceding year while the number of applications for orders by state authorities grew by 13% (19 jurisdictions reporting, 4 fewer than in 2003). The states reporting the most applications were New York, California, New Jersey, and Florida. Under the amended 18 U.S.C. § 2519(2)(b) authorities are now required to report the number of wiretap applications in which encryption was encountered. Two such instaces were reported, one federal and one state, but in neither case did encryption bar successful interception by law enforcement authorities. The vast majority of cases in which authorities sought wiretaps were narcotics cases (1,308) followed by racketeering (108). As in prior years, the risk of rejection was low. In 2004, 1,710 authorizations were sought and 1,710 authorizations were issued. None were refused, though a number were amended and not all were installed. 2004 Report of the Director of the Administrative Office of the United States Courts on Applications for Orders Authorizing or Approving the Interception of Wire, Oral or Electronic Communications http://www.uscourts.gov/wiretap04/contents.html.

Page 353. Add to end of note 4 on page 353:

As this supplement was being prepared, Congress was considering the Patriot Act again. The House approved a bill that would make all but two of the "temporary" provisions (those that would sunset) permanent. The Senate was scheduled to take up the bill.

CHAPTER 5

THE LAW OF ARREST, SEARCH AND SEIZURE

B. PROBABLE CAUSE

Page 408. Add at the end of note 3(a) Probable Cause for What? after *Illinois v. Gates*:

Probable cause for an offense defined by a statute that is later held to be unconstitutional nevertheless will suffice to establish probable cause. See *Michigan v. DeFillippo*, 443 U.S. 31, 99 S.Ct. 2627 (1979).

Similarly, if police arrest for offense A, but ultimately charge the defendant with offense B, probable cause can be established even though the two offenses are not closely related. When a defendant brought a civil action under 42 U.S.C. § 1983 against a police officer for wrongful arrest, he claimed a lack of probable cause. Without probable cause, the arrest would be unconstitutional. The police arrested the defendant for taping a traffic stop. Later the defendant was charged with impersonating an officer and obstruction of justice. The Court held that the arrest for the impersonating an officer or obstruction of justice could be supported by probable cause even when those offenses were not closely related to the offense stated by the officer as the reason for the arrest. Devenpeck v. Alford, ___ U.S. ___, 125 S.Ct. 588 (2004).

Page 409. Add note 3(d) to the end of note 3:

(d) How specific does the probable cause have to be? Suppose officers have clear probable cause to believe a crime has been committed, but it is unclear which, if any, of multiple suspects committed it?

How does an officer measure probable cause when multiple parties are involved? The United States Supreme Court addressed this question in *Maryland v. Pringle*, 540 U.S. 366, 124 S.Ct. 795 (2003). There, officers pulled over a passenger car in the early morning hours for speeding. There were three occupants in the car, two in front and one in the back seat. A consent search turned up $763 in the front glove compartment and five glassine baggies of cocaine between the back seat and the back seat armrest. When none of the occupants claimed ownership of the drugs, the officers placed all three under arrest. Later defendant Pringle, who had been the front seat passenger, confessed (after waiving his *Miranda* rights) and claimed ownership of the contraband. He moved to suppress his confession as the fruit of an illegal arrest, arguing that the officers lacked probable cause to arrest him. The trial court denied his motion and he was convicted and sentenced to 10 years incarceration.

On appeal, his conviction was reversed by a divided court. The Court of Appeals of Maryland held that "there was not probable cause to arrest petitioner, who was not the owner of the vehicle, when petitioner was merely the front seat passenger and the only evidence supporting the arrest was a sum of money in the closed front glove compartment and drugs that were hidden from view in the armrest in the backseat of the vehicle." 370 Md. 525, 531, 805 A.2d 1016, 1019 (2002).

The United States Supreme Court disagreed and held that the arresting officer did have sufficient probable cause. First, all agreed that on these facts, the discovery of the illegal drugs constituted unquestionable probable cause to believe a crime had been committed. There was only the issue of whether there was sufficient probable cause that this defendant had committed it. Relying on *Wyoming v. Houghton*, 526 U.S. 295, 119 S.Ct. 1297 (1999), the Court found that it was reasonable for the officer to have inferred a common criminal enterprise in this situation. The Court rejected the defendant's argument based on *Ybarra v. Illinois*, 444 U.S. 85, 100 S.Ct. 338 (1979) that ''mere propinquity'' was not enough.

C.   The Issuance of Warrants

Page 412. Add to note 3:

In *Groh v. Ramirez*, 540 U.S. 551, 124 S.Ct. 1284 (2004), although the affidavit in support of the warrant set forth probable cause, the warrant itself lacked particularity and did not describe the items to be seized at all. The agent inserted a description of the place to be searched in the warrant space provided for the items to be seized. Thus, no items were listed in the warrant itself. The Supreme Court held that the search violated the Fourth Amendment. The Court further determined on these facts that the agent was not entitled to a good faith defense and further, the agent would not receive qualified immunity in this civil action for the violation of constitutional rights.

D.   The Execution of Search Warrants

Page 418. Add after paragraph 5 of note 5:

The Supreme Court revisited the issues in *Michigan v. Summers* this term in the *Muehler v. Mena* case that follows.

Page 418. Add after note 5:

Muehler v. Mena

United States Supreme Court
___ U.S. ___, 125 S.Ct. 1465 (2005).

■ OPINION: Chief Justice Rehnquist delivered the opinion of the Court.

Respondent Iris Mena was detained in handcuffs during a search of the premises that she and several others occupied. Petitioners were lead members of a police detachment executing a search warrant of these premises. She sued the officers under Rev Stat § 1979, 42 U.S.C. § 1983, and the District Court found in her favor. The Court of Appeals affirmed the judgment, holding that the use of handcuffs to detain Mena during the search violated the Fourth Amendment and that the officers' questioning of Mena about her immigration status during the detention constituted an independent Fourth Amendment violation. *Mena* v. *Simi Valley*, 332 F.3d 1255 (CA9 2003). We hold that Mena's detention in handcuffs for the length of the search was consistent with our opinion in *Michigan* v. *Summers*, 452 U.S. 692, 101 S. Ct. 2587 (1981), and that the officers' questioning during that detention did not violate her Fourth Amendment rights.

* * *

Based on information gleaned from the investigation of a gang-related, driveby shooting, petitioners Muehler and Brill had reason to believe at least one member of a gang—the West Side Locos—lived at 1363 Patricia Avenue. They also suspected that the individual was armed and dangerous, since he had recently been involved in the driveby shooting. As a result, Muehler obtained a search warrant for 1363 Patricia Avenue that authorized a broad search of the house and premises for, among other things, deadly weapons and evidence of gang membership. In light of the high degree of risk involved in searching a house suspected of housing at least one, and perhaps multiple, armed gang members, a Special Weapons and Tactics (SWAT) team was used to secure the residence and grounds before the search.

At 7 a.m. on February 3, 1998, petitioners, along with the SWAT team and other officers, executed the warrant. Mena was asleep in her bed when the SWAT team, clad in helmets and black vests adorned with badges and the word "POLICE," entered her bedroom and placed her in handcuffs at gunpoint. The SWAT team also handcuffed three other individuals found on the property. The SWAT team then took those individuals and Mena into a converted garage, which contained several beds and some other bedroom furniture. While the search proceeded, one or two officers guarded the four detainees, who were allowed to move around the garage but remained in handcuffs.

Aware that the West Side Locos gang was composed primarily of illegal immigrants, the officers had notified the Immigration and Naturalization Service (INS) that they would be conducting the search, and an INS officer accompanied the officers executing the warrant. During their detention in the garage, an officer asked for each detainee's name, date of birth, place of birth, and immigration status. The INS officer later asked the detainees for their immigration documentation. Mena's status as a permanent resident was confirmed by her papers.

The search of the premises yielded a .22 caliber handgun with .22 caliber ammunition, a box of .25 caliber ammunition, several baseball bats with gang writing, various additional gang paraphernalia, and a bag of marijuana. Before the officers left the area, Mena was released.

In her § 1983 suit against the officers she alleged that she was detained "for an unreasonable time and in an unreasonable manner" in violation of the Fourth Amendment. App. 19. In addition, she claimed that the warrant and its execution were overbroad, that the officers failed to comply with the "knock and announce" rule, and that the officers had needlessly destroyed property during the search. The officers moved for summary judgment, asserting that they were entitled to qualified immunity, but the District Court denied their motion. The Court of Appeals affirmed that denial, *except* for Mena's claim that the warrant was overbroad; on this claim the Court of Appeals held that the officers were entitled to qualified immunity. *Mena* v. *Simi Valley*, 226 F.3d 1031 (CA9

2000). After a trial, a jury, pursuant to a special verdict form, found that Officers Muehler and Brill violated Mena's Fourth Amendment right to be free from unreasonable seizures by detaining her both with force greater than that which was reasonable and for a longer period than that which was reasonable. The jury awarded Mena $10,000 in actual damages and $20,000 in punitive damages against each petitioner for a total of $60,000.

The Court of Appeals affirmed the judgment on two grounds. 332 F.3d 1255 (CA9 2003). Reviewing the denial of qualified immunity *de novo, id.,* at 1261, n. 2, it first held that the officers' detention of Mena violated the Fourth Amendment because it was objectively unreasonable to confine her in the converted garage and keep her in handcuffs during the search, *id.,* at 1263–1264. In the Court of Appeals' view, the officers should have released Mena as soon as it became clear that she posed no immediate threat. *Id.,* at 1263. The court additionally held that the questioning of Mena about her immigration status constituted an independent Fourth Amendment violation. *Id.,* at 1264–1266. The Court of Appeals went on to hold that those rights were clearly established at the time of Mena's questioning, and thus the officers were not entitled to qualified immunity. *Id.,* at 1266–1267. We granted certiorari, 542 U.S. ___, 160 L. Ed. 2d 221, 125 S. Ct. 317 (2004), and now vacate and remand.

* * *

In *Michigan v. Summers,* 452 U.S. 692, 101 S. Ct. 2587 (1981), we held that officers executing a search warrant for contraband have the authority "to detain the occupants of the premises while a proper search is conducted." *Id.,* at 705, 101 S. Ct. 2587. Such detentions are appropriate, we explained, because the character of the additional intrusion caused by detention is slight and because the justifications for detention are substantial. *Id.,* at 701–705, 101 S. Ct. 2587. We made clear that the detention of an occupant is "surely less intrusive than the search itself," and the presence of a warrant assures that a neutral magistrate has determined that probable cause exists to search the home. *Id.,* at 701, 101 S. Ct. 2587. Against this incremental intrusion, we posited three legitimate law enforcement interests that provide substantial justification for detaining an occupant: "preventing flight in the event that incriminating evidence is found"; "minimizing the risk of harm to the officers"; and facilitating "the orderly completion of the search," as detainees' "self-interest may induce them to open locked doors or locked containers to avoid the use of force." *Id.,* at 702–703, 101 S. Ct. 2587.

Mena's detention was, under *Summers,* plainly permissible.[1] An officer's authority to detain incident to a search is categorical; it does not depend on the "quantum of proof justifying detention or the extent of the intrusion to be imposed by the seizure." *Id.,* at 705, n. 19, 101 S. Ct. 2587. Thus, Mena's detention for the duration of the search was reasonable

---

1. In determining whether a Fourth Amendment violation occurred we draw all reasonable factual inferences in favor of the jury verdict, but as we made clear in *Ornelas v. United States,* 517 U.S. 690, 697–699, 134 L. Ed. 2d 911, 116 S. Ct. 1657 (1996), we do not defer to the jury's legal conclusion that those facts violate the Constitution.

under *Summers* because a warrant existed to search 1363 Patricia Avenue and she was an occupant of that address at the time of the search.

Inherent in *Summers'* authorization to detain an occupant of the place to be searched is the authority to use reasonable force to effectuate the detention. See *Graham v. Connor,* 490 U.S. 386, 396, 109 S. Ct. 1865 (1989) ("Fourth Amendment jurisprudence has long recognized that the right to make an arrest or investigatory stop necessarily carries with it the right to use some degree of physical coercion or threat thereof to effect it"). Indeed, *Summers* itself stressed that the risk of harm to officers and occupants is minimized "if the officers routinely exercise unquestioned command of the situation." 452 U.S., at 703, 101 S. Ct. 2587.

The officers' use of force in the form of handcuffs to effectuate Mena's detention in the garage, as well as the detention of the three other occupants, was reasonable because the governmental interests outweigh the marginal intrusion. See *Graham, supra,* at 396–397, 109 S. Ct. 1865. The imposition of correctly applied handcuffs on Mena, who was already being lawfully detained during a search of the house, was undoubtedly a separate intrusion in addition to detention in the converted garage.[2] The detention was thus more intrusive than that which we upheld in *Summers.* See 452 U.S., at 701–702, 101 S. Ct. 2587 (concluding that the additional intrusion in the form of a detention was less than that of the warrant-sanctioned search); *Maryland* v. *Wilson,* 519 U.S. 408, 413–414, 117 S. Ct. 882 (1997) (concluding that the additional intrusion from ordering passengers out of a car, which was already stopped, was minimal).

But this was no ordinary search. The governmental interests in not only detaining, but using handcuffs, are at their maximum when, as here, a warrant authorizes a search for weapons and a wanted gang member resides on the premises. In such inherently dangerous situations, the use of handcuffs minimizes the risk of harm to both officers and occupants. Cf. *Summers, supra,* at 702–703, 101 S. Ct. 2587 (recognizing the execution of a warrant to search for drugs "may give rise to sudden violence or frantic efforts to conceal or destroy evidence"). Though this safety risk inherent in executing a search warrant for weapons was sufficient to justify the use of handcuffs, the need to detain multiple occupants made the use of handcuffs all the more reasonable. Cf. *Maryland* v. *Wilson, supra,* at 414, 117 S. Ct. 882 (noting that "danger to an officer from a traffic stop is likely to be

---

2. In finding the officers should have released Mena from the handcuffs, the Court of Appeals improperly relied upon the fact that the warrant did not include Mena as a suspect. See *Mena v. Simi Valley,* 332 F.3d 1255, 1263, n. 5 (CA9 2003). The warrant was concerned not with individuals but with locations and property. In particular, the warrant in this case authorized the search of 1363 Patricia Avenue and its surrounding grounds for, among other things, deadly weapons and evidence of street gang membership. In this respect, the warrant here resembles that at issue in *Michigan* v. *Summers,* 452 U.S. 692, 101 S. Ct. 2587 (1981), which allowed the search of a residence for drugs without mentioning any individual, including the owner of the home whom police ultimately arrested. (Cites omitted). *Summers* makes clear that when a neutral magistrate has determined police have probable cause to believe contraband exists, "[t]he connection of an occupant to [a] home" alone "justifies a detention of that occupant." 452 U.S., at 703–704, 101 S. Ct. 2587.

greater when there are passengers in addition to the driver in the stopped car'').

Mena argues that, even if the use of handcuffs to detain her in the garage was reasonable as an initial matter, the duration of the use of handcuffs made the detention unreasonable. The duration of a detention can, of course, affect the balance of interests under *Graham*. However, the 2–to 3–hour detention in handcuffs in this case does not outweigh the government's continuing safety interests. As we have noted, this case involved the detention of four detainees by two officers during a search of a gang house for dangerous weapons. We conclude that the detention of Mena in handcuffs during the search was reasonable.

The Court of Appeals also determined that the officers violated Mena's Fourth Amendment rights by questioning her about her immigration status during the detention. 332 F.3d, at 1264–1266. This holding, it appears, was premised on the assumption that the officers were required to have independent reasonable suspicion in order to question Mena concerning her immigration status because the questioning constituted a discrete Fourth Amendment event. But the premise is faulty. We have "held repeatedly that mere police questioning does not constitute a seizure." *Florida* v. *Bostick,* 501 U.S. 429, 434, 111 S. Ct. 2382 (1991); see also *INS* v. *Delgado,* 466 U.S. 210, 212, 104 S. Ct. 1758 (1984). "[E]ven when officers have no basis for suspecting a particular individual, they may generally ask questions of that individual; ask to examine the individual's identification; and request consent to search his or her luggage." *Bostick, supra,* at 434–435, 111 S. Ct. 2382 (citations omitted). As the Court of Appeals did not hold that the detention was prolonged by the questioning, there was no additional seizure within the meaning of the Fourth Amendment. Hence, the officers did not need reasonable suspicion to ask Mena for her name, date and place of birth, or immigration status.

Our recent opinion in *Illinois* v. *Caballes,* 543 U.S. ___, 125 S. Ct. 834 (2005), is instructive. There, we held that a dog sniff performed during a traffic stop does not violate the Fourth Amendment. We noted that a lawful seizure "can become unlawful if it is prolonged beyond the time reasonably required to complete that mission," but accepted the state court's determination that the duration of the stop was not extended by the dog sniff. *Id.,* at ___, 125 S. Ct., at 837. Because we held that a dog sniff was not a search subject to the Fourth Amendment, we rejected the notion that "the shift in purpose" "from a lawful traffic stop into a drug investigation" was unlawful because it "was not supported by any reasonable suspicion." *Id.,* at ___, 125 S. Ct., at 837. Likewise here, the initial *Summers* detention was lawful; the Court of Appeals did not find that the questioning extended the time Mena was detained. Thus no additional Fourth Amendment justification for inquiring about Mena's immigration status was required. [3]

---

3. The Court of Appeals' reliance on *United States* v. *Brignoni-Ponce,* 422 U.S. 873, 95 S. Ct. 2574 (1975), is misplaced. *Brignoni-Ponce* held that stops by roving patrols near the border "may be justified on facts that do not amount to the probable cause require[ment] for an arrest." *Id.,* at 880, 95 S. Ct. 2574. We considered only whether the patrols had the "authority to *stop* automobiles in areas near the Mexican border," *id.,* at 874, 95 S. Ct. 2574 (emphasis added), and expressed no opinion as to the appropriate-

In summary, the officers' detention of Mena in handcuffs during the execution of the search warrant was reasonable and did not violate the Fourth Amendment. Additionally, the officers' questioning of Mena did not constitute an independent Fourth Amendment violation. Mena has advanced in this Court, as she did before the Court of Appeals, an alternative argument for affirming the judgment below. She asserts that her detention extended beyond the time the police completed the tasks incident to the search. Because the Court of Appeals did not address this contention, we too decline to address it. See *Pierce County* v. *Guillen,* 537 U.S. 129, 148, n. 10, 154 L. Ed. 2d 610, 123 S. Ct. 720 (2003); *NCAA* v. *Smith,* 525 U.S. 459, 469–470, 142 L. Ed. 2d 929, 119 S. Ct. 924 (1999).

The judgment of the Court of Appeals is therefore vacated, and the case is remanded for further proceedings consistent with this opinion.

It is so ordered.

■ CONCUR: JUSTICE KENNEDY, concurring.

I concur in the judgment and in the opinion of the Court. It does seem important to add this brief statement to help ensure that police handcuffing during searches becomes neither routine nor unduly prolonged.

The safety of the officers and the efficacy of the search are matters of first concern, but so too is it a matter of first concern that excessive force is not used on the persons detained, especially when these persons, though lawfully detained under *Michigan* v. *Summers,* 452 U.S. 692, 101 S. Ct. 2587 (1981), are not themselves suspected of any involvement in criminal activity. The use of handcuffs is the use of force, and such force must be objectively reasonable under the circumstances, *Graham* v. *Connor,* 490 U.S. 386, 109 S. Ct. 1865 (1989).

The reasonableness calculation under *Graham* is in part a function of the expected and actual duration of the search. If the search extends to the point when the handcuffs can cause real pain or serious discomfort, provision must be made to alter the conditions of detention at least long enough to attend to the needs of the detainee. This is so even if there is no question that the initial handcuffing was objectively reasonable. The restraint should also be removed if, at any point during the search, it would be readily apparent to any objectively reasonable officer that removing the handcuffs would not compromise the officers' safety or risk interference or substantial delay in the execution of the search. The time spent in the search here, some two to three hours, certainly approaches, and may well exceed, the time beyond which a detainee's Fourth Amendment interests require revisiting the necessity of handcuffing in order to ensure the restraint, even if permissible as an initial matter, has not become excessive.

That said, under these circumstances I do not think handcuffing the detainees for the duration of the search was objectively unreasonable. As I understand the record, during much of this search 2 armed officers were available to watch over the 4 unarmed detainees, while the other 16 officers

ness of questioning when an individual was already seized. See *United States* v. *Martinez-Fuerte,* 428 U.S. 543, 556–562, 96 S. Ct. 3074 (1976). We certainly did not, as the Court of Appeals suggested, create a "requirement of particularized reasonable suspicion for purposes of inquiry into citizenship status." 332 F.3d, at 1267.

on the scene conducted an extensive search of a suspected gang safe house. Even if we accept as true—as we must—the factual assertions that these detainees posed no readily apparent danger and that keeping them handcuffed deviated from standard police procedure, it does not follow that the handcuffs were unreasonable. Where the detainees outnumber those supervising them, and this situation could not be remedied without diverting officers from an extensive, complex, and time-consuming search, the continued use of handcuffs after the initial sweep may be justified, subject to adjustments or temporary release under supervision to avoid pain or excessive physical discomfort. Because on this record it does not appear the restraints were excessive, I join the opinion of the Court.

■ JUSTICE STEVENS, with whom JUSTICE SOUTER, JUSTICE GINSBURG, and JUSTICE BREYER join, concurring in the judgment.

The jury in this case found that the two petitioners violated Iris Mena's Fourth Amendment right to be free from unreasonable seizure by detaining her with greater force and for a longer period of time than was reasonable under the circumstances.... the jury's award of punitive damages. The trial judge's thoughtful explanation of his reasons for denying the motion does not address either of the issues the Court discusses today....

In my judgment, however, the Court's discussion of the amount of force used to detain Iris pursuant to *Michigan* v. *Summers*, 452 U.S. 692, 101 S. Ct. 2587 (1981), is analytically unsound. Although the Court correctly purports to apply the "objective reasonableness" test announced in *Graham* v. *Connor*, 490 U.S. 386, 109 S. Ct. 1865 (1989), it misapplies that test. Given the facts of this case—and the presumption that a reviewing court must draw all reasonable inferences in favor of supporting the verdict—I think it clear that the jury could properly have found that this 5–foot–2–inch young lady posed no threat to the officers at the scene, and that they used excessive force in keeping her in handcuffs for up to three hours. Although *Summers* authorizes the detention of any individual who is present when a valid search warrant is being executed, that case does not give officers *carte blanche* to keep individuals who pose no threat in handcuffs throughout a search, no matter how long it may last. On remand, I would therefore instruct the Court of Appeals to consider whether the evidence supports Mena's contention that the petitioners used excessive force in detaining her when it considers the length of the *Summers* detention.

I

As the Court notes, the warrant in this case authorized the police to enter the Mena home to search for a gun belonging to Raymond Romero that may have been used in a gang-related driveby shooting. Romero, a known member of the West Side Locos gang, rented a room from the Mena family. The house, described as a " 'poor house,' " was home to several unrelated individuals who rented from the Menas. Brief for Petitioners 4. Each resident had his or her own bedroom, which could be locked with a padlock on the outside, and each had access to the living room and kitchen. In addition, several individuals lived in trailers in the back yard and also had access to the common spaces in the Mena home. *Id.*, at 5.

In addition to Romero, police had reason to believe that at least one other West Side Locos gang member had lived at the residence, although Romero's brother told police that the individual had returned to Mexico. The officers in charge of the search, petitioners Muehler and Brill, had been at the same residence a few months earlier on an unrelated domestic violence call, but did not see any other individuals they believed to be gang members inside the home on that occasion.

In light of the fact that the police believed that Romero possessed a gun and that there might be other gang members at the residence, petitioner Muehler decided to use a Special Weapons and Tactics (SWAT) team to execute the warrant. As described in the majority opinion, eight members of the SWAT team forcefully entered the home at 7 a.m. In fact, Iris Mena was the only occupant of the house and she was asleep in her bedroom. The police woke her up at gunpoint, and immediately handcuffed her. At the same time, officers served another search warrant at the home of Romero's mother, where Romero was known to stay several nights each week. In part because Romero's mother had previously cooperated with police officers, they did not use a SWAT team to serve that warrant. Romero was found at his mother's house; after being cited for possession of a small amount of marijuana, he was released.

Meanwhile, after the SWAT team secured the Mena residence and gave the "all clear," police officers transferred Iris and three other individuals (who had been in trailers in the back yard) to a converted garage.[4] To get to the garage, Iris, who was still in her bedclothes, was forced to walk barefoot through the pouring rain. The officers kept her and the other three individuals in the garage for up to three hours while they searched the home. Although she requested them to remove the handcuffs, they refused to do so. For the duration of the search, two officers guarded Iris and the other three detainees. A .22 caliber handgun, ammunition, and gang-related paraphernalia were found in Romero's bedroom, and other gang-related paraphernalia was found in the living room. Officers found nothing of significance in Iris' bedroom.[5] *Id.,* at 6–9.

II

In analyzing the quantum of force used to effectuate the *Summers* detention, the Court rightly employs the "objective reasonableness" test of *Graham.* Under *Graham,* the trier of fact must balance " 'the nature and quality of the intrusion on the individual's Fourth Amendment interests' against the countervailing governmental interests at stake." 490 U.S., at

---

4. The other individuals were a 55-year-old Latina female, a 40-year-old Latino male who was removed from the scene by the Immigration and Naturalization Service (INS), and a white male who appears to be in his early 30's and who was cited for possession of a small amount of marijuana.

5. One of the justifications for our decision in *Michigan v. Summers,* 452 U.S. 692, 101 S. Ct. 2587 (1981), was the fact that the occupants may be willing to "open locked doors or locked containers to avoid the use of force that is not only damaging to property but may also delay the completion of the task at hand." *Id.,* at 703, 101 S. Ct. 2587. Iris, however, was never asked to assist the officers, although she testified that she was willing to do so. See 3 Tr. 42 (June 14, 2001). Instead, officers broke the locks on several cabinets and dressers to which Iris possessed the keys.

396, 109 S. Ct. 1865. The District Court correctly instructed the jury to take into consideration such factors as " 'the severity of the suspected crime, whether the person being detained is the subject of the investigation, whether such person poses an immediate threat to the security of the police or others or to the ability of the police to conduct the search, and whether such person is actively resisting arrest or attempting to flee.' " The District Court also correctly instructed the jury to consider whether the detention was prolonged and whether Iris was detained in handcuffs after the search had ended. Many of these factors are taken from *Graham* itself, and the jury instruction reflects an entirely reasonable construction of the objective reasonableness test in the *Summers* context.

Considering those factors, it is clear that the SWAT team's initial actions were reasonable. When officers undertake a dangerous assignment to execute a warrant to search property that is presumably occupied by violence-prone gang members, it may well be appropriate to use both overwhelming force and surprise in order to secure the premises as promptly as possible. In this case the decision to use a SWAT team of eight heavily armed officers and to execute the warrant at 7 a.m. gave the officers maximum protection against the anticipated risk. As it turned out, there was only one person in the house—Iris Mena–and she was sound asleep. Nevertheless, "[t]he 'reasonableness' of a particular use of force must be judged from the perspective of a reasonable officer on the scene, rather than with the 20/20 vision of hindsight." *Graham,* 490 U.S., at 396, 109 S. Ct. 1865. At the time they first encountered Iris, the officers had no way of knowing her relation to Romero, whether she was affiliated with the West Side Locos, or whether she had any weapons on her person. Further, the officers needed to use overwhelming force to immediately take command of the situation; by handcuffing Iris they could more quickly secure her room and join the other officers. It would be unreasonable to expect officers, who are entering what they believe to be a high risk situation, to spend the time necessary to determine whether Iris was a threat before they handcuffed her. To the extent that the Court of Appeals relied on the initial actions of the SWAT team to find that there was sufficient evidence to support the jury's verdict, it was in error.

Whether the well-founded fears that justified the extraordinary entry into the house should also justify a prolonged interruption of the morning routine of a presumptively innocent person, however, is a separate question and one that depends on the specific facts of the case. This is true with respect both to how the handcuffs were used, and to the totality of the circumstances surrounding the detention, including whether Mena was detained in handcuffs after the search had concluded. With regard to the handcuffs, police may use them in different ways. [6]Here, the cuffs kept Iris' arms behind her for two to three hours. She testified that they were " 'real uncomfortable' " and that she had asked the officers to remove them, but

---

6. For instance, a suspect may be handcuffed to a fixed object, to a custodian, or her hands may simply be linked to one another. The cuffs may join the wrists either in the front or the back of the torso. They can be so tight that they are painful, particularly when applied for prolonged periods. While they restrict movement, they do not necessarily preclude flight if the prisoner is not kept under constant surveillance.

that they had refused. App. 105. Moreover, she was continuously guarded by two police officers who obviously made flight virtually impossible even if the cuffs had been removed.

A jury could reasonably have found a number of facts supporting a conclusion that the prolonged handcuffing was unreasonable. No contraband was found in Iris' room or on her person. There were no indications suggesting she was or ever had been a gang member, which was consistent with the fact that during the police officers' last visit to the home, no gang members were present. She fully cooperated with the officers and the INS agent, answering all their questions. She was unarmed, and given her small size, was clearly no match for either of the two armed officers who were guarding her. In sum, there was no evidence that Mena posed any threat to the officers or anyone else.

The justifications offered by the officers are not persuasive. They have argued that at least six armed officers were required to guard the four detainees, even though all of them had been searched for weapons. Since there were 18 officers at the scene, and since at least 1 officer who at one point guarded Mena and the other three residents was sent home after offering to assist in the search, it seems unlikely that lack of resources was really a problem. While a court should not ordinarily question the allocation of police officers or resources, a jury could have reasonably found that this is a case where ample resources were available.

The Court suggests that officers are under "no duty to divert resources from the search to make a predictive judgment about whether a particular occupant can be freed from handcuffs." In reality, the officers *did* make such an inquiry when they filled out the field identification cards, the use of which is standard police practice and takes less than five minutes. Further, the armed officers who guarded Iris had, of course, already been diverted from other search activities. It is therefore difficult to see what additional resources would have been required to determine that she posed no threat to the officers that would justify handcuffing her for two to three hours.

The jury may also have been skeptical of testimony that the officers in fact feared for their safety given that the actual suspect of the shooting had been found at the other location and promptly released. Additionally, while the officers testified that as a general matter they would not release an individual from handcuffs while searching a residence, the SWAT team's tactical plan for this particular search arguably called for them to do just that, since it directed that "[a]ny subjects encountered will be handcuffed and detained until they can be patted down, their location noted, [field identified], and released by Office Muehler or Officer R. Brill." 2 Record 53. The tactical plan suggests that they can, and often do, release individuals who are not related to the search. The SWAT team leader testified that handcuffs are not always required when executing a search.

In short, under the factors listed in *Graham* and those validly presented to the jury in the jury instructions, a jury could have reasonably found from the evidence that there was no apparent need to handcuff Iris for the entire duration of the search and that she was detained for an unreasonably prolonged period. She posed no threat whatsoever to the officers at the scene. She was not suspected of any crime and was not a person targeted by the search warrant. She had no reason to flee the scene and gave no indication that she desired to do so. Viewing the facts in the light most favorable to the jury's verdict, as we are required to do, there is certainly no obvious factual basis for rejecting the jury's verdict that the officers acted unreasonably, and no obvious basis for rejecting the conclusion that, on these facts, the quantum of force used was unreasonable as a matter of law.

III

Police officers' legitimate concern for their own safety is always a factor that should weigh heavily in balancing the relevant *Graham* factors. But, as Officer Brill admitted at trial, if that justification were always sufficient, it would authorize the handcuffing of every occupant of the premises for the duration of every *Summers* detention. Nothing in either the *Summers* or the *Graham* opinion provides any support for such a result. Rather, the decision of what force to use must be made on a case-by-case basis. There is evidence in this record that may well support the conclusion that it was unreasonable to handcuff Iris Mena throughout the search. On remand, therefore, I would instruct the Ninth Circuit to consider that evidence, as well as the possibility that Iris was detained after the search was completed, when deciding whether the evidence in the record is sufficient to support the jury's verdict.

E.   The Law of Arrest and of Search Incident to Arrest

Page 444. Add in new paragraph at end of quote from New York v. Belton, 453 U.S. 454, 101 S.Ct. 2860 (1981) in section on *Special Rules for Searches Beyond the Person of Motor Vehicle Driver or Passenger Arrestees*:

The United States Supreme Court has further expanded the search incident to arrest exception when vehicles are involved:

Thornton v. United States

United States Supreme Court.
540 U.S. 1102, 124 S.Ct. 1129 (2004).

■ JUDGES: REHNQUIST, C. J., delivered the opinion of the Court except as to footnote 4. KENNEDY, THOMAS, and BREYER, JJ., joined that opinion in full, and O'CONNOR, J., joined as to all but footnote 4. O'CONNOR, J., filed an opinion concurring in part. SCALIA, J., filed an opinion concurring in the judgment, in which GINSBURG, J., joined. STEVENS, J., filed a dissenting opinion, in which SOUTER, J., joined.

■ OPINION: CHIEF JUSTICE REHNQUIST delivered the opinion of the Court except as to footnote 4.

In *New York* v. *Belton,* 453 U.S. 454, 101 S. Ct. 2860 (1981), we held that when a police officer has made a lawful custodial arrest of an occupant of an automobile, the Fourth Amendment allows the officer to search the passenger compartment of that vehicle as a contemporaneous incident of arrest. We have granted certiorari twice before to determine whether *Belton*'s rule is limited to situations where the officer makes contact with the occupant while the occupant is inside the vehicle, or whether it applies as well when the officer first makes contact with the arrestee after the latter has stepped out of his vehicle. We did not reach the merits in either of those two cases. *Arizona v. Gant*, 540 U.S. 963, 124 S. Ct. 461 (2003) (vacating and remanding for reconsideration in light of *State v. Dean*, 206 Ariz. 158, 76 P. 3d 429 (2003)); *Florida* v. *Thomas*, 532 U.S. 774, 121 S. Ct. 1905 (2001) (dismissing for lack of jurisdiction). We now reach that question and conclude that *Belton* governs even when an officer does not make contact until the person arrested has left the vehicle.

Officer Deion Nichols of the Norfolk, Virginia, Police Department, who was in uniform but driving an unmarked police car, first noticed petitioner Marcus Thornton when petitioner slowed down so as to avoid driving next to him. Nichols suspected that petitioner knew he was a police officer and for some reason did not want to pull next to him. His suspicions aroused, Nichols pulled off onto a side street and petitioner passed him. After petitioner passed him, Nichols ran a check on petitioner's license tags, which revealed that the tags had been issued to a 1982 Chevy two-door and not to a Lincoln Town Car, the model of car petitioner was driving. Before Nichols had an opportunity to pull him over, petitioner drove into a parking lot, parked, and got out of the vehicle. Nichols saw petitioner leave his vehicle as he pulled in behind him. He parked the patrol car, accosted petitioner, and asked him for his driver's license. He also told him that his license tags did not match the vehicle that he was driving.

Petitioner appeared nervous. He began rambling and licking his lips; he was sweating. Concerned for his safety, Nichols asked petitioner if he had any narcotics or weapons on him or in his vehicle. Petitioner said no. Nichols then asked petitioner if he could pat him down, to which petitioner agreed. Nichols felt a bulge in petitioner's left front pocket and again asked himif he had any illegal narcotics on him. This time petitioner stated that he did, and he reached into his pocket and pulled out two individual bags, one containing three bags of marijuana and the other containing a large amount of crack cocaine. Nichols handcuffed petitioner, informed him that he was under arrest, and placed him in the back seat of the patrol car. He then searched petitioner's vehicle and found a BryCo .9–millimeter hand-gun under the driver's seat.

A grand jury charged petitioner with possession with intent to distrib-ute cocaine base, 84 Stat. 1260, 21 U.S.C. § 841(a)(1), possession of a firearm after having been previously convicted of a crime punishable by a term of imprisonment exceeding one year, 18 U.S.C. § 922(g)(1), and possession of a firearm in furtherance of a drug trafficking crime, § 924(c)(1). Petitioner sought to suppress, *inter alia*, the firearm as the fruit of an unconstitutional search. After a hearing, the District Court denied petitioner's motion to suppress, holding that the automobile search was valid under *New York* v. *Belton, supra,* and alternatively that Nichols could have conducted an inventory search of the automobile. A jury convicted petitioner on all three counts; he was sentenced to 180 months' imprisonment and 8 years of supervised release.

Petitioner appealed, challenging only the District Court's denial of the suppression motion. He argued that *Belton* was limited to situations where the officer initiated contact with an arrestee while he was still an occupant of the car. The United States Court of Appeals for the Fourth Circuit affirmed. 325 F.3d 189 (2003). It held that "the historical rationales for the search incident to arrest doctrine—'the need to disarm the suspect in order to take him into custody' and 'the need to preserve evidence for later use at trial,' " *id.*, at 195 (quoting *Knowles* v. *Iowa,* 525 U.S. 113, 116, 119 S. Ct. 484 (1998)), did not require *Belton* to be limited solely to situations in which suspects were still in their vehicles when approached by the police. Noting that petitioner conceded that he was in "close proximity, both temporally and spatially," to his vehicle, the court concluded that the car was within petitioner's immediate control, and thus Nichols' search was reasonable under *Belton*.[1] 325 F.3d at 196. We granted certiorari, 540 U.S. 963, 124 S. Ct. 461 (2003), and now affirm.

In *Belton*, an officer overtook a speeding vehicle on the New York Thruway and ordered its driver to pull over (cites omitted). Suspecting that the occupants possessed marijuana, the officer directed them to get out of the car and arrested them for unlawful possession. He searched them and then searched the passenger compartment of the car. We considered the constitutionally permissible scope of a search in these circumstances and sought to lay down a workable rule governing that situation.

We first referred to *Chimel* v. *California,* 395 U.S. 752, 89 S. Ct. 2034 (1969), a case where the arrestee was arrested in his home, and we had described the scope of a search incident to a lawful arrest as the person of the arrestee and the area immediately surrounding him (cites omitted) This rule was justified by the need to remove any weapon the arrestee might seek to use to resist arrest or to escape, and the need to prevent the concealment or destruction of evidence (cite omitted). Although easily stated, the *Chimel* principle had proved difficult to apply in specific cases. We pointed out that in *United States* v. *Robinson,* 414 U.S. 218, 94 S. Ct. 467 (1973), a case dealing with the scope of the search of the arrestee's person, we had rejected a suggestion that " 'there must be litigated in each case the issue of whether or not there was present one of the reasons supporting the authority' " to conduct such a search (cite omitted). Similarly, because "courts had found no workable definition of the 'area within the immediate control of the arrestee' when that area arguably included the interior of an automobile and the arrestee was its recent occupant," (cite omitted), we sought to set forth a clear rule for police officers and citizens alike. We therefore held that "when a policeman has made a lawful custodial arrest of the occupant of an automobile, he may, as a contemporaneous incident of that arrest, search the passenger compartment of that automobile." (footnotes omitted).

---

1. The Court of Appeals did not reach the District Court's alternative holding that Nichols could have conducted a lawful inventory search. 325 F.3d at 196.

In so holding, we placed no reliance on the fact that the officer in *Belton* ordered the occupants out of the vehicle, or initiated contact with them while they remained within it. Nor do we find such a factor persuasive in distinguishing the current situation, as it bears no logical relationship to *Belton*'s rationale. There is simply no basis to conclude that the span of the area generally within the arrestee's immediate control is determined by whether the arrestee exited the vehicle at the officer's direction, or whether the officer initiated contact with him while he remained in the car. We recognized as much, albeit in dicta, in *Michigan* v. *Long,* (cite omitted), where officers observed a speeding car swerve into a ditch. The driver exited and the officers met him at the rear of his car. Although there was no indication that the officers initiated contact with the driver while he was still in the vehicle, we observed that "it is clear . . . that if the officers had arrested [respondent] . . . they could have searched the passenger compartment under *New York* v. *Belton*." (cite omitted).

In all relevant aspects, the arrest of a suspect who is next to a vehicle presents identical concerns regarding officer safety and the destruction of evidence as the arrest of one who is inside the vehicle. An officer may search a suspect's vehicle under *Belton* only if the suspect is arrested (cite omitted). A custodial arrest is fluid and "the danger to the police officer flows from *the fact of the arrest*, and its attendant proximity, stress, and uncertainty," *Robinson, supra,*(cites omitted). (emphasis added). See *Washington* v. *Chrisman*, 455 U.S. 1, 7, 102 S. Ct. 812 (1982) ("Every arrest must be presumed to present a risk of danger to the arresting officer"). The stress is no less merely because the arrestee exited his car before the officer initiated contact, nor is an arrestee less likely to attempt to lunge for a weapon or to destroy evidence if he is outside of, but still in control of, the vehicle. In either case, the officer faces a highly volatile situation. It would make little sense to apply two different rules to what is, at bottom, the same situation.

In some circumstances it may be safer and more effective for officers to conceal their presence from a suspect until he has left his vehicle. Certainly that is a judgment officers should be free to make. But under the strictures of petitioner's proposed "contact initiation" rule, officers who do so would be unable to search the car's passenger compartment in the event of a custodial arrest, potentially compromising their safety and placing incriminating evidence at risk of concealment or destruction. The Fourth Amendment does not require such a gamble.

Petitioner argues, however, that *Belton* will fail to provide a "brightline" rule if it applies to more than vehicle "occupants." Brief for Petitioner 29–34. But *Belton* allows police to search the passenger compartment of a vehicle incident to a lawful custodial arrest of both "occupants" and "recent occupants" (cite omitted). Indeed, the respondent in *Belton* was not inside the car at the time of the arrest and search; he was standing on the highway. In any event, while an arrestee's status as a "recent occupant" may turn on his temporal or spatial relationship to the car at the time of the arrest and search,[2] it certainly does not turn on whether he was inside

---

2. Petitioner argues that if we reject his proposed "contact initiation" rule, we should limit the scope of *Belton* to "recent distance" of the car. Brief for Petitioner 35–26. We

or outside the car at the moment that the officer first initiated contact with him.

To be sure, not all contraband in the passenger compartment is likely to be readily accessible to a "recent occupant." It is unlikely in this case that petitioner could have reached under the driver's seat for his gun once he was outside of his automobile. But the firearm and the passenger compartment in general were no more inaccessible than were the contraband and the passenger compartment in *Belton*. The need for a clear rule, readily understood by police officers and not depending on differing estimates of what items were or were not within reach of an arrestee at any particular moment, justifies the sort of generalization which *Belton* enunciated.[3]

Once an officer determines that there is probable cause to make an arrest, it is reasonable to allow officers to ensure their safety and to preserve evidence by searching the entire passenger compartment.

Rather than clarifying the constitutional limits of a *Belton* search, petitioner's "contact initiation" rule would obfuscate them. Under petitioner's proposed rule, an officer approaching a suspect who has just alighted from his vehicle would have to determine whether he actually confronted or signaled confrontation with the suspect while he remained in the car, or whether the suspect exited his vehicle unaware of, and for reasons unrelated to, the officer's presence. This determination would be inherently subjective and highly fact specific, and would require precisely the sort of ad hoc determinations on the part of officers in the field and reviewing courts that *Belton* sought to avoid. (cite omitted). Experience has shown that such a rule is impracticable, and we refuse to adopt it. So long as an arrestee is the sort of "recent occupant" of a vehicle such as petitioner was here, officers may search that vehicle incident to the arrest.[4]

decline to address petitioner's argument, however, as it is outside the question on which we granted certiorari, (cite omitted)....

3. Justice Stevens contends that *Belton*'s bright-line rule "is not needed for cases in which the arrestee is first accosted when he is a pedestrian, because *Chimel* [v. *California*, 395 U.S. 752, 89 S. Ct. 2034 (1969),] itself provides all the guidance that is necessary." (dissenting opinion). Under Justice Stevens' approach, however, even if the car itself was within the arrestee's reaching distance under *Chimel*, police officers and courts would still have to determine whether a particular object within the passenger compartment was also within an arrestee's reaching distance under *Chimel*. This is exactly the type of unworkable and fact-specific inquiry that *Belton* rejected by holding that the entire passenger compartment may be searched when "'the area within the immediate con-

trol of the arrestee' ... arguably includes the interior of an automobile and the arrestee is its recent occupant" (cite omitted).

4. Whatever the merits of Justice Scalia opinion concurring in the judgment, this is the wrong case in which to address them. Petitioner has never argued that *Belton* should be limited "to cases where it is reasonable to believe evidence relevant to the crime of arrest might be found in the vehicle," nor did any court below consider Justice Scalia's reasoning. See *Pennsylvania Dept. of Corrections* v. *Yeskey*, 524 U.S. 206, 212–213, 118 S. Ct. 1952 (1998) (" 'Where issues are neither raised before nor considered by the Court of Appeals, this Court will not ordinarily consider them' " (cite omitted).) The question presented—"whether the bright-line rule announced in *New York* v. *Belton* is confined to situations in which the police initiate contact with the occupant of a vehicle while that person is in the vehicle," Pet. for

The judgment of the Court of Appeals is affirmed.

It is so ordered.

■ CONCUR: Justice O'Connor, concurring in part

I join all but footnote 4 of the Court's opinion. Although the opinion is a logical extension of the holding of *New York* v. *Belton,* (cite omitted). I write separately to express my dissatisfaction with the state of the law in this area. As Justice Scalia forcefully argues, (opinion concurring in judgment), lower court decisions seem now to treat the ability to search a vehicle incident to the arrest of a recent occupant as a police entitlement rather than as an exception justified by the twin rationales of *Chimel* v. *California,* (cite omitted). That erosion is a direct consequence of *Belton's* shaky foundation. While the approach Justice Scalia proposes appears to be built on firmer ground, I am reluctant to adopt it in the context of a case in which neither the Government nor the petitioner has had a chance to speak to its merit.

■ Justice Scalia, with whom Justice Ginsburg joins, concurring in the judgment.

In *Chimel* v. *California,* (cite omitted), we held that a search incident to arrest was justified only as a means to find weapons the arrestee might use or evidence he might conceal or destroy. We accordingly limited such searches to the area within the suspect's " 'immediate control' "—*i.e.,* "the area into which an arrestee might reach in order to grab a weapon or evidentiary item" (cite omitted). In *New York* v. *Belton,*(cite omitted), we set forth a bright-line rule for arrests of automobile occupants, holding that, because the vehicle's entire passenger compartment is "in fact generally, even if not inevitably," within the arrestee's immediate control, a search of the whole compartment is justified in every case.

When petitioner's car was searched in this case, he was neither in, nor anywhere near, the passenger compartment of his vehicle. Rather, he was handcuffed and secured in the back of the officer's squad car. The risk that he would nevertheless "grab a weapon or evidentiary item" from his car was remote in the extreme. The Court's effort to apply our current doctrine to this search stretches it beyond its breaking point, and for that reason I cannot join the Court's opinion.

I

I see three reasons why the search in this case might have been justified to protect officer safety or prevent concealment or destruction of evidence. None ultimately persuades me.

The first is that, despite being handcuffed and secured in the back of a squad car, petitioner might have escaped and retrieved a weapon or

Cert.—does not fairly encompass Justice Scalia's analysis. See this Court's Rule 14.1(a) ("Only the questions set out in the petition, or fairly included therein, will be considered by the Court"). And the United States has never had an opportunity to respond to such an approach. See *Yee* v. *Escondido,* 503 U.S. 519, 536,112 S. Ct. 1522 (1992). Under these circumstances, it would be imprudent to overrule, for all intents and purposes, our established constitutional precedent, which governs police authority in a common occurrence such as automobile searches pursuant to arrest, and we decline to do so at this time.

evidence from his vehicle—a theory that calls to mind Judge Goldberg's reference to the mythical arrestee "possessed of the skill of Houdini and the strength of Hercules." *United States* v. *Frick*, 490 F.2d 666, 673 (CA5 1973) (opinion concurring in part and dissenting in part). The United States, endeavoring to ground this seemingly speculative fear in reality, points to a total of seven instances over the past 13 years in which state or federal officers were attacked with weapons by handcuffed or formerly handcuffed arrestees. (cite omitted). These instances do not, however, justify the search authority claimed. . . .

Of course, the Government need not document specific instances in order to justify measures that avoid obvious risks. But the risk here is far from obvious, and in a context as frequently recurring as roadside arrests, the Government's inability to come up with even a single example of a handcuffed arrestee's retrieval of arms or evidence from his vehicle undermines its claims. The risk that a suspect handcuffed in the back of a squad car might escape and recover a weapon from his vehicle is surely no greater than the risk that a suspect handcuffed in his residence might escape and recover a weapon from the next room—a danger we held insufficient to justify a search in *Chimel* (cite omitted).

The second defense of the search in this case is that, since the officer could have conducted the search at the time of arrest (when the suspect was still near the car), he should not be penalized for having taken the sensible precaution of securing the suspect in the squad car first. As one Court of Appeals put it: " 'It does not make sense to prescribe a constitutional test that is entirely at odds with safe and sensible police procedures' " (cites omitted). The weakness of this argument is that it assumes that, one way or another, the search must take place. But conducting a *Chimel* search is not the Government's right; it is an exception—justified by necessity—to a rule that would otherwise render the search unlawful. If "sensible police procedures" require that suspects be handcuffed and put in squad cars, then police should handcuff suspects, put them in squad cars, and not conduct the search. Indeed, if an officer leaves a suspect unrestrained nearby just to manufacture authority to search, one could argue that the search is unreasonable *precisely because* the dangerous conditions justifying it existed only by virtue of the officer's failure to follow sensible procedures.

The third defense of the search is that, even though the arrestee posed no risk here, *Belton* searches in general are reasonable, and the benefits of a bright-line rule justify upholding that small minority of searches that, on their particular facts, are not reasonable. The validity of this argument rests on the accuracy of *Belton*'s claim that the passenger compartment is "in fact generally, even if not inevitably," within the suspect's immediate control (cite omitted). By the United States' own admission, however, "the practice of restraining an arrestee on the scene before searching a car that he just occupied is so prevalent that holding that *Belton* does not apply in that setting would . . . 'largely render *Belton* a dead letter.' " (cites omitted). Reported cases involving this precise factual scenario—a motorist handcuffed and secured in the back of a squad car when the search takes place—are legion (cites omitted). Some courts uphold such searches even when the squad car carrying the handcuffed arrestee has already left the scene (cite omitted).

The popularity of the practice is not hard to fathom. If *Belton* entitles an officer to search a vehicle upon arresting the driver despite having taken measures that eliminate any danger, what rational officer would not take those measures? Cf. Moskovitz, A Rule in Search of a Reason: An Empirical Reexamination of *Chimel* and *Belton*, 2002 Wis. L. Rev. 657, 665–666 (citing police training materials). If it was ever true that the passenger compartment is "in fact generally, even if not inevitably," within the arrestee's immediate control at the time of the search, (cite omitted), it certainly is not true today. As one judge has put it: "In our search for clarity, we have now abandoned our constitutional moorings and floated to a place where the law approves of purely exploratory searches of vehicles during which officers with no definite objective or reason for the search are allowed to rummage around in a car to see what they might find." *McLaughlin* supra, at 894 (Trott, J., concurring). I agree entirely with that assessment.

II

If *Belton* searches are justifiable, it is not because the arrestee might grab a weapon or evidentiary item from his car, but simply because the car might contain evidence relevant to the crime for which he was arrested. This more general sort of evidence-gathering search is not without antecedent. For example, in *United States* v. *Rabinowitz,* 339 U.S. 56, 70 S. Ct. 430 (1950), we upheld a search of the suspect's place of business after he was arrested there. We did not restrict the officers' search authority to "the area into which [the] arrestee might reach in order to grab a weapon or evidentiary item," *Chimel*, (cite omitted), and we did not justify the search as a means to prevent concealment or destruction of evidence. Rather, we relied on a more general interest in gathering evidence relevant to the crime for which the suspect had been arrested (cite omitted).

Numerous earlier authorities support this approach, referring to the general interest in gathering evidence related to the crime of arrest with no mention of the more specific interest in preventing its concealment or destruction (cites omitted). . . . Only in the years leading up to *Chimel* did we start consistently referring to the narrower interest in frustrating concealment or destruction of evidence (cite omitted).

There is nothing irrational about broader police authority to search for evidence when and where the perpetrator of a crime is lawfully arrested. The fact of prior lawful arrest distinguishes the arrestee from society at large, and distinguishes a search for evidence of *his* crime from general rummaging. Moreover, it is not illogical to assume that evidence of a crime is most likely to be found where the suspect was apprehended.

Nevertheless, *Chimel*'s narrower focus on concealment or destruction of evidence also has historical support (cites omitted) . . .

In short, both *Rabinowitz* and *Chimel* are plausible accounts of what the Constitution requires, and neither is so persuasive as to justify departing from settled law. But if we are going to continue to allow *Belton* searches on *stare decisis* grounds, we should at least be honest about why we are doing so. *Belton* cannot reasonably be explained as a mere application of *Chimel*. Rather, it is a return to the broader sort of search incident to arrest that we allowed before *Chimel*—limited, of course, to searches of motor vehicles, a category of "effects" which give rise to a reduced expectation of privacy, see *Wyoming* v. *Houghton,* 526 U.S. 295, 303, 119 S. Ct. 1297 (1999), and heightened law enforcement needs, see 526 U.S. at 304, 119 S. Ct. 1297; *Rabinowitz*, 339 U.S., at 73, 70 S. Ct. 430 (Frankfurter, J., dissenting).

Recasting *Belton* in these terms would have at least one important practical consequence. In *United States* v. *Robinson,* (cite omitted), we held that authority to search an arrestee's person does not depend on the actual presence of one of *Chimel*'s two rationales in the particular case; rather, the fact of arrest alone justifies the search. That holding stands in contrast to *Rabinowitz*, where we did not treat the fact of arrest alone as sufficient, but upheld the search only after noting that it was "not general or exploratory for whatever might be turned up" but reflected a reasonable belief that evidence would be found (cites omitted) The two different rules make sense: When officer safety or imminent evidence concealment or destruction is at issue, officers should not have to make fine judgments in the heat of the moment. But in the context of a general evidence-gathering search, the state interests that might justify any overbreadth are far less compelling. A motorist may be arrested for a wide variety of offenses; in many cases, there is no reasonable basis to believe relevant evidence might be found in the car. See *Atwater* v. *Lago Vista,* (cite omitted). I would therefore limit *Belton* searches to cases where it is reasonable to believe evidence relevant to the crime of arrest might be found in the vehicle.

In this case, as in *Belton*, petitioner was lawfully arrested for a drug offense. It was reasonable for Officer Nichols to believe that further contraband or similar evidence relevant to the crime for which he had been arrested might be found in the vehicle from which he had just alighted and which was still within his vicinity at the time of arrest. I would affirm the decision below on that ground.

■ DISSENT: Justice Stevens, with whom Justice Souter joins, dissenting.

Prior to our decision in *New York* v. *Belton,* (cite omitted), there was a widespread conflict among both federal and state courts over the question "whether, in the course of a search incident to the lawful custodial arrest of the occupants of an automobile, police may search inside the automobile after the arrestees are no longer in it" (cite omitted). In answering that question, the Court expanded the authority of the police in two important respects. It allowed the police to conduct a broader search than our decision in *Chimel* v. *California,* (cite omitted), would have permitted, and it authorized them to open closed containers that might be found in the vehicle's passenger compartment.

The bright-line rule crafted in *Belton* is not needed for cases in which the arrestee is first accosted when he is a pedestrian, because *Chimel* itself provides all the guidance that is necessary. The only genuine justification for extending *Belton* to cover such circumstances is the interest in uncovering potentially valuable evidence. In my opinion, that goal must give way to the citizen's constitutionally protected interest in privacy when there is already in place a well-defined rule limiting the permissible scope of a search of an arrested pedestrian. The *Chimel* rule should provide the same protection to a "recent occupant" of a vehicle as to a recent occupant of a house.

Unwilling to confine the *Belton* rule to the narrow class of cases it was designed to address, the Court extends *Belton*'s reach without supplying any guidance for the future application of its swollen rule. We are told that officers may search a vehicle incident to arrest "so long as [the] arrestee is the sort of 'recent occupant' of a vehicle such as petitioner was here" (cite omitted). But we are not told how recent is recent, or how close is close, perhaps because in this case "the record is not clear" (cite omitted). As the Court cautioned in *Belton* itself, "when a person cannot know how a court will apply a settled principle to a recurring factual situation, that person cannot know the scope of his constitutional protection, nor can a policeman know the scope of his authority" (cite omitted). Without some limiting principle, I fear that today's decision will contribute to "a massive broadening of the automobile exception," *Robbins*, 453 U.S., at 452, 101 S. Ct. 2841 (Stevens, J., dissenting), when officers have probable cause to arrest an individual but not to search his car.

Accordingly, I respectfully dissent.

G.   EXIGENT CIRCUMSTANCES, HOT PURSUIT, AND EMERGENCY SEARCHES

Page 469. Add as note 1 after the *Patrick* case and renumber the following notes accordingly:

1.   In *United States v. McGough*, 412 F.3d 1232 (11th Cir. 2005), police responded to a 911 call placed accidentally by a five year old left in an apartment alone–she dialed 911 then hung up quickly. The police began to forcibly enter through burglar bars and a heavy door to remove the child for her own protection. Her father arrived and opened the door for them. The police arrested the father on a charge related to leaving the child unattended. The police placed the father and child into a police car. Noticing the child was barefoot, one officer returned to the apartment to get her shoes. While doing so, he observed a bag of marijuana and a revolver. The officer used this information to get a warrant to search the apartment.

At the hearing on the motion to suppress, the prosecution argued that the warrantless entries that preceded the warrant were justified under the community caretaking function.

The Eleventh Circuit rejected this argument, noting that even if there is a community caretaking function, there was insufficient urgency to enter to get shoes. Thus, the community caretaking function was not applicable.

H.   MOTOR VEHICLE SEARCHES

Page 476. Add to note (2)(c):

Note that many states have laws that create a presumption that if contraband is found within a car, all the occupants are presumed to possess the contraband unless there is other evidence to the contrary. See e.g. *Maryland v. Pringle*, 540 U.S. 366, 124 S.Ct. 795 (2003). Thus there may be some overlap between a motor vehicle search and a search incident to the arrest of an occupant within a vehicle.

K.   STOP-AND-FRISK AND OTHER LIMITED INVESTIGATIVE DETENTIONS

Page 512. Add at end of note 2:

In *Florida v. J.L.*, 529 U.S. 266, 120 S.Ct. 1375 (2000) the police frisked a defendant after receiving an anonymous tip that a young black male standing at a particular bus stop and wearing a plaid shirt was carrying a gun. They saw no firearm or unusual movements prior to their action. The Court held that this was insufficient to justify the frisk and thus the gun that was recovered from the defendant's pocket was the fruit of an illegal stop and frisk. The Court refrained from converting *Terry* into a "firearms exception" to the Fourth Amendment.

Page 516. Add after note 4:

Illinois v. Caballes

United States Supreme Court.
543 U.S. ___, 125 S.Ct. 834 (2005).

■ JUSTICE STEVENS delivered the opinion of the Court.

Illinois State Trooper Daniel Gillette stopped respondent for speeding on an interstate highway. When Gillette radioed the police dispatcher to report the stop, a second trooper, Craig Graham, a member of the Illinois State Police Drug Interdiction Team, overheard the transmission and immediately headed for the scene with his narcotics-detection dog. When they arrived, respondent's car was on the shoulder of the road and respondent was in Gillette's vehicle. While Gillette was in the process of writing a warning ticket, Graham walked his dog around respondent's car. The dog alerted at the trunk. Based on that alert, the officers searched the trunk, found marijuana, and arrested respondent. The entire incident lasted less than 10 minutes.

Respondent was convicted of a narcotics offense and sentenced to 12 years' imprisonment and a $256,136 fine. The trial judge denied his motion to suppress the seized evidence and to quash his arrest. He held that the officers had not unnecessarily prolonged the stop and that the dog alert was sufficiently reliable to provide probable cause to conduct the search. Although the Appellate Court affirmed, the Illinois Supreme Court reversed, concluding that because the canine sniff was performed without any " 'specific and articulable facts' " to suggest drug activity, the use of the dog "unjustifiably enlarg[ed] the scope of a routine traffic stop into a drug investigation."

The question on which we granted certiorari is narrow: "Whether the Fourth Amendment requires reasonable, articulable suspicion to justify using a drug-detection dog to sniff a vehicle during a legitimate traffic stop." Pet. for Cert. I. Thus, we proceed on the assumption that the officer conducting the dog sniff had no information about respondent except that he had been stopped for speeding; accordingly, we have omitted any reference to facts about respondent that might have triggered a modicum of suspicion.

Here, the initial seizure of respondent when he was stopped on the highway was based on probable cause, and was concededly lawful. It is nevertheless clear that a seizure that is lawful at its inception can violate the Fourth Amendment if its manner of execution unreasonably infringes interests protected by the Constitution. *United States* v. Jacobsen, 466 U.S. 109 (1984) (1984). A seizure that is justified solely by the interest in issuing a warning ticket to the driver can become unlawful if it is prolonged beyond the time reasonably required to complete that mission. In an earlier case involving a dog sniff that occurred during an unreasonably prolonged traffic stop, the Illinois Supreme Court held that use of the dog and the subsequent discovery of contraband were the product of an unconstitutional seizure. *People* v. *Cox*, 782 N.E.2d 275,(2002). We may assume that a similar result would be warranted in this case if the dog sniff had been conducted while respondent was being unlawfully detained.

In the state-court proceedings, however, the judges carefully reviewed the details of Officer Gillette's conversations with respondent and the precise timing of his radio transmissions to the dispatcher to determine whether he had improperly extended the duration of the stop to enable the dog sniff to occur. We have not recounted those details because we accept the state court's conclusion that the duration of the stop in this case was entirely justified by the traffic offense and the ordinary inquiries incident to such a stop.

Despite this conclusion, the Illinois Supreme Court held that the initially lawful traffic stop became an unlawful seizure solely as a result of the canine sniff that occurred outside respondent's stopped car. That is, the court characterized the dog sniff as the cause rather than the consequence of a constitutional violation. In its view, the use of the dog converted the citizen-police encounter from a lawful traffic stop into a drug investigation, and because the shift in purpose was not supported by any reasonable suspicion that respondent possessed narcotics, it was unlawful. In our view, conducting a dog sniff would not change the character of a traffic stop that is lawful at its inception and otherwise executed in a reasonable manner, unless the dog sniff itself infringed respondent's constitutionally protected interest in privacy. Our cases hold that it did not.

Official conduct that does not "compromise any legitimate interest in privacy" is not a search subject to the Fourth Amendment. *Jacobsen,* 466 U.S., at 123. We have held that any interest in possessing contraband cannot be deemed "legitimate," and thus, governmental conduct that *only* reveals the possession of contraband "compromises no legitimate privacy interest." *Ibid.* This is because the expectation "that certain facts will not come to the attention of the authorities" is not the same as an interest in "privacy that society is prepared to consider reasonable." *Id.,* at 122 (punctuation omitted). In *United States* v. *Place,* 462 U.S. 696 (1983), we treated a canine sniff by a well-trained narcotics-detection dog as "*sui generis*" because it "discloses only the presence or absence of narcotics, a contraband item." *Id.,* at 707, see also *Indianapolis* v. *Edmond,* 531 U.S. 32, 40 (2000). Respondent likewise concedes that "drug sniffs are designed, and if properly conducted are generally likely, to reveal only the presence of contraband." Brief for Respondent 17. Although respondent argues that the error rates, particularly the existence of false positives, call into question the premise that drug-detection dogs alert only to contraband, the record contains no evidence or findings that support his argument. Moreover, respondent does not suggest that an erroneous alert, in and of itself, reveals any legitimate private information, and, in this case, the trial judge found that the dog sniff was sufficiently reliable to establish probable cause to conduct a full-blown search of the trunk.

Accordingly, the use of a well-trained narcotics-detection dog—one that "does not expose noncontraband items that otherwise would remain hidden from public view," *Place,* 462 U.S., at 707—during a lawful traffic stop, generally does not implicate legitimate privacy interests. In this case, the dog sniff was performed on the exterior of respondent's car while he was lawfully seized for a traffic violation. Any intrusion on respondent's privacy expectations does not rise to the level of a constitutionally cognizable infringement.

This conclusion is entirely consistent with our recent decision that the use of a thermal-imaging device to detect the growth of marijuana in a home constituted an unlawful search. *Kyllo* v. *United States,* 533 U.S. 27, (2001). Critical to that decision was the fact that the device was capable of detecting lawful activity—in that case, intimate details in a home, such as "at what hour each night the lady of the house takes her daily sauna and bath." *Id.,* at 38. The legitimate expectation that information about perfectly lawful activity will remain private is categorically distinguishable from respondent's hopes or expectations concerning the nondetection of contraband in the trunk of his car. "A dog sniff conducted during a concededly lawful traffic stop that reveals no information other than the location of a substance that no individual has any right to possess does not violate the Fourth Amendment."

The judgment of the Illinois Supreme Court is vacated, and the case is remanded for further proceedings not inconsistent with this opinion.

■ THE CHIEF JUSTICE took no part in the decision of this case.

■ DISSENT: JUSTICE SOUTER, dissenting.

I would hold that using the dog for the purposes of determining the presence of marijuana in the car's trunk was a search unauthorized as an incident of the speeding stop and unjustified on any other ground. I would accordingly affirm the judgment of the Supreme Court of Illinois, and I respectfully dissent.

In *United States* v. *Place,* 462 U.S. 696 (1983), we categorized the sniff of the narcotics-seeking dog as *"sui generis"* under the Fourth Amendment and held it was not a search. *Id.,* at 707 . The classification rests not only upon the limited nature of the intrusion, but on a further premise that experience has shown to be untenable, the assumption that trained sniffing dogs do not err. What we have learned about the fallibility of dogs in the years since *Place* was decided would itself be reason to call for reconsidering *Place*'s decision against treating the intentional use of a trained dog as a search. The portent of this very case, however, adds insistence to the call, for an uncritical adherence to *Place* would render the Fourth Amendment indifferent to suspicionless and indiscriminate sweeps of cars in parking garages and pedestrians on sidewalks; if a sniff is not preceded by a seizure subject to Fourth Amendment notice, it escapes Fourth Amendment review entirely unless it is treated as a search. We should not wait for these developments to occur before rethinking *Place*'s analysis, which invites such untoward consequences.[4]

At the heart both of *Place* and the Court's opinion today is the proposition that sniffs by a trained dog are *sui generis* because a reaction by the dog in going alert is a response to nothing but the presence of contraband.[5] See *ibid.* ("[T]he sniff discloses only the presence or absence of narcotics, a contraband item"); ante (assuming "that a canine sniff by a well-trained narcotics dog will only reveal 'the presence or absence of narcotics, a contraband item'" (quoting *Place, supra,* at 707)). Hence, the argument goes, because the sniff can only reveal the presence of items devoid of any legal use, the sniff "does not implicate legitimate privacy interests" and is not to be treated as a search. Ante.

The infallible dog, however, is a creature of legal fiction. Although the Supreme Court of Illinois did not get into the sniffing averages of drug dogs, their supposed infallibility is belied by judicial opinions describing well-trained animals sniffing and alerting with less than perfect accuracy, whether owing to errors by their handlers, the limitations of the dogs themselves, or even the pervasive contamination of currency by cocaine. See, *e.g.*, United States v. *Kennedy*, 131 F.3d 1371, 1378 (CA10 1997) (describing a dog that had a 71% accuracy rate); *United States* v. *Scarborough*, 128 F.3d 1373, 1378, n. 3 (CA10 1997) (describing a dog that erroneously alerted 4 times out of 19 while working for the postal service and 8% of the time over its entire career); *United States* v. *Limares*, 269 F.3d 794, 797 (CA7 2001) (accepting as reliable a dog that gave false positives between 7 and 38% of the time); *Laime* v. *State*, 347 Ark. 142, 159, 60 S. W. 3d 464, 476 (2001) (speaking of a dog that made between 10 and 50 errors); *United States* v. *$242,484.00*, 351 F.3d 499, 511 (CA11 2003) (noting that because as much as 80% of all currency in circulation contains drug residue, a dog alert "is of little value"), vacated on other grounds by rehearing en banc, 357 F.3d 1225 (CA11 2004); *United States* v. *Carr*, 25 F.3d 1194, 1214–1217 (CA3 1994) (Becker, J., concurring in part and dissenting in part) ("[A] substantial portion of United States currency ... is tainted with sufficient traces of controlled substances to cause a trained canine to alert to their presence"). Indeed, a study cited by Illinois in this case for the proposition that dog sniffs are "generally reliable"

4. I also join Justice Ginsburg's dissent, post. Without directly reexamining the soundness of the Court's analysis of government dog sniffs in *Place*, she demonstrates that investigation into a matter beyond the subject of the traffic stop here offends the rule in *Terry* v. *Ohio*, 392 U.S. 1 (1968), the analysis I, too, adopt.

5. Another proffered justification for *sui generis* status is that a dog sniff is a particularly nonintrusive procedure. *United States* v. *Place*, 462 U.S. 696, 707 (1983). I agree with Justice Ginsburg that the introduction of a dog to a traffic stop (let alone an encounter with someone walking down the street) can in fact be quite intrusive.

shows that dogs in artificial testing situations return false positives anywhere from 12.5 to 60% of the time, depending on the length of the search. See Reply Brief for Petitioner 13; K. Garner et al., Duty Cycle of the Detector Dog: A Baseline Study 12 (Apr. 2001) (prepared under Federal Aviation Administration grant by the Institute for Biological Detection Systems of Auburn University). In practical terms, the evidence is clear that the dog that alerts hundreds of times will be wrong dozens of times.

Once the dog's fallibility is recognized, however, that ends the justification claimed in *Place* for treating the sniff as *sui generis* under the Fourth Amendment: the sniff alert does not necessarily signal hidden contraband, and opening the container or enclosed space whose emanations the dog has sensed will not necessarily reveal contraband or any other evidence of crime. This is not, of course, to deny that a dog's reaction may provide reasonable suspicion, or probable cause, to search the container or enclosure; the Fourth Amendment does not demand certainty of success to justify a search for evidence or contraband. The point is simply that the sniff and alert cannot claim the certainty that *Place* assumed, both in treating the deliberate use of sniffing dogs as *sui generis* and then taking that characterization as a reason to say they are not searches subject to Fourth Amendment scrutiny. And when that aura of uniqueness disappears, there is no basis in *Place*'s reasoning, and no good reason otherwise, to ignore the actual function that dog sniffs perform. They are conducted to obtain information about the contents of private spaces beyond anything that human senses could perceive, even when conventionally enhanced. The information is not provided by independent third parties beyond the reach of constitutional limitations, but gathered by the government's own officers in order to justify searches of the traditional sort, which may or may not reveal evidence of crime but will disclose anything meant to be kept private in the area searched. Thus in practice the government's use of a trained narcotics dog functions as a limited search to reveal undisclosed facts about private enclosures, to be used to justify a further and complete search of the enclosed area. And given the fallibility of the dog, the sniff is the first step in a process that may disclose "intimate details" without revealing contraband, just as a thermal-imaging device might do, as described in *Kyllo* v. *United States,* 533 U.S. 27 (2001).[6]

It makes sense, then, to treat a sniff as the search that it amounts to in practice, and to rely on the body of our Fourth Amendment cases, including

---

6. *Kyllo* was concerned with whether a search occurred when the police used a thermal-imaging device on a house to detect heat emanations associated with high-powered marijuana-growing lamps. In concluding that using the device was a search, the Court stressed that the "Government [may not] us[e] a device . . . to explore details of the home that would previously have been unknowable without physical intrusion." 533 U.S., at 40. Any difference between the dwelling in *Kyllo* and the trunk of the car here may go to the issue of the reasonableness of the respective searches, but it has no bearing on the question of search or no search. Nor is it significant that *Kyllo*'s imaging device would disclose personal details immediately, whereas they would be revealed only in the further step of opening the enclosed space following the dog's alert reaction; in practical terms the same values protected by the Fourth Amendment are at stake in each case. The justifications required by the Fourth Amendment may or may not differ as between the two practices, but if constitutional scrutiny is in order for the imager, it is in order for the dog.

Kyllo, in deciding whether such a search is reasonable. As a general proposition, using a dog to sniff for drugs is subject to the rule that the object of enforcing criminal laws does not, without more, justify suspicionless Fourth Amendment intrusions. See *Indianapolis* v. *Edmond*, 531 U.S. 32, 41–42 (2000). Since the police claim to have had no particular suspicion that Caballes was violating any drug law,[7] this sniff search must stand or fall on its being ancillary to the traffic stop that led up to it. It is true that the police had probable cause to stop the car for an offense committed in the officer's presence, which Caballes concedes could have justified his arrest. See Brief for Respondent 31. There is no occasion to consider authority incident to arrest, however, see *Knowles* v. *Iowa,* 525 U.S. 113 (1998), for the police did nothing more than detain Caballes long enough to check his record and write a ticket. As a consequence, the reasonableness of the search must be assessed in relation to the actual delay the police chose to impose, and as Justice Ginsburg points out in her opinion, the Fourth Amendment consequences of stopping for a traffic citation are settled law.

In *Berkemer v. McCarty*, 468 U.S. 420, 439–440 (1984), followed in *Knowles, supra,* at 117, we held that the analogue of the common traffic stop was the limited detention for investigation authorized by *Terry* v. *Ohio,* 392 U.S. 1 (1968). While *Terry* authorized a restricted incidental search for weapons when reasonable suspicion warrants such a safety measure, the Court took care to keep a *Terry* stop from automatically becoming a foot in the door for all investigatory purposes; the permissible intrusion was bounded by the justification for the detention.[8] Although facts disclosed by enquiry within this limit might give grounds to go further, the government could not otherwise take advantage of a suspect's immobility to search for evidence unrelated to the reason for the detention. That has to be the rule unless *Terry* is going to become an open-sesame for general searches, and that rule requires holding that the police do not have reasonable grounds to conduct sniff searches for drugs simply because they have stopped someone to receive a ticket for a highway offense. Since the police had no indication of illegal activity beyond the speed of the car in this case, the sniff search should be held unreasonable under the Fourth Amendment and its fruits should be suppressed.

Nothing in the case relied upon by the Court, *United States v. Jacobsen*, 466 U.S. 109 (1984), unsettled the limit of reasonable enquiry adopted in *Terry*. In *Jacobsen*, the Court found that no Fourth Amendment search occurred when federal agents analyzed powder they had already lawfully obtained. The Court noted that because the test could only reveal whether the powder was cocaine, the owner had no legitimate privacy interest at stake. As already explained, however, the use of a sniffing dog in cases like

---

7. Despite the remarkable fact that the police pulled over a car for going 71 miles an hour on I–80, the State maintains that excessive speed was the only reason for the stop, and the case comes to us on that assumption.

8. Thus, in *Place* itself, the Government officials had independent grounds to suspect that the luggage in question contained contraband before they employed the dog sniff. 462 U.S., at 698 (describing how Place had acted suspiciously in line at the airport and had labeled his luggage with inconsistent and fictional addresses).

this is significantly different and properly treated as a search that does indeed implicate Fourth Amendment protection.

In *Jacobsen*, once the powder was analyzed, that was effectively the end of the matter: either the powder was cocaine, a fact the owner had no legitimate interest in concealing, or it was not cocaine, in which case the test revealed nothing about the powder or anything else that was not already legitimately obvious to the police. But in the case of the dog sniff, the dog does not smell the disclosed contraband; it smells a closed container. An affirmative reaction therefore does not identify a substance the police already legitimately possess, but informs the police instead merely of a reasonable chance of finding contraband they have yet to put their hands on. The police will then open the container and discover whatever lies within, be it marijuana or the owner's private papers. Thus, while *Jacobsen* could rely on the assumption that the enquiry in question would either show with certainty that a known substance was contraband or would reveal nothing more, both the certainty and the limit on disclosure that may follow are missing when the dog sniffs the car.[9]

The Court today does not go so far as to say explicitly that sniff searches by dogs trained to sense contraband always get a free pass under the Fourth Amendment, since it reserves judgment on the constitutional significance of sniffs assumed to be more intrusive than a dog's walk around a stopped car, *ante*. For this reason, I do not take the Court's reliance on *Jacobsen* as actually signaling recognition of a broad authority to conduct suspicionless sniffs for drugs in any parked car, about which Justice Ginsburg is rightly concerned, post, or on the person of any pedestrian minding his own business on a sidewalk. But the Court's stated reasoning provides no apparent stopping point short of such excesses. For the sake of providing a workable framework to analyze cases on facts like these, which are certain to come along, I would treat the dog sniff as the familiar search it is in fact, subject to scrutiny under the Fourth Amendment.[10]

---

9. It would also be error to claim that some variant of the plain-view doctrine excuses the lack of justification for the dog sniff in this case. When an officer observes an object left by its owner in plain view, no search occurs because the owner has exhibited "no intention to keep [the object] to himself." *Katz* v. *United States*, 389 U.S. 347, 361 (1967) (Harlan, J., concurring). In contrast, when an individual conceals his possessions from the world, he has grounds to expect some degree of privacy. While plain view may be enhanced somewhat by technology, see, e.g., *Dow Chemical Co.* v. *United States,* 476 U.S. 227, 90 L. Ed. 2d 226, 106 S. Ct. 1819 (1986) (allowing for aerial surveillance of an industrial complex), there are limits. As *Kyllo* v. *United States,* 533 U.S. 27, 33 (2001), explained in treating the thermal-imaging device as outside the plain-view doctrine, "[w]e have previously reserved judgment as to how much technological enhancement of ordinary perception" turns mere observation into a Fourth Amendment search. While *Kyllo* laid special emphasis on the heightened privacy expectations that surround the home, closed car trunks are accorded some level of privacy protection. See, *e.g.*, *New York* v. *Belton*, 453 U.S. 454, 460, n. 4 (1981) (holding that even a search incident to arrest in a vehicle does not itself permit a search of the trunk). As a result, if Fourth Amendment protections are to have meaning in the face of superhuman, yet fallible, techniques like the use of trained dogs, those techniques must be justified on the basis of their reasonableness, lest everything be deemed in plain view.

10. I should take care myself to reserve judgment about a possible case significantly unlike this one. All of us are concerned not to prejudge a claim of authority to detect explo-

■ JUSTICE GINSBURG, with whom JUSTICE SOUTER joins, dissenting.

Illinois State Police Trooper Daniel Gillette stopped Roy Caballes for driving 71 miles per hour in a zone with a posted speed limit of 65 miles per hour. Trooper Craig Graham of the Drug Interdiction Team heard on the radio that Trooper Gillette was making a traffic stop. Although Gillette requested no aid, Graham decided to come to the scene to conduct a dog sniff. Gillette informed Caballes that he was speeding and asked for the usual documents—driver's license, car registration, and proof of insurance. Caballes promptly provided the requested documents but refused to consent to a search of his vehicle. After calling his dispatcher to check on the validity of Caballes' license and for outstanding warrants, Gillette returned to his vehicle to write Caballes a warning ticket. Interrupted by a radio call on an unrelated matter, Gillette was still writing the ticket when Trooper Graham arrived with his drug-detection dog. Graham walked the dog around the car, the dog alerted at Caballes' trunk, and, after opening the trunk, the troopers found marijuana.

The Supreme Court of Illinois held that the drug evidence should have been suppressed. Adhering to its decision in *People* v. Cox, 782 N.E.2d 275 (2002), the court employed a two-part test taken from *Terry* v. *Ohio,* 392 U.S. 1 (1968), to determine the overall reasonableness of the stop. The court asked first "whether the officer's action was justified at its inception," and second "whether it was reasonably related in scope to the circumstances which justified the interference in the first place." *Ibid.* (Cites omitted). "[I]t is undisputed," the court observed, "that the traffic stop was properly initiated"; thus, the dispositive inquiry trained on the "second part of the *Terry* test," in which "[t]he State bears the burden of establishing that the conduct remained within the scope of the stop." 802 N. E. 2d, at 204.

The court concluded that the State failed to offer sufficient justification for the canine sniff: "The police did not detect the odor of marijuana in the car or note any other evidence suggesting the presence of illegal drugs." Lacking "specific and articulable facts" supporting the canine sniff, *ibid.* (quoting *Cox,* 782 N. E. 2d, at 281), the court ruled, "the police impermissibly broadened the scope of the traffic stop in this case into a drug investigation." 802 N. E. 2d, at 204.[11] I would affirm the Illinois Supreme

sives and dangerous chemical or biological weapons that might be carried by a terrorist who prompts no individualized suspicion. Suffice it to say here that what is a reasonable search depends in part on demonstrated risk. Unreasonable sniff searches for marijuana are not necessarily unreasonable sniff searches for destructive or deadly material if suicide bombs are a societal risk.

11. The Illinois Supreme Court held insufficient to support a canine sniff Gillette's observations that (1) Caballes said he was moving to Chicago, but his only visible belongings were two sport coats in the backseat; (2) the car smelled o The *Berkemer*

Court cautioned that by analogizing a traffic stop to a *Terry* stop, it did "not suggest that a traffic stop supported by probable cause may not exceed the bounds set by the Fourth Amendment on the scope of a *Terry* stop." 468 U.S., at 439, n. 29. This Court, however, looked to *Terry* earlier in deciding that an officer acted reasonably when he ordered a motorist stopped for driving with expired license tags to exit his car, *Pennsylvania* v. *Mimms,* 434 U.S. 106, 109–110, 54 L. Ed. 2d 331, 98 S. Ct. 330 (1977) *(per curiam),* and later reaffirmed the *Terry* analogy when evaluating a police officer's authority to search a vehicle during a routine traffic stop, *Knowles,* 525 U.S., at 117.

Court's judgment and hold that the drug sniff violated the Fourth Amendment.

In *Terry* v *Ohio*, the Court upheld the stop and subsequent frisk of an individual based on an officer's observation of suspicious behavior and his reasonable belief that the suspect was armed. See 392 U.S., at 27–28, In a *Terry*-type investigatory stop, "the officer's action [must be] justified at its inception, and . . . reasonably related in scope to the circumstances which justified the interference in the first place." *Id.*, at 20, 20 L. Ed. 2d 889, 88 S. Ct. 1868. In applying *Terry*, the Court has several times indicated that the limitation on "scope" is not confined to the duration of the seizure; it also encompasses the manner in which the seizure is conducted. See, *e.g.*, *Hiibel* v. Sixth Judicial Dist. Court, 542 U.S. 177, ___ (2004) (an officer's request that an individual identify himself "has an immediate relation to the purpose, rationale, and practical demands of a *Terry* stop"); *United States* v. *Hensley*, 469 U.S. 221, 235 (1985) (examining, under *Terry*, both "the length and intrusiveness of the stop and detention"); *Florida* v. *Royer*, 460 U.S. 491, 500 (1983) (plurality opinion) ("[A]n investigative detention must be temporary and last no longer than is necessary to effectuate the purpose of the stop [and] . . . the investigative methods employed should be the least intrusive means reasonably available to verify or dispel the officer's suspicion. . . .").

"A routine traffic stop," the Court has observed, "is a relatively brief encounter and 'is more analogous to a so-called *Terry* stop . . . than to a formal arrest.' " *Knowles* v. *Iowa,* 525 U.S. 113, 117 (1998). (quoting *Berkemer* v. *McCarty*, 468 U.S. 420, 439 (1984)); see also *ante* (Souter, J., dissenting) (The government may not "take advantage of a suspect's immobility to search for evidence unrelated to the reason for the detention.").[12] I would apply *Terry*'s reasonable-relation test, as the Illinois Supreme Court did, to determine whether the canine sniff impermissibly expanded the scope of the initially valid seizure of Caballes.

It is hardly dispositive that the dog sniff in this case may not have lengthened the duration of the stop. Cf. *ante* ("A seizure . . . can become unlawful if it is prolonged beyond the time reasonably required to complete [the initial] mission."). *Terry*, it merits repetition, instructs that any investigation must be "reasonably related in *scope* to the circumstances which justified the interference in the first place." 392 U.S., at 20, (emphasis added). The unwarranted and nonconsensual expansion of the seizure here from a routine traffic stop to a drug investigation broadened the scope of the investigation in a manner that, in my judgment, runs afoul of the Fourth Amendment.[13]

---

12.   The *Berkemer* Court cautioned that by analogizing a traffic stop to a *Terry* stop, it did "not suggest that a traffic stop supported by probable cause may not exceed the bounds set by the Fourth Amendment on the scope of a *Terry* stop." 468 U.S., at 439, n. 29. This Court, however, looked to *Terry* earlier in deciding that an officer acted reasonably when he ordered a motorist stopped for driving with expired license tags to exit his car,

Pennsylvania v. *Mimms,* 434 U.S. 106, 109–110, 54 L. Ed. 2d 331, 98 S. Ct. 330 (1977) *(per curiam),* and later reaffirmed the *Terry* analogy when evaluating a police officer's authority to search a vehicle during a routine traffic stop, *Knowles*, 525 U.S., at 117.

13.   The question whether a police officer inquiring about drugs without reasonable suspicion unconstitutionally broadens a traf-

In my view, the Court diminishes the Fourth Amendment's force by abandoning the second *Terry* inquiry (was the police action "reasonably related in scope to the circumstances [justifying] the [initial] interference"). 392 U.S., at 20. A drug-detection dog is an intimidating animal. Cf. *United States* v. *Williams,* 356 F.3d 1268, 1276 (CA10 2004) (McKay, J., dissenting) ("drug dogs are not lap dogs"). Injecting such an animal into a routine traffic stop changes the character of the encounter between the police and the motorist. The stop becomes broader, more adversarial, and (in at least some cases) longer. Caballes—who, as far as Troopers Gillette and Graham knew, was guilty solely of driving six miles per hour over the speed limit—was exposed to the embarrassment and intimidation of being investigated, on a public thoroughfare, for drugs. Even if the drug sniff is not characterized as a Fourth Amendment "search," cf. *Indianapolis* v. *Edmond,* 531 U.S. 32, 40 (2000); *United States* v. *Place,* 462 U.S. 696, 707 (1983), the sniff surely broadened the scope of the traffic-violation-related seizure.

The Court has never removed police action from Fourth Amendment control on the ground that the action is well calculated to apprehend the guilty. See, *e.g., United States* v. *Karo,* 468 U.S. 705, 717 (1984) (Fourth Amendment warrant requirement applies to police monitoring of a beeper in a house even if "the facts [justify] believing that a crime is being or will be committed and that monitoring the beeper wherever it goes is likely to produce evidence of criminal activity."); see also *Minnesota* v. *Carter,* 525 U.S. 83, 110 (1998) (Ginsburg, J., dissenting) ("Fourth Amendment protection, reserved for the innocent only, would have little force in regulating police behavior toward either the innocent or the guilty."). Under today's decision, every traffic stop could become an occasion to call in the dogs, to the distress and embarrassment of the law-abiding population.

The Illinois Supreme Court, it seems to me, correctly apprehended the danger in allowing the police to search for contraband despite the absence of cause to suspect its presence. Today's decision, in contrast, clears the way for suspicionless, dog-accompanied drug sweeps of parked cars along sidewalks and in parking lots ... Nor would motorists have constitutional grounds for complaint should police with dogs, stationed at long traffic lights, circle cars waiting for the red signal to turn green.

Today's decision also undermines this Court's situation-sensitive balancing of Fourth Amendment interests in other contexts. For example, in *Bond* v. *United States,* 529 U.S. 334, 338–339 (2000), the Court held that a bus passenger had an expectation of privacy in a bag placed in an overhead bin and that a police officer's physical manipulation of the bag constituted an illegal search. If canine drug sniffs are entirely exempt from Fourth Amendment inspection, a sniff could substitute for an officer's request to a bus passenger for permission to search his bag, with this significant difference: The passenger would not have the option to say "No."

---

fic investigation is not before the Court. Cf. *Florida* v. *Bostick,* 501 U.S. 429, 434 (1991) (police questioning of a bus passenger, who might have just said "No," did not constitute a seizure).

The dog sniff in this case, it bears emphasis, was for drug detection only. A dog sniff for explosives, involving security interests not presented here, would be an entirely different matter. Detector dogs are ordinarily trained not as all-purpose sniffers, but for discrete purposes. For example, they may be trained for narcotics detection or for explosives detection or for agricultural products detection. See, *e.g.,* U. S. Customs & Border Protection, Canine Enforcement Training Center, Training Program Course Descriptions, http://www.cbp.gov/xp/cgov/border_security/canines/training_program.xml (all Internet materials as visited Dec. 16, 2004, and available in the Clerk of Court's case file) (describing Customs training courses in narcotics detection); Transportation Security Administration, Canine and Explosives Program, http://www.tsa.gov/public/display? theme=32 (describing Transportation Security Administration's explosives detection canine program); U. S. Dept. of Agriculture, Animal and Plant Health Inspection Service, USDA's Detector Dogs: Protecting American Agriculture (Oct. 2001), available at http://www.aphis.usda.gov/oa/pubs/detdogs.pdf (describing USDA Beagle Brigade detector dogs trained to detect prohibited fruits, plants, and meat); see also Jennings, Origins and History of Security and Detector Dogs, in Canine Sports Medicine and Surgery 16, 18–19 (M. Bloomberg, J. Dee, & R. Taylor eds. 1998) (describing narcotics detector dogs used by Border Patrol and Customs, and bomb detector dogs used by the Federal Aviation Administration and the Secret Service, but noting the possibility in some circumstances of cross training dogs for multiple tasks); S. Chapman, Police Dogs in North America 64, 70–79 (1990) (describing narcotics-and explosives-detection dogs and noting the possibility of cross training). There is no indication in this case that the dog accompanying Trooper Graham was trained for anything other than drug detection. ("Trooper Graham arrived with his drug-detection dog...."); Brief for Petitioner 3 ("Trooper Graham arrived with a drug-detection dog....").

This Court has distinguished between the general interest in crime control and more immediate threats to public safety. In Michigan Dep't of State Police v. Sitz, 496 U.S. 444 (1990), this Court upheld the use of a sobriety traffic checkpoint. Balancing the State's interest in preventing drunk driving, the extent to which that could be accomplished through the checkpoint program, and the degree of intrusion the stops involved, the Court determined that the State's checkpoint program was consistent with the Fourth Amendment. *Id, at 455* . Ten years after *Sitz*, in *Indianapolis* v. *Edmond,* 531 U.S. 32, this Court held that a drug interdiction checkpoint violated the Fourth Amendment. Despite the illegal narcotics traffic that the Nation is struggling to stem, the Court explained, a "general interest in crime control" did not justify the stops. *Id.,* at 43–44. The Court distinguished the sobriety checkpoints in *Sitz* on the ground that those checkpoints were designed to eliminate an "immediate, vehicle-bound threat to life and limb." 531 U.S., at 43.

The use of bomb-detection dogs to check vehicles for explosives without doubt has a closer kinship to the sobriety checkpoints in *Sitz* than to the drug checkpoints in *Edmond.* As the Court observed in *Edmond:* "[T]he Fourth Amendment would almost certainly permit an appropriately tailored roadblock set up to thwart an imminent terrorist attack.... " 531

U.S., at 44. Even if the Court were to change course and characterize a dog sniff as an independent Fourth Amendment search, see *ante* (Souter, J., dissenting), the immediate, present danger of explosives would likely justify a bomb sniff under the special needs doctrine. See, e.g., *ante* (Souter, J., dissenting); *Griffin* v. *Wisconsin,* 483 U.S. 868, 873, 97 L. Ed. 2d 709, 107 S. Ct. 3164 (1987) (permitting exceptions to the warrant and probable-cause requirements for a search when "special needs, beyond the normal need for law enforcement," make those requirements impracticable (quoting *New Jersey* v. *T. L. O.,* 469 U.S. 325, 351 (1985) (Blackmun, J., concurring in judgment))).

For the reasons stated, I would hold that the police violated Caballes' Fourth Amendment rights when, without cause to suspect wrongdoing, they conducted a dog sniff of his vehicle. I would therefore affirm the judgment of the Illinois Supreme Court.

* * *

NOTE

Not every court agrees with the majority's reasoning in *Caballes*. Several state courts have relied on state constitutional grounds to reach an opposite result. See, e.g. *State v. Carter*, 697 N.W.2d 199 (Minn. 2005). ("Although we conclude that the dog sniff was not a "search" within the meaning of the Fourth Amendment to the United States Constitution, we hold that the dog sniff was a 'search' within the meaning of Article I, Section 10 of the Minnesota Constitution. Because the governmental interest in the use of drug-detection dogs to aid law enforcement is significant, we hold that a dog sniff is an unreasonable search unless police have at least reasonable, articulable suspicion of criminal activity before conducting it. And because the police did not have such suspicion here, and there was no probable cause to issue the warrant without the results of the dog sniff, we reverse appellant's conviction and grant a new trial.")

Page 522. Add after note E:

May police require that a suspect provide a name? Identification? A video of the events that form the basis of the case that follows is available on the defendant's website at http://papersplease.org/hiibel/index2.html.

Hiibel v. Sixth Judicial District Court of Nevada, Humboldt County, et. al.

United States Supreme Court.
542 U.S. 177, 124 S.Ct. 2451 (2004).

■ JUSTICE KENNEDY delivered the opinion of the Court.

The petitioner was arrested and convicted for refusing to identify himself during a stop allowed by *Terry v. Ohio*, 392 U.S. 1, 88 S. Ct.1868 (1968). He challenges his conviction under the Fourth and Fifth Amendments to the United States Constitution, applicable to the States through the Fourteenth Amendment.

I

The sheriff's department in Humboldt County, Nevada, received an afternoon telephone call reporting an assault. The caller reported seeing a man a woman in a red and silver GMC truck on Grass Valley Road. Deputy Sheriff Lee Dove was dispatched to investigate. When the officer arrived at the scene, he found the truck parked on the side of the road. A man was standing by the truck, and a young woman was sitting inside it. The officer observed skid marks in the gravel behind the vehicle, leading him to believe it had come to a sudden stop.

The officer approached the man and explained that he was investigating a report of a fight. The man appeared to be intoxicated. The officer asked him if he had "any identification on [him]," which we understand as a request to produce a driver's license or some other form of written identification. The man refused and asked why the officer wanted to see identification. The officer responded that he was conducting an investigation and needed to see some identification. The unidentified man became agitated and insisted he had done nothing wrong. The officer explained that he wanted to find out who the man was and what he was doing there. After continued refusals to comply with the officer's request for identification, the man began to taunt the officer by placing his hands behind his back and telling the officer to arrest him and take him to jail. This routine kept up for several minutes: the officer asked for identification 11 times and was refused each time. After warning the man that he would be arrested is he continued to refuse to comply, the officer placed him under arrest.

We now know that the man arrested on Grass Valley Road is Larry Dudley Hiibel. Hiibel was charged with "willfully resisting, delaying, or obstructing a public officer in discharging or attempting to discharge any legal duty of his office" in violation of Nev. Rev. Stat. (NRS) § 199.280 (2003). The government reasoned that Hiibel had obstructed the officer in carrying out his duties under § 171.123, a Nevada statute that defines the legal rights and duties of a police officer in the context of an investigative stop. Section 171.123 provides in relevant part:

> 1. Any peace officer may detain any person whom the officer encounters under circumstances which reasonably indicate that the person has committed, is committing or is about to commit a crime.
>
> . . .
>
> 3. The officer may detain the person pursuant to this section only to ascertain his identity and the suspicious circumstances surrounding his presence aboard. Any person so detained shall identify himself, but may not be compelled to answer any other inquiry of any peace officer.

Hiibel was tried in the Justice Court of Union Township. The court agreed that Hiibel's refusal to identify himself as required by § 171.123 "obstructed and delayed Dove as a public officer in attempting to discharge his duty" in violation of § 199.280.... Hiibel was convicted and fined $250. The Sixth Judicial District Court affirmed, rejecting Hiibel's argument that the application of § 171.123 to his case violated the Fourth and Fifth Amendments. On review the Supreme Court of Nevada rejected the Fourth Amendment challenge in a divided opinion. Hiibel petitioned for rehearing, seeking explicit resolution of his Fifth Amendment challenge. The petition was denied without opinion. We granted certiorari.

II

NRS § 171.123(3) is an enactment sometimes referred to as a "stop and identify" statute (cites omitted).

Stop and identify statutes often combine elements of traditional vagrancy laws with provisions intended to regulate police behavior in the course of investigatory stops. The statutes vary from State to State, but all permit an officer to ask or require a suspect to disclose his identity. . . . In some States, a suspect's refusal to identify himself is a misdemeanor offense or civil violation; in others, it is a factor to be considered in whether the suspect has violated loitering laws. In other States, a suspect may decline to identify himself without penalty.

Stop and identify statutes have their root in early English vagrancy laws that required suspected vagrants to face arrest unless they gave a "a good Account of themselves," (cite omitted) a power that itself reflected common-law rights of private persons to "arrest any suspicious night-walker, and detain him till he gave a good account of himself . . . ." (cite omitted) In recent decades, the Court has found constitutional infirmity in traditional vagrancy laws. In *Papachristou v. Jacksonville*, 405 U.S. 156, 92 S.Ct. 839 (1972), the Court held that a traditional vagrancy law was void for vagueness. Its broad scope and imprecise terms denied proper notice to potential offenders and permitted police officers to exercise unfettered discretion in the enforcement of the law.

The Court has recognized similar constitutional limitations on the scope and operation of stop and identify statutes. In Brown v. Texas, 443 U.S. 47, 99 S.Ct. 2637 (1979), the Court invalidated a conviction for violating a Texas stop and identify statute on Fourth Amendment grounds. The Court ruled that the initial stop was not based on specific, objective facts establishing reasonable suspicion to believe the suspect was involved in criminal activity (cite omitted). Absent that factual basis for detaining the defendant, the Court held, the risk of "arbitrary and abusive police practices" was too great and the stop was impermissible(cite omitted). Four Terms later, the Court invalidated a modified stop and identify statute of vagueness grounds. See *Kolender v. Lawson*, 461 U.S. 352 , 103 S.Ct. 1855 (1983). The California law in *Kolender* required a suspect to give an officer " 'credible and reliable' " identification when asked to identify himself. The Court held that the statute was void because it provided no standard for determining what a suspect must do to comply with it, resulting in " 'virtually unrestrained power to arrest and charge persons with a violation' " (cite omitted).

The present case begins where our prior cases left off. Here there is no question that the initial stop was based on reasonable suspicion, satisfying the Fourth Amendment requirements noted in *Brown*. Further, the petitioner has not alleged that the statute is unconstitutionally vague, as in *Kolender*. Here the Nevada statute is narrower and more precise. The statute in Kolender has been interpreted to require a suspect to give the officer "credible and reliable" identification. In contrast, the Nevada Supreme Court has interpreted NRS § 171.123(3) to require only that a suspect disclose his name.... As we understand it, the statute does not require a suspect to give the officer a driver's license or any other document. Provided that the suspect either states his name or communicates it to officer by other means–a choice, we assume, that the suspect may make–the statute is satisfied and no violation occurs (cite omitted).

III

Hiibel argues that his conviction cannot stand because the officer's conduct violated his Fourth Amendment rights. We disagree.

Asking questions is an essential part of police investigations. In the ordinary course a police officer is free to ask a person for identification without implicating the Fourth Amendment. "Interrogation relating to one's identity or a request for identification by the police does not by itself constitute a Fourth Amendment seizure." *INS v. Delgado*, 466 U.S. 210, 104 S.Ct. 1758 (1984). Beginning with *Terry v. Ohio* (cite omitted) (1968), the Court has recognized that a law enforcement officer's reasonable suspicion that a person may be involved in criminal activity permits the officer to stop the person for a brief time and take additional steps to investigate further, *Delgado*, (cite omitted), *United States v. Brignoni-Ponce*, 422 U.S. 873, 95 S.Ct. 2574 (1975). To ensure that the resulting seizure is constitutionally reasonable, a *Terry* stop must be limited. The officer's action must be " 'justified at its inception, and.... reasonably related in scope to the circumstances which justified the interference in the first place.' " *United States v. Sharpe*, 470 U.S. 675, 105 S. Ct. 1568 (1985)(quoting *Terry*, (cite omitted)). For example, the seizure cannot continue for an excessive period of time, see *United States* v. *Place,* 462 U.S. 696, 709, 103 S. Ct. 2637 (1983), or resemble a traditional arrest, see *Dunaway* v. *New York,* 442 U.S. 200, 212, 99 S. Ct. 2248 (1979).

Our decisions make clear that questions concerning a suspect's identity are a routine and accepted part of many *Terry* stops. See *United States v. Hensley,* 469 U.S. 221, 105 S.Ct. 675 (1985) ("The ability to briefly stop [a suspect], ask questions, or check identification in the absence of probable cause promotes the strong government interest in solving crimes and bringing offenders to justice"); *Hayes v. Florida,* 470 U.S. 811, 816, 105 S. Ct. 1643 (1985) ("If there are articulable facts supporting a reasonable suspicion that a person has committed a criminal offense, that person may be stopped in order to identify him, to question him briefly, or to detain him briefly while attempting to obtain additional information"); *Adams v. Williams,* 407 U.S. 143, 92 S.Ct. 1921 (1972) ("A brief stop of a suspicious individual, in order to determine his ability or to maintain the status quo momentarily while obtaining more information, may be most reasonable in light of the facts known to the officer at the time").

Obtaining a suspect's name in the course of a *Terry* stops serves important government interests. Knowledge of identity may inform an officer that a suspect is wanted for another offense, or has a record of violence or mental disorder. On the other hand, knowing identity may help clear a suspect and allow the police to concentrate their efforts elsewhere. Identity may prove particularly important in cases such as this, where the police are investigating what appears to be a domestic assault. Officers called to investigate domestic disputes need to know whom they are dealing with in order to assess the situation, the threat to their own safety, and possible danger to the potential victim.

Although it is well established that an officer may ask a suspect to identify himself in the course of a *Terry* stop, it has been an open question whether the suspect can be arrested and prosecuted for refusal to answer. See Brown (cite omitted) Petitioner draws our attention to statements in prior opinions that, according to him, answer the question in his favor. In *Terry*, Justice White stated in a concurring opinion that a person detained in an investigative stop can be questioned but is "not obliged to answer, answers may not be compelled, and refusal to answer furnishes no basis for an arrest." 392 U.S. 1, at 34, 88 S.Ct. 1868. The Court cited this opinion in dicta in *Berkemer v. McCarty*, 468 U.S. 420, 104 S.Ct. 3138 (1984), a decision holding that a routine traffic stop is not a custodial stop requiring the protections of *Miranda v. Arizona*, (cite omitted). In the course of explaining why *Terry* stops have not been subject to *Miranda*, the Court suggested reasons why *Terry* stops have a "nonthreatening character," among them the fact that a suspect detained during a *Terry* stop "is not obliged to respond" to questions (cite omitted). According to petitioner, these statements establish a right to refuse to answer questions during a *Terry* stop.

We do not read these statements as controlling. The passages recognize that the Fourth Amendment does not impose obligations on the citizen but instead provides rights against the government. As a result, the Fourth Amendment itself cannot require a suspect to answer questions. This case concerns a different issue, however. Here, the source of the legal obligation arises from Nevada state law, not the Fourth Amendment. Further, the statutory obligation does not go beyond answering an officer's request to disclose a name. See NRS § 171.123(3)("Any person so detained shall identify himself, but may not be compelled to answer any other inquiry of any peace officer"). As a result, we cannot view the dicta in *Berkemer* of Justice White's concurrence in *Terry* as answering the question whether a State can compel a suspect to disclose his name during a *Terry* stop.

The principles of *Terry* permits a State to require a suspect to disclose his name in the course of a *Terry* stop. The reasonableness of a seizure under the Fourth Amendment is determined "by balancing its intrusion on the individual's Fourth Amendment interests against its promotion of legitimate government interest." *Delaware v. Prouse*, 440 U.S. 648, 99 S.Ct. 1391 (1979). The Nevada statute satisfies that standard. The request for identity has an immediate relation to the purpose, rationale, and practical demands of a *Terry* stop. The threat of criminal sanction helps ensure that the request for identity does not become a legal nullity. On the other hand, the Nevada statute does not alter the nature of the stop itself: it does not change its duration. A state law requiring a suspect to disclose his name in the course of a valid *Terry* stop is consistent with Fourth Amendment prohibitions against unreasonable searches and seizures.

Petitioner argues that the Nevada statute circumvents the probable cause requirement, in effect allowing an officer to arrest a person for being suspicious. According to petitioner, this creates a risk of arbitrary police conduct that the Fourth Amendment does not permit. Brief for Petitioner 28–33. These are familiar concerns; they were central to the opinion in *Papachristou*, and also to the decisions limiting the operation of stop and identify statutes in *Kolender* and *Brown*. Petitioner's concerns are met by the requirement that a *Terry* stop must be justified at its inception and "reasonably related in scope to the circumstances which justified" the initial stop. 392 U.S.1, at 20. Under these principles, an officer may not arrest a suspect for failure to identify himself if the request for identification is not reasonably related to the circumstances justifying the stop. The Court noted a similar limitation in *Hayes*, where it suggested that *Terry* may permit an officer to determine a suspect's identity by compelling the suspect to submit to fingerprinting only if there is "reasonable basis for believing that fingerprinting will establish or negate the suspect's connection with that crime"(cite omitted). It is clear in this case that the request for identification was "reasonably related in scope to the circumstances which justified" the stop. *Terry* (cite omitted). The officer's request was a commonsense inquiry, not an effort to obtain an arrest for failure to identify after a Terry stop yielded insufficient evidence. The stop, the request, and the State's requirement of a response did not contravene the guarantees of the Fourth Amendment.

IV

Petitioner further contends that his conviction violates the Fifth Amendment's prohibition on compelled self-incrimination. The Fifth Amendment states that."no person . . . shall be compelled in any criminal case to be a witness against himself." To qualify for the Fifth Amendment privilege, a communication must be testimonial, incriminating, and compelled. See *United States* v. *Hubbell,* (cite omitted).

Respondents urge us to hold that the statements NRS § 171.123(3) requires are nontestimonial, and so outside the Clause's scope. We decline to resolve the case on that basis. "To be testimonial, an accused's communication must itself, explicitly or implicitly, relate a factual assertion or disclose information." *Doe v. United States*, 487 U.S. 201, 108 S. Ct. 2341 (1988). Stating one's name may qualify as an assertion of fact relating to identity. Production of identity documents might meet the definition as well. As we noted in *Hubbell*, acts of production may yield testimony establishing "the existence, authenticity, and custody of items [the police seek]" (cite omitted). Even if these required actions are testimonial, however, petitioner's challenge must fail because in his case disclosure of his name presented no reasonable danger of incrimination.

The Fifth Amendment prohibits only compelled testimony that is incriminating. . . .

In this case petitioner's refusal to disclose his name was not based on any articulated real and appreciable fear that his name would be used to incriminate him, or that it "would furnish a link in the chain of evidence needed to prosecute" him. Hoffman v. United States, 341 U.S. 479, 71 S.Ct.

814 (1951). As best we can tell, petitioner refused to identify himself only because he thought his name was none of the officer's business. Even today, petitioner does not explain how the disclosure of his name could have been used against him in a criminal case. While we recognize petitioner's strong belief that he should not have to disclose his identity, the Fifth Amendment does not override the Nevada Legislature's judgment to the contrary absent a reasonable belief that the disclosure would tend to incriminate him.

The narrow scope of the disclosure requirement is also important. One's identity is, by definition, unique; yet it is, in another sense, a universal characteristic. Answering a request to disclose a name is likely to be so insignificant in the scheme of things as to be incriminating only in unusual circumstances (cites omitted).... Even witnesses who plan to invoke the Fifth Amendment privilege answer when their names are called to take the stand. Still, a case may arise where there is a substantial allegation that furnishing identity at the time of a stop would have given the police a link in the chain of evidence needed to convict the individual of a separate offense. In that case, the court can then consider whether the privilege applies, and, if the Fifth Amendment has been violated, what remedy must follow. We need not resolve those questions here.

The judgment of the Nevada Supreme Court is

Affirmed.

■ JUSTICE STEVENS, dissenting.

The Nevada law at issue in this case imposes a narrow duty to speak upon a specific class of individuals. The class includes only those persons detained by a police officer "under circumstances which reasonably indicate that the person has committed, is committing or is about to commit a crime"–persons who are, in other words, targets of a criminal investigation. The statute therefore is directed not "at the public at large," but rather "at a highly selective group inherently suspect of criminal activities"(cite omitted).

Under the Nevada law, a member of the targeted class "may not be compelled to answer" any inquiry except a command that he "identify himself." Refusal to identify oneself upon request is punishable as a crime. Presumably the statute does not require the detainee to answer any other question because the Nevada Legislature realized that the Fifth Amendment prohibits compelling the target of a criminal investigation to make any other statement. In my judgment, the broad constitutional right to remain silent, which derives from the Fifth Amendment's guarantee that "no person ... shall be compelled in any criminal case to be a witness against himself." U.S. Const. Amdt. 5, is not as circumscribed as the Court suggests, and does not admit even of the narrow exception defined by the Nevada statute.

"There can be no doubt that the Fifth Amendment privilege is available outside of criminal court proceedings and serves to protect persons in all settings in which their freedom of action is curtailed in any significant way from being compelled to incriminate themselves." *Miranda v. Arizona*, (cite omitted). It is a "settled principle" that "the police have the right to request citizens to answer voluntarily questions concerning unsolved crimes," but "they have no right to compel them to answer." *Davis v. Mississippi*, 394 U.S. 721, 89 S.Ct. 1394 (1969). The protections of the Fifth Amendment are directed squarely toward those who are the focus of the government's investigative and prosecutorial powers. In a criminal trial, the indicted defendant has an unqualified right to refuse to testify and not be punished for invoking that right (cites omitted). The unindicted target of a grand jury investigation enjoys the same constitutional protection even if he has been served with a subpoena (cite omitted). So does an arrested suspect during custodial interrogation in a police station (cite omitted).

There is no reason why the subject of police interrogation based on mere suspicion, rather than probable cause, should have any lesser protection. Indeed, we have said that the Fifth Amendment's protections apply with equal force in the context of *Terry* stops (cite omitted), where an officer's inquiry "must be reasonably related in scope to the justification for [the stop's] initiation." *Berkemer v. McCarty*, 468 U.S. 420, 439, 104 S.Ct. 3138 (1984) [some internal quotation marks omitted in original]. "Typically this means that the officer may ask the detainee a moderate number of questions to determine his identity and to try to obtain information confirming or dispelling the officer's suspicions. But the detainee is not obliged to respond." See also *Terry*, (cite omitted) (White, J., concurring) ("Of course, the person stopped is not obliged to answer, answers may not be compelled, and refusal to answer furnishes no basis for arrest, although it may alert the officer to the need for continued observation"). Given our statements to the effect that citizens are not required respond to police officers' questions during a Terry stop, it is no surprise that petitioner assumed, as have we, that he had a right not to disclose his identity.

The Court correctly observes that a communication does not enjoy the Fifth Amendment privilege unless it is testimonial. Although the Court declines to resolve this question, I think it clear that this case concerns a testimonial communication. Recognizing that whether a communication is testimonial is sometimes a "difficult question," *Doe v. United States*, (cite omitted), we have stated generally that "it is the 'extortion of information from the accused,' the attempt to force him 'to disclose the contents of his own mind,' that implicates the Self–Incrimination Clause," (cite with citations omitted). While "the vast majority of verbal statements thus will be testimonial and, to that extent at least, will fall within the privilege," (cite omitted), certain acts and physical evidence fall outside the privilege.[1] In all instances, we have afforded Fifth Amendment protection if the disclosure in question was being admitted because of its content rather than some other aspect of the communication.

Considered in light of these precedents, the compelled statement at issue in this case is clearly testimonial. It is significant that the communication must be made in response to a question posed by a police officer. Surely police questioning during a *Terry* stop qualifies as an interrogation,

---

1. A suspect may be made, for example, to provide a blood sample, *Schmerber* v. *California*, 384 U.S. 757, 765, 86 S. Ct. 1826 (1966), a voice exemplar, *United States* v. *Dionisio*, 410 U.S. 1, 7, 93 S. Ct. 764 (1973), or a handwriting sample, *Gilbert* v. *California*, 388 U.S. 263, 266–267, 87 S. Ct. 1951 (1967).

and it follows that response to such questions are testimonial in nature. As we recently explained, albeit in the different context of the Sixth Amendment's Confrontation Clause, "whatever else the term ['testimonial'] covers, it applies at a minimum ... to police interrogations." *Crawford* v. *Washington,* 541 U.S. 36, ___, 124 S. Ct. 1354 (2004). Surely police questioning during a *Terry* stop qualifies as an interrogation, and it follows that responses to such questions are testimonial in nature.

Rather than determining whether the communication at issue is testimonial, the Court instead concludes that the State can compel the disclosure of one's identity because it is not "incriminating." But our cases have afforded Fifth Amendment protection to statements that are "incriminating" in a much broader sense than the Court suggests. It has "long been settled that [the Fifth Amendment's] protection encompasses compelled statements that lead to the discovery of incriminating evidence even though the statements themselves are not incriminating and are not introduced into evidence" (cite omitted).... Thus, "compelled testimony that communicates information that may 'lead to incriminating evidence' is privileged even if the information itself is not inculpatory" (cites omitted).

Given a proper understanding of the category of "incriminating" communications that fall within the Fifth Amendment privilege, it is clear that the disclosure of petitioner's identity is protected. The Court reasons that we should not assume that the disclosure of petitioner's name would be used to incriminate him or that it would furnish a link in a chain of evidence needed to prosecute him. But why else would an officer ask for it? And why else would the Nevada Legislature require its disclosure only when circumstances "reasonably indicate that the person has committed, is committing or is about to commit a crime"? If the Court is correct, then petitioner's refusal to cooperate did not impede the police investigation. Indeed, if we accept the predicate for the Court's holding, the statute requires nothing more than a useless invasion of privacy. I think that, on the contrary, the Nevada Legislature intended to provide its police officers with a useful law enforcement tool, and that the very existence of the statute demonstrates the value of the information it demands.

A person's identity obviously bears informational and incriminating worth, "even if the [name] itself is not inculpatory" (cite omitted). A name can provide the key to a broad array of information about the person, particularly in the hands of a police officer with access to a range of law enforcement databases. And that information, in turn, can be tremendously useful in a criminal prosecution. It is therefore quite wrong to suggest that a person's identity provides a link in the chain to incriminating evidence "only in unusual circumstances."

The officer in the case told petitioner, in the Court's words, that "he was conducting an investigation and needed to see some identification." As the target of that investigation, petitioner, in my view, acted well within his rights when he opted to stand mute. According, I respectfully dissent.

■ JUSTICE BREYER, with whom JUSTICE SOUTER and JUSTICE GINSBURG join, dissenting.

Notwithstanding the vagrancy statutes to which the majority refers, this Court's Fourth Amendment precedents make clear that police may conduct a *Terry* stop only within circumscribed limits. And one of those limits invalidates laws that compel responses to police questioning.

In *Terry v. Ohio*, (cite omitted), the Court considered whether police, in the absence of probable cause, can stop, questions, or frisk an individual at all.... At the same time, it recognized that in certain circumstances, public safety might require a limited "seizure," or stop, of an individual against his will. The Court consequently set forth conditions circumscribing when and how the police might conduct a *Terry* stop. They include what has become known as the "reasonable suspicion" standard (cite omitted). Justice White, in a separate concurring opinion, set forth further conditions. Justice White wrote: "Of course, the person stopped is not obliged to answer, answer may not be compelled, and refusal to answer furnishes no basis for an arrest, although it may alert the officer to the need for continued observation." (cite omitted).

About 10 years later, the Court, in *Brown v. Texas* (cite omitted) held that police lacked "any reasonable suspicion" to detain the particular petitioner and require him to identify himself. The Court noted that the trial judge had asked the following: "I'm sure [officers conducting a *Terry* stop] should ask everything they possibly could find out. *What I'm asking is what's the State's interest in putting a man in jail because he doesn't want to answer*...." (cite omitted)(emphasis in the original).... The Court referred to Justice White's *Terry* concurrence (cite omitted). 443 U.S. 47, at 53, n. 3. And it said that it "need not decide" the matter.

Then, five years later, the Court wrote that an "officer may ask the [*Terry*] detainee a moderate number of questions to determine his identity and to try to obtain information confirming or dispelling the officer's suspicions. *But the detainee is not obliged to respond.*" *Berkemer v. McCarty*, (cite omitted) (emphasis added in original). See also *Kolender v. Lawson*, (cite omitted) (Brennan, J., concurring) (Terry suspect "must be free to ... decline to answer the questions put to him); *Illinois v. Wardlow*, (cite omitted)('stating that allowing officers to stop and question a fleeing person' is quite consistent with the individual's right to go about his business or to stay put and remain silent in the fact of police questioning").

This lengthy history–of concurring opinions, of references, and of clear explicit statements–means that the Court's statement in *Berkemer,* while technically dicta, is the kind of strong dicta that the legal community typically takes as a statement of the law. And that law has remained undisturbed for more than 20 years.

There is no good reason now to reject this generation-old statement of the law. There are sound reasons rooted in Fifth Amendment considerations for adhering to this Fourth Amendment legal condition circumscribing police authority to stop an individual against his will. Administrative considerations also militate against change. Can a State, in addition to requiring a stopped individual to answer "What's your name?" also require an answer to "What's your license number?" or "Where do you live?" Can a police officer, who must know how to make a Terry stop, keep track of the constitutional answers? After all, answers to any of these questions may, or may not, incriminate, depending upon the circumstances.

Indeed, as the majority points out, a name itself–even if it not "Killer Bill" or "Rough 'em up Harry"–will sometimes provide the police with a link in the chain of evidence needed to convict the individual of a separate offense. The majority reserves judgment about whether compulsion is permissible in such instances. How then is a police officer in the midst of a *Terry* stop to distinguish between the majority's ordinary case and this special case where the majority reserves judgment?

The majority presents no evidence that the rule enunciated by Justice White and then by the *Berkemer* Court, which for nearly a generation has set forth a settled *Terry* stop condition, has significantly interfered with law enforcement. Nor has the majority presented any other convincing justification for change. I would not begin to erode a clear rule with special exceptions.

I consequently dissent.

L. ADMINISTRATIVE AND "SPECIAL NEEDS" SEARCHES

Page 545. Add before the first full paragraph:

1.b. *Drug Testing of Students*

Page 547. Add at the end of note 3:

The Court has approved highway checkpoints vehicle roadblocks established to ask motorists if they had information about a crime that had occurred earlier at the location.

Illinois v. Lidster

540 U.S. 419, 124 S.Ct. 885 (2004).

■ JUDGES: BREYER, J., delivered the opinion of the Court, in which REHNQUIST, C. J., and O'CONNOR, SCALIA, KENNEDY, and THOMAS, JJ., joined, and in which STEVENS, SOUTER, and GINSBURG, JJ., joined as to Parts I and II. STEVENS, J., filed an opinion concurring in part and dissenting in part, in which SOUTER and GINSBURG, JJ., joined.

■ JUSTICE BREYER delivered the opinion of the Court.

This Fourth Amendment case focuses upon a highway checkpoint where police stopped motorists to ask them for information about a recent hit-and-run accident. We hold that the police stops were reasonable, hence, constitutional.

I

The relevant background is as follows: On Saturday, August 23, 1997, just after midnight, an unknown motorist traveling eastbound on a highway in Lombard, Illinois, struck and killed a 70–year-old bicyclist. The motorist drove off without identifying himself. About one week later at about the same time of night and at about the same place, local police set up a highway checkpoint designed to obtain more information about the accident from the motoring public.

Police cars with flashing lights partially blocked the eastbound lanes of the highway. The blockage forced traffic to slow down, leading to lines of up to 15 cars in each lane. As each vehicle drew up to the checkpoint, an officer would stop it for 10 to 15 seconds, ask the occupants whether they had seen anything happen there the previous weekend, and hand each driver a flyer. The flyer said "ALERT ... FATAL HIT & RUN ACCIDENT" and requested "assistance in identifying the vehicle and driver in this accident which killed a 70 year old bicyclist."

Robert Lidster, the respondent, drove a minivan toward the checkpoint. As he approached the checkpoint, his van swerved, nearly hitting one of the officers. The officer smelled alcohol on Lidster's breath. He directed Lidster to a side street where another officer administered a sobriety test and then arrested Lidster. Lidster was tried and convicted in Illinois state court of driving under the influence of alcohol.

Lidster challenged the lawfulness of his arrest and conviction on the ground that the government had obtained much of the relevant evidence through use of a checkpoint stop that violated the Fourth Amendment. The trial court rejected that challenge. But an Illinois appellate court reached the opposite conclusion (cite omitted). The Illinois Supreme Court agreed with the appellate court. It held (by a vote of 4 to 3) that our decision in *Indianapolis* v. *Edmond,* 531 U.S. 32, 121 S. Ct. 447 (2000), required it to find the stop unconstitutional (cite omitted).

Because lower courts have reached different conclusions about this matter, we granted certiorari (cite omitted).

II

The Illinois Supreme Court basically held that our decision in *Edmond* governs the outcome of this case. We do not agree. *Edmond* involved a checkpoint at which police stopped vehicles to look for evidence of drug crimes committed by occupants of those vehicles. After stopping a vehicle at the checkpoint, police would examine (from outside the vehicle) the vehicle's interior; they would walk a drug-sniffing dog around the exterior; and, if they found sufficient evidence of drug (or other) crimes, they would arrest the vehicle's occupants. 531 U.S., at 35, 121 S. Ct. 447. We found that police had set up this checkpoint primarily for general "crime control" purposes, *i.e.*, "to detect evidence of ordinary criminal wrongdoing" (cite omitted). We noted that the stop was made without individualized suspicion. And we held that the Fourth Amendment forbids such a stop, in the absence of special circumstances (cite omitted).

The checkpoint stop here differs significantly from that in *Edmond.* The stop's primary law enforcement purpose was *not* to determine whether a vehicle's occupants were committing a crime, but to ask vehicle occupants, as members of the public, for their help in providing information about a crime in all likelihood committed by others. The police expected the information elicited to help them apprehend, not the vehicle's occupants, but other individuals.

Edmond's language, as well as its context, makes clear that the constitutionality of this latter, information-seeking kind of stop was not then before the Court. *Edmond* refers to the subject matter of its holding as "stops justified only by the generalized and ever-present possibility that interrogation and inspection may reveal that *any given motorist has committed some crime.*" (emphasis added). We concede that *Edmond* describes the law enforcement objective there in question as a "general interest in crime control," but it specifies that the phrase "general interest in crime control" does not refer to every "law enforcement" objective (cite omitted). We must read this and related general language in *Edmond* as we often read general language in judicial opinions—as referring in context to circumstances similar to the circumstances then before the Court and not referring to quite different circumstances that the Court was not then considering.

Neither do we believe, *Edmond* aside, that the Fourth Amendment would have us apply an *Edmond*-type rule of automatic unconstitutionality to brief, information-seeking highway stops of the kind now before us. For one thing, the fact that such stops normally lack individualized suspicion cannot by itself determine the constitutional outcome. As in *Edmond,* the stop here at issue involves a motorist. The Fourth Amendment does not treat a motorist's car as his castle (cites omitted). And special law enforcement concerns will sometimes justify highway stops without individualized suspicion. See *Michigan Dept. of State Police* v. *Sitz,* 496 U.S. 444, 110 S. Ct. 2481 (1990) (sobriety checkpoint); *Martinez-Fuerte, supra* (Border Patrol checkpoint). Moreover, unlike *Edmond,* the context here (seeking information from the public) is one in which, by definition, the concept of individualized suspicion has little role to play. Like certain other forms of police activity, say, crowd control or public safety, an information-seeking stop is not the kind of event that involves suspicion, or lack of suspicion, of the relevant individual.

For another thing, information-seeking highway stops are less likely to provoke anxiety or to prove intrusive. The stops are likely brief. The police are not likely to ask questions designed to elicit self-incriminating information. And citizens will often react positively when police simply ask for their help as "responsible citizen[s]" to "give whatever information they may have to aid in law enforcement." *Miranda* v. *Arizona,* (cite omitted).

Further, the law ordinarily permits police to seek the voluntary cooperation of members of the public in the investigation of a crime. "[L]aw enforcement officers do not violate the Fourth Amendment by merely approaching an individual on the street or in another public place, by asking him if he is willing to answer some questions, [or] by putting questions to him if the person is willing to listen." *Florida* v. *Royer,* 460 U.S. 491, 497, 103 S. Ct. 1319 (1983). See also ALI, Model Code of Pre–Arraignment Procedure § 110.1(1) (1975) ("[L]aw enforcement officer may . . . request any person to furnish information or otherwise cooperate in the investigation or prevention of crime"). That, in part, is because voluntary requests play a vital role in police investigatory work. See, *e.g., Haynes* v. *Washington,* 373 U.S. 503, 515, 83 S. Ct. 1336 (1963) ("[I]nterrogation of witnesses . . . is undoubtedly an essential tool in effective law enforcement''); U. S. Dept. of Justice, Eyewitness Evidence: A Guide for Law Enforcement 14–15 (1999) (instructing law enforcement to gather information from witnesses near the scene).

The importance of soliciting the public's assistance is offset to some degree by the need to stop a motorist to obtain that help—a need less likely present where a pedestrian, not a motorist, is involved. The difference is significant in light of our determinations that such an involuntary stop amounts to a ''seizure'' in Fourth Amendment terms. *E.g., Edmond* (cite omitted). That difference, however, is not important enough to justify an *Edmond*-type rule here. After all, as we have said, the motorist stop will likely be brief. Any accompanying traffic delay should prove no more onerous than many that typically accompany normal traffic congestion. And the resulting voluntary questioning of a motorist is as likely to prove important for police investigation as is the questioning of a pedestrian. Given these considerations, it would seem anomalous were the law (1) ordinarily to allow police freely to seek the voluntary cooperation of pedestrians but (2) ordinarily to forbid police to seek similar voluntary cooperation from motorists.

Finally, we do not believe that an *Edmond*-type rule is needed to prevent an unreasonable proliferation of police checkpoints. Cf. *Lidster*, 202 Ill. 2d, at 9–10, 779 N. E. 2d, at 859–860 (expressing that concern). Practical considerations—namely, limited police resources and community hostility to related traffic tie-ups—seem likely to inhibit any such proliferation. See Fell, Ferguson, Williams, & Fields, Why Aren't Sobriety Checkpoints Widely Adopted as an Enforcement Strategy in the United States?, 35 Accident Analysis & Prevention 897 (Nov. 2003) (finding that sobriety checkpoints are not more widely used due to the lack of police resources and the lack of community support). And, of course, the Fourth Amendment's normal insistence that the stop be reasonable in context will still provide an important legal limitation on police use of this kind of information-seeking checkpoint.

These considerations, taken together, convince us that an *Edmond*-type presumptive rule of unconstitutionality does not apply here. That does not mean the stop is automatically, or even presumptively, constitutional. It simply means that we must judge its reasonableness, hence, its constitutionality, on the basis of the individual circumstances. And as this Court said in *Brown* v. *Texas,* 443 U.S. 47, 51, 99 S. Ct. 2637 (1979),''in judging reasonableness, we look to 'the gravity of the public concerns served by the seizure, the degree to which the seizure advances the public interest, and the severity of the interference with individual liberty.' '' See also *Sitz, supra,* at 450–455, 110 S. Ct. 2481 (balancing these factors in determining reasonableness of a checkpoint stop) *Martinez-Fuerte* (cite omitted), (same).

III

We now consider the reasonableness of the checkpoint stop before us in light of the factors just mentioned, an issue that, in our view, has been fully argued here. We hold that the stop was constitutional.

The relevant public concern was grave. Police were investigating a crime that had resulted in a human death. No one denies the police's need to obtain more information at that time. And the stop's objective was to help find the perpetrator of a specific and known crime, not of unknown crimes of a general sort. Cf. *Edmond*, (cite omitted)

The stop advanced this grave public concern to a significant degree. The police appropriately tailored their checkpoint stops to fit important criminal investigatory needs. The stops took place about one week after the hit-and-run accident, on the same highway near the location of the accident, and at about the same time of night. And police used the stops to obtain information from drivers, some of whom might well have been in the vicinity of the crime at the time it occurred. See App. 28–29 (describing police belief that motorists routinely leaving work after night shifts at nearby industrial complexes might have seen something relevant).

Most importantly, the stops interfered only minimally with liberty of the sort the Fourth Amendment seeks to protect. Viewed objectively, each stop required only a brief wait in line—a very few minutes at most. Contact with the police lasted only a few seconds. Cf. *Martinez-Fuerte*, (cite omitted)(upholding stops of three-to-five minutes); *Sitz*, (cite omitted) (upholding delays of 25 seconds). Police contact consisted simply of a request for information and the distribution of a flyer. Cf. *Martinez-Fuerte* (cite omitted) (upholding inquiry as to motorists' citizenship and immigration status); *Sitz*, (cite omitted) (upholding examination of all drivers for signs of intoxication). Viewed subjectively, the contact provided little reason for anxiety or alarm. The police stopped all vehicles systematically. Cf. *Martinez-Fuerte*, (cite omitted); *Sitz*, (cite omitted). And there is no allegation here that the police acted in a discriminatory or otherwise unlawful manner while questioning motorists during stops.

For these reasons we conclude that the checkpoint stop was constitutional.

The judgment of the Illinois Supreme Court is reversed.

■ Concurring in part and dissenting in part: Justice Stevens, with whom Justice Souter and Justice Ginsburg join, concurring in part and dissenting in part.

There is a valid and important distinction between seizing a person to determine whether she has committed a crime and seizing a person to ask whether she has any information about an unknown person who committed a crime a week earlier. I therefore join Parts I and II of the Court's opinion explaining why our decision in *Indianapolis* v. *Edmond*, (cite omitted), is not controlling in this case. However, I find the issue discussed in Part III of the opinion closer than the Court does and believe it would be wise to remand the case to the Illinois state courts to address that issue in the first instance.

In contrast to pedestrians, who are free to keep walking when they encounter police officers handing out flyers or seeking information, motorists who confront a roadblock are required to stop, and to remain stopped for as long as the officers choose to detain them. Such a seizure may seem relatively innocuous to some, but annoying to others who are forced to wait for several minutes when the line of cars is lengthened—for example, by a surge of vehicles leaving a factory at the end of a shift. Still other drivers may find an unpublicized roadblock at midnight on a Saturday somewhat alarming.

On the other side of the equation, the likelihood that questioning a random sample of drivers will yield useful information about a hit-and-run accident that occurred a week earlier is speculative at best. To be sure, the sample in this case was not entirely random: The record reveals that the police knew that the victim had finished work at the Post Office shortly before the fatal accident, and hoped that other employees of the Post Office or the nearby industrial park might work on similar schedules and, thus, have been driving the same route at the same time the previous week. That is a plausible theory, but there is no evidence in the record that the police did anything to confirm that the nearby businesses in fact had shift changes at or near midnight on Saturdays, or that they had reason to believe that a roadblock would be more effective than, say, placing flyers on the employees' cars.

In short, the outcome of the multifactor test prescribed in *Brown* v. *Texas* (cite omitted), is by no means clear on the facts of this case. Because the Illinois Appellate Court and the State Supreme Court held that the Lombard roadblock was *per se* unconstitutional under *Indianapolis* v *Edmond*, neither court attempted to apply the *Brown* test. "We ordinarily do not decide in the first instance issues not resolved below." (cite omitted) We should be especially reluctant to abandon our role as a court of review in a case in which the constitutional inquiry requires analysis of local conditions and practices more familiar to judges closer to the scene. I would therefore remand the case to the Illinois courts to undertake the initial analysis of the issue that the Court resolves in Part III of its opinion. To that extent, I respectfully dissent.

M. Border and Immigration Searches

Add to end of first note on page 551 and before note 2:

Agents may conduct border searches without any probable cause or reasonable suspicion.

United States v. Manuel Flores–Montano

541 U.S. 149, 124 S.Ct. 1582 (2004).

■ JUDGES: REHNQUIST, C. J., delivered the opinion for a unanimous Court. BREYER, J., filed a concurring opinion.

Customs officials seized 37 kilograms—a little more than 81 pounds— of marijuana from respondent Manuel Flores–Montano's gas tank at the international border. The Court of Appeals for the Ninth Circuit, relying on an earlier decision by a divided panel of that court, *United States* v. *Molina-Tarazon*, 279 F.3d 709 (2002), held that the Fourth Amendment forbade the fuel tank search absent reasonable suspicion (cite omitted). We hold that the search in question did not require reasonable suspicion.

Respondent, driving a 1987 Ford Taurus station wagon, attempted to enter the United States at the Otay Mesa Port of Entry in southern California. A customs inspector conducted an inspection of the station wagon, and requested respondent to leave the vehicle. The vehicle was then taken to a secondary inspection station.

At the secondary station, a second customs inspector inspected the gas tank by tapping it, and noted that the tank sounded solid. Subsequently, the inspector requested a mechanic under contract with Customs to come to the border station to remove the tank. Within 20 to 30 minutes, the mechanic arrived. He raised the car on a hydraulic lift, loosened the straps and unscrewed the bolts holding the gas tank to the undercarriage of the vehicle, and then disconnected some hoses and electrical connections. After the gas tank was removed, the inspector hammered off bondo (a putty-like hardening substance that is used to seal openings) from the top of the gas tank. The inspector opened an access plate underneath the bondo and found 37 kilograms of marijuana bricks. The process took 15 to 25 minutes.

A grand jury for the Southern District of California indicted respondent on one count of unlawfully importing marijuana, in violation of 21 U.S.C. § 952 [21 USCS § 952], and one count of possession of marijuana with intent to distribute, in violation of § 841(a)(1). Relying on *Molina-Tarazon*, respondent filed a motion to suppress the marijuana recovered from the gas tank. In *Molina-Tarazon*, a divided panel of the Court of Appeals held, *inter alia*, that removal of a gas tank requires reasonable suspicion in order to be consistent with the Fourth Amendment. 279 F.3d, at 717.

The Government advised the District Court that it was not relying on reasonable suspicion as a basis for denying respondent's suppression motion, but that it believed *Molina-Tarazon* was wrongly decided. The District Court, relying on *Molina-Tarazon*, held that reasonable suspicion was required to justify the search and, accordingly, granted respondent's motion to suppress. The Court of Appeals, citing *Molina-Tarazon*, summarily affirmed the District Court's judgment (cite omitted). We granted certiorari, (cite omitted), and now reverse.

In *Molina-Tarazon*, the Court of Appeals decided a case presenting similar facts to the one at bar. It asked "whether [the removal and dismantling of the defendant's fuel tank] is a 'routine' border search for which no suspicion whatsoever is required"(cite omitted). The Court of Appeals stated that "[i]n order to conduct a search that goes beyond the routine, an inspector must have reasonable suspicion," and the "critical factor" in determining whether a search is "routine" is the "degree of intrusiveness" (cite omitted).

The Court of Appeals seized on language from our opinion in *United States* v. *Montoya de Hernandez*, (cite omitted), in which we used the word "routine" as a descriptive term in discussing border searches (cite omitted).("Routine searches of the persons and effects of entrants are not subject to any requirement of reasonable suspicion, probable cause, or warrant"); (cite omitted) ("Because the issues are not presented today we suggest no view on what level of suspicion, if any, is required for nonroutine border searches such as strip, body-cavity, or involuntary x-ray searches"). The Court of Appeals took the term "routine," fashioned a new balancing test, and extended it to searches of vehicles. But the reasons that might support a requirement of some level of suspicion in the case of highly intrusive searches of the person—dignity and privacy interests of the person being searched—simply do not carry over to vehicles. Complex balancing tests to determine what is a "routine" search of a vehicle, as opposed to a more "intrusive" search of a person, have no place in border searches of vehicles.

The Government's interest in preventing the entry of unwanted persons and effects is at its zenith at the international border. Time and again, we have stated that "searches made at the border, pursuant to the longstanding right of the sovereign to protect itself by stopping and examining persons and property crossing into this country, are reasonable simply by virtue of the fact that they occur at the border." *United States* v. *Ramsey,* 431 U.S. 606, 616, 97 S. Ct. 1972 (1977). Congress, since the beginning of our Government, "has granted the Executive plenary authority to conduct routine searches and seizures at the border, without probable cause or a warrant, in order to regulate the collection of duties and to prevent the introduction of contraband into this country." *United States v. Montoya de Hernandez,* (citations omitted) The modern statute that authorized the search in this case, 46 Stat 747, 19 U.S.C. § 1581(a)[19 USCS § 1581(a)],[1] derived from a statute passed by the First Congress, the Act of Aug. 4, 1790, ch 35, § 31, 1 Stat 164, see *United States* v. *Villamonte-Marquez,* 462 U.S. 579, 584, 103 S. Ct. 2573 (1983), and reflects the "impressive historical pedigree" of the Government's power and interest, (citation omitted). It is axiomatic that the United States, as sovereign, has the inherent authority to protect, and a paramount interest in protecting, its territorial integrity.

That interest in protecting the borders is illustrated in this case by the evidence that smugglers frequently attempt to penetrate our borders with contraband secreted in their automobiles' fuel tank. Over the past 5 1/2 fiscal years, there have been 18,788 vehicle drug seizures at the southern California ports of entry. App. to Pet. for Cert. 12a. Of those 18,788, gas tank drug seizures have accounted for 4,619 of the vehicle drug seizures, or approximately 25%. *Ibid.* In addition, instances of persons smuggled in and around gas tank compartments are discovered at the ports of entry of San Ysidro and Otay Mesa at a rate averaging 1 approximately every 10 days. (cite omitted).

Respondent asserts two main arguments with respect to his Fourth Amendment interests. First, he urges that he has a privacy interest in his fuel tank, and that the suspicion less disassembly of his tank is an invasion of his privacy. But on many occasions, we have noted that "the expectation

---

1. Section 1581(a) provides: "Any officer of the customs may at any time go on board of any vessel or vehicle at any place in the United States or within the customs waters or, as he may be authorized, within a customs-enforcement area established under the Anti–Smuggling Act, or at any other authorized place, without as well as within his district, and examine the manifest and other documents and papers and examine, inspect, and search the vessel or vehicle and every part thereof and any person, trunk, package, or cargo on board, and to this end may hail and stop such vessel or vehicle, and use all necessary force to compel compliance."

of privacy is less at the border than it is in the interior." *Montoya de Hernandez*, (cite omitted). We have long recognized that automobiles seeking entry into this country may be searched. See *Carroll* v. *United States,* 267 U.S. 132, 154, 45 S. Ct. 280 (1925) ("Travellers may be so stopped in crossing an international boundary because of national self protection reasonably requiring one entering the country to identify himself as entitled to come in, and his belongings as effects which may be lawfully brought in"). It is difficult to imagine how the search of a gas tank, which should be solely a repository for fuel, could be more of an invasion of privacy than the search of the automobile's passenger compartment.

Second, respondent argues that the Fourth Amendment "protects property as well as privacy," *Soldal* v. *Cook County,* 506 U.S. 56, 62, 113 S. Ct. 538 (1992), and that the disassembly and reassembly of his gas tank is a significant deprivation of his property interest because it may damage the vehicle. He does not, and on the record cannot, truly contend that the procedure of removal, disassembly, and reassembly of the fuel tank in this case or any other has resulted in serious damage to, or destruction of, the property.[2] According to the Government, for example, in fiscal year 2003, 348 gas tank searches conducted along the southern border were negative (*i.e.,* no contraband was found), the gas tanks were reassembled, and the vehicles continued their entry into the United States without incident. Brief for United States 31.

Respondent cites not a single accident involving the vehicle or motorist in the many thousands of gas tank disassemblies that have occurred at the border. A gas tank search involves a brief procedure that can be reversed without damaging the safety or operation of the vehicle. If damage to a vehicle were to occur, the motorist might be entitled to recovery. While the interference with a motorist's possessory interest is not insignificant when the Government removes, disassembles, and reassembles his gas tank, it nevertheless is justified by the Government's paramount interest in protecting the border.[3]

---

2. Respondent's reliance on cases involving exploratory drilling searches is misplaced. See *United States* v. *Rivas*, 157 F.3d 364 (CA5 1998) (drilling into body of trailer required reasonable suspicion); *United States* v. *Robles*, 45 F.3d 1 (CA1 1995) (drilling into machine part required reasonable suspicion); *United States* v. Carreon, 872 F.2d 1436 (CA10 1989) (drilling into camper required reasonable suspicion). We have no reason at this time to pass on the reasonableness of drilling, but simply note the obvious factual difference that this case involves the procedure of removal, disassembly, and reassembly of a fuel tank, rather than potentially destructive drilling. We again leave open the question "whether, and under what circumstances, a border search might be deemed 'unreasonable' because of the particularly offensive manner it is carried out." *United States v. Ramsey* (cite omitted).

3. Respondent also argued that he has some sort of Fourth Amendment right not to be subject to delay at the international border and that the need for the use of specialized labor, as well as the hour actual delay here and the potential for even greater delay for reassembly are an invasion of that right. Respondent points to no cases indicating the Fourth Amendment shields entrants from inconvenience or delay at the international border.

The procedure in this case took about an hour (including the wait for the mechanic). At oral argument, the Government advised us that, depending on the type of car, a search involving the disassembly and reassembly of a gas tank may take one to two hours. Tr. of Oral Arg. 10. We think it clear that delays of one to two hours at international borders are to be expected.

For the reasons stated, we conclude that "the Government's authority to conduct suspicionless inspections at the border includes the authority to remove, disassemble, and reassemble a vehicle's fuel tank." While it may be true that some searches of property are so destructive as to require a different result, this was not one of them. The judgment of the United States Court of Appeals for the Ninth Circuit is therefore reversed, and the case is remanded for further proceedings consistent with this opinion.

It is so ordered.

■ CONCUR: JUSTICE BREYER, CONCURRING.

I join the Court's opinion in full. I also note that Customs keeps track of the border searches its agents conduct, including the reasons for the searches. Tr. of Oral Arg. 53–54. This administrative process should help minimize concerns that gas tank searches might be undertaken in an abusive manner.

CHAPTER 6

EXCLUSIONARY PRINCIPLES & ALTERNATIVE REMEDIES

C. THE GOOD–FAITH EXCEPTION

Add after note 1 on page 598:

In a more recent case, the Court rejected a good faith exception argument and held that evidence seized on the basis of a facially deficient warrant violated the Fourth Amendment:

Groh v. Ramirez

540 U.S. 551, 124 S.Ct. 1284 (2004)

■ JUSTICE STEVENS delivered the opinion of the Court.

Petitioner conducted a search of respondents' home pursuant to a warrant that failed to describe the "persons or things to be seized." U.S. Const., Amdt 4. The questions presented are (1) whether the search violated the Fourth Amendment, and (2) if so, whether petitioner nevertheless is entitled to qualified immunity, given that a Magistrate Judge (Magistrate), relying on an affidavit that particularly described the items in question, found probable cause to conduct the search.

I

Respondents, Joseph Ramirez and members of his family, live on a large ranch in Butte–Silver Bow County, Montana. Petitioner, Jeff Groh, has been a Special Agent for the Bureau of Alcohol, Tobacco and Firearms (ATF) since 1989. In February 1997, a concerned citizen informed petitioner that on a number of visits to respondents' ranch the visitor had seen a large stock of weaponry, including an automatic rifle, grenades, a grenade launcher, and a rocket launcher. Based on that information, petitioner prepared and signed an application stated that the search was for "any automatic firearms or parts to automatic weapons, destructive devices to include but not limited to grenades, grenade launchers, rocket launchers, and any and all receipts pertaining to the purchase or manufacture of automatic weapons or explosive devices or launchers." Petitioner supported the application with a detailed affidavit, which he also prepared and executed, that set forth the basis for his belief that the listed items were concealed on the ranch. Petitioner then presented these documents to a Magistrate, along with a warrant form that petitioner also had completed. The Magistrate signed the warrant form.

Although the application particularly described the place to be searched and the contraband petitioner expected to find, the warrant itself was less specific; it failed to identify any of the items that petitioner intended to seize. In the portion of the form that called for a description of the "person or property" to be seized, petitioner typed a description of respondents' two-story blue house rather than the alleged stockpile of firearms.[1] The warrant did not incorporate by reference the itemized list contained in the application. It did, however, recite that the Magistrate was satisfied the affidavit established probable cause to believe that contraband was concealed on the premises, and that sufficient grounds existed for the warrant's issuance.[2]

The day after the Magistrate issued the warrant, petitioner led a team of law enforcement officers, including both federal agents and members of the local sheriff's department, in the search of respondents' premises. Although respondent Joseph Ramirez was not home, his wife and children were. Petitioner states that he orally described the objects of the search to Mrs. Ramirez in person and to Mr. Ramirez by telephone. According to Mrs. Ramirez, however, petitioner explained only that he was searching for "an explosive device in a box." *Ramirez v. Butte–Silver Bow County*, 298 F.3d 1022, 1026 (CA2002). At any rate, the officers' search uncovered no illegal weapons or explosives. When the officers left, petitioner gave Mrs. Ramirez a copy of the search warrant, but not a copy of the application, which had been sealed. The following day, in response to a request from respondents' attorney, petitioner faxed the attorney a copy of the page of the application that listed the items to be seized. No charges were filed against the Ramirezes.

Respondents sued petitioner and the other officers under *Bivens v. Six Unknown Fed. Narcotics Agents*, 403 U.S. 388, 91 S.Ct. 1999 (1971) raising eight claims, including violation of the Fourth Amendment. The District Court entered summary judgment for all defendants. The court found on the Fourth Amendment violation, because it considered the case comparable to one in which the warrant contained an inaccurate address, and in such a case, the court reasoned, the warrant is sufficiently detailed if the executing officers can locate the correct house. The court added that even if a constitutional violation occurred, the defendants were entitled to qualified immunity because the failure of the warrant to describe the objects of the search amounted to a mere "typographical error."

The Court of Appeals affirmed the judgment with respect to all defendants and all claims, with respect to all defendants and all claims, with the exception of respondents' Fourth Amendment claim against petitioner. On that claim, the court held that the warrant was invalid because it did not "describe with particularity the place to be searched and the items to be seized," and that oral statements by petitioner during or after the search could not cure the omission. The court observed that the

---

1. The warrant stated: "[T]here is now concealed [on the specified premise] a certain person or property, namely [a] single dwelling residence two story in height which is blue in color and has two additions attached to the east. The front entrance to the residence faces in a southerly direction." App. To Pet. for Cert. 26a.

2. The affidavit was sealed. Its sufficiency is not disputed.

warrant's facial defect "increased the likelihood and degree of confrontation between Ramirezes and the police" and deprived respondents of the means "to challenge officers who might have exceeded the limits imposed by the magistrate." The court also expressed concern that "permitting officers to expand the scope of the warrant by oral statements would broaden the area of dispute between the parties in subsequent litigation." The court nevertheless concluded that all of the officers except petitioner were protected by qualified immunity. With respect to petitioner, the court read our opinion in *United States v. Leon*, 468 U.S. 897, 104 S.Ct. 3405 (1984) as precluding qualified immunity for the leader of a search who fails to "read the warrant and satisfy [himself] that [he] understand[s] its scope and limitations, and it is not defective in some obvious way." The court added that "[t]he leaders of the search team must also make sure that a copy of the warrant is available to give to the person whose property is being searched at the commencement of the search, and that such copy has no missing pages or other obvious defects" (cites omitted).

II

The warrant was plainly invalid. The Fourth Amendment states unambiguously that "no Warrants shall issue, but upon probable cause, supported by Oath or affirmation, and particularly describing the place to be searched, and *the persons or things to be seized*." (Emphasis added.) The warrant in this case complied with the first three of these requirements: It is based on probable cause and supported by a sworn affidavit, and it described particularly the place of the search. On the fourth requirement, however, the warrant failed altogether. Indeed, petitioner concedes that "the warrant ... was deficient in particularity because it provided no description of the type of evidence sought." Brief for Petitioner 10.

The fact that the application adequately described the "things to be seized" does not save the *warrant* from its facial invalidity. The Fourth Amendment by its terms requires particularity in the warrant, not in the supporting documents. See *Massachusetts v. Sheppard*, 468 U.S. 981, 104 S.Ct. 3424 (1984) ("[A] warrant that fails to conform to the particularity requirement of the Fourth Amendment is unconstitutional").... But in case the warrant did not incorporate other documents by reference, nor did either the affidavit or the application (which had been placed under seal) accompany the warrant. Hence, we need not further explore the matter of incorporation.

Petitioner argues that even though the warrant was invalid, the search nevertheless was "reasonable" within the meaning of the Fourth Amendment. He notes that a Magistrate authorized the search on the basis of adequate evidence of probable cause, that petitioner orally described to respondents the items to be seized, and that the search did not exceed the limits intended by the Magistrate and described by petitioner. Thus, petitioner maintains, his search of respondents' ranch was functionally equivalent to a search authorized by a valid warrant.

We disagree. This warrant did not simply omit a few items from a list of many to be seized, or misdescribe a few of several items. Nor did it make what fairly could be characterized as a mere technical mistake or typographical error. Rather, in the space set aside for a description of the items to be seized, the warrant stated that the items consisted of a "single dwelling residence . . . blue in color." In other words, the warrant did not describe the items to be seized *at* all (emphasis in original). In this respect the warrant was so obviously deficient that we must regard the search as "warrantless" within the meaning of our case law (cites omitted). Our cases have firmly established the "basic principle of Fourth Amendment law that searches and seizures inside a home without a warrant are presumptively unreasonable," *Payton v. New York*, 445 U.S. 573, 586, 100 S.Ct. 1371 (1980) (footnote omitted). . . . Thus, "absent exigent circumstances, a warrantless entry to search for weapons or contraband is unconstitutional even when a felony has been committed and there is probable cause to believe that incriminating evidence will be found within." *Id.*, 445 U.S. at 587–88, 1010 S.Ct. 1371 (footnote omitted) (further cites omitted).

We have clearly stated that the presumptive rule against warrantless searches applies with equal force to searches whose only defect is a lack of particularity in the warrant. In *Sheppard*, for instance, the petitioner argued that even though the warrant was invalid for lack of particularity, "the search was constitutional because it was reasonable within the meaning of the Fourth Amendment." 468 U.S., at 988, n. 5. In squarely rejecting that position, we explained:

> The uniformly applied rule is that a search conducted pursuant to a warrant that fails to conform to the particularity requirement of the Fourth Amendment is unconstitutional. (cites omitted). That rule is in keeping with the well-established principle that 'except in certain carefully defined classes of cases, a search of private property without proper consent is "unreasonable" unless it has been authorized by a valid search warrant' (cites omitted).

Petitioner asks us to hold that a search conducted pursuant to a warrant lacking particularity should be exempt from the presumption of unreasonableness if the goals served by the particularity requirement are otherwise satisfied. He maintains that the requirement are otherwise satisfied. He maintains that the search in this case satisfied those goals–which he says are "to prevent general searches, to prevent the seizure of one thing under a warrant describing another, and to prevent warrants from being issued o vague or dubious information ," Brief for Petitioner 16–because the scope of the search did not exceed the limits set forth in the application. But unless the particular items described in the affidavit are also set forth in the warrant itself (or at least incorporated by reference, and the affidavit present at the search), there can be no written assurance that the Magistrate actually found probable cause to search for, and to seize, every item mentioned in the affidavit (cite omitted). In this case, for example, it is at least theoretically possible that the Magistrate was satisfied that the search for weapons and explosives was justified by the showing in the affidavit, but not convinced that any evidentiary basis existed for rummaging through respondents' files and papers for receipts pertaining to the purchase or manufacture of such items. Cf. *Stanford* v. *Texas,* 379 U.S. 476, 485–486, 85 S. Ct. 506 (1965). Or, conceivably, the Magistrate might have believed that some of the weapons mentioned in the affidavit could have been lawfully possessed and therefore should not be seized. See 26 USC § 5861 [26 USCS § 5861] (requiring registration, but not banning possession of, certain firearms). The mere fact that the Magistrate issued a warrant does not necessarily establish that he agreed that the scope of the search should be as broad as the affiant's request. Even though petitioner acted with restraint in conducting the search, "the inescapable fact is that this restraint was imposed by the agents themselves, not by a judicial officer." *Katz* v. *United States,* 389 U.S. 347, 356, 88 S. Ct. 507 (1967).[3]

We have long held, moreover, that the purpose of the particularity requirement is not limited to the prevention of general searches (cite omitted). A particular warrant also "assures the individual whose property is searched or seized of the lawful authority of the executing officer, his need to search, and the limits of his power to search"(cites omitted)....

It is incumbent on the officer executing a search warrant to ensure the search is lawfully authorized and lawfully conducted. Because petitioner did not have in his possession a warrant particularly describing the things he intended to seize, proceeding with the search was clearly "unreasonable" under the Fourth Amendment. The Court of Appeals correctly held that the search was unconstitutional.

III

Having concluded that a constitutional violation occurred, we turn to the question whether petitioner is entitled to qualified immunity despite that violation. See *Wilson* v. *Layne,* 526 U.S. 603, 609, 119 S. Ct. 1692 (1999). The answer depends on whether the right that was transgressed was " 'clearly established' "—that is, "whether it would be clear to a reasonable officer that his conduct was unlawful in the situation he confronted." *Saucier* v. *Katz,* 533 U.S. 194, 202, 150 L. Ed. 2d 272, 121 S. Ct. 2151 (2001). Given that the particularity requirement is set forth in the text of the Constitution, no reasonable officer could believe that a warrant that plainly did not comply with that requirement was valid. See *Harlow* v. *Fitzgerald,* 457 U.S. 800, 818–819, 102 S. Ct. 2727 (1982) ("If the law was clearly established, the immunity defense ordinarily should fail, since a reasonably competent public official should know the law governing his conduct"). Moreover, because petitioner himself prepared the invalid warrant, he may not argue that he reasonably relied on the Magistrate's

---

3. For this reason petitioner's argument that any constitutional error was committed by the Magistrate, not petitioner, is misplaced. In *Massachusetts v. Sheppard,* 468 U.S. 981, 104 S. Ct. 3424 (1984), we suggested that "the judge, not the police officers," may have committed "[a]n error of constitutional dimension," *id.,* 468 U.S. at 990, 104 S. Ct. 3424, because the judge had assured the officers requesting the warrant that he would take the steps necessary to conform the warrant to constitutional requirements, *id.,* 468 U.S. at 968, 104 S. Ct. 3424. Thus, "it was not unreasonable for the police in [that] case to rely on the judge's assurances that the warrant authorized the search they had requested." *id.,* 468 U.S. at 900, n. 6, 1024 S. Ct. 3424. In this case, by contrast, the petitioner did not alert the Magistrate to the defect in the warrant the petitioner had drafted, and we therefore cannot know whether the Magistrate was aware of the search he was authorizing. Nor would it have been reasonable for petitioner to rely on a warrant that was so patently defective, even if the Magistrate was aware of the deficiency. See United States v. Leon, 468 U.S. 897, 915, 922, n. 23, 104 S. Ct. 3405 (1984).

assurance that the warrant contained an adequate description of the things to be seized and was therefore valid. Cf. *Sheppard*, 468 U.S., at 989–990, 104 S. Ct. 3424. In fact, the guidelines of petitioner's own department placed him on notice that he might be liable for executing a manifestly invalid warrant. An ATF directive in force at the time of this search warned: "Special agents are liable if they exceed their authority while executing a search warrant and must be sure that a search warrant is sufficient on its face even when issued by a magistrate." Searches and Examinations, ATF Order O 3220.1(7)(d) (Feb. 13, 1997). See also *id.*, at 3220.1(23)(b) ("If any error or deficiency is discovered and there is a reasonable probability that it will invalidate the warrant, such warrant shall not be executed. The search shall be postponed until a satisfactory warrant has been obtained").[4] And even a cursory reading of the warrant in this case—perhaps just a simple glance—would have revealed a glaring deficiency that any reasonable police officer would have known was constitutionally fatal.

No reasonable officer could claim to be unaware of the basic rule, well established by our cases, that, absent consent or exigency, a warrantless search of the home is presumptively unconstitutional. See *Payton*, 445 U.S., at 586–588, 100 S. Ct. 1371. Indeed, as we noted nearly 20 years ago in *Sheppard*: "The uniformly applied rule is that a search conducted pursuant to a warrant that fails to conform to the particularity requirement of the Fourth Amendment is unconstitutional." 468 U.S., at 988, n. 5, 104 S. Ct. 3424.[5] Because not a word in any of our cases would suggest to a reasonable officer that this case fits within any exception to that fundamental tenet, petitioner is asking us, in effect, to craft a new exception. Absent any support for such an exception in our cases, he cannot reasonably have relied on an expectation that we would do so.

Petitioner contends that the search in this case was the product, at worst, of a lack of due care, and that our case law requires more than negligent behavior before depriving an official of qualified immunity. See *Malley* v. *Briggs*, 475 U.S. 335, 341, 106 S. Ct. 1092 (1986). But as we observed in the companion case to *Sheppard*, "a warrant may be so facially deficient—*i.e.*, in failing to particularize the place to be searched or the things to be seized—that the executing officers cannot reasonably presume it to be valid." *Leon*, 468 U.S., at 923, 104 S. Ct. 3405 . This is such a case.[6]

---

4. We do not suggest that an official is deprived of qualified immunity whenever he violates an internal guideline. We refer to the ATF Order only to underscore that petitioner should have known that he should not execute a patently defective warrant.

5. Although both *Sheppard* and *Leon* involved the application of the "good faith" exception to the Fourth Amendment's general exclusionary rule, we have explained that "the same standard of objective reasonableness that we applied in the context of a suppression hearing in *Leon* defines the qualified immunity accorded an officer." *Malley* v.

Briggs, 475 U.S. 335, 344, 106 S. Ct. 1092 (1986) (citation omitted).

6. Justice Kennedy argues in dissent that we have not allowed " 'ample room for mistaken judgments,' " *post*, at __, 157 L. Ed. 2d, at 1087 (quoting *Malley*, 475 U.S., at 343, 271, 106S. Ct. 1092), because "difficult and important tasks demand the officer's full attention in the heat of an ongoing and often dangerous criminal investigation." In this case, however, petitioner does not contend that any sort of exigency existed when he drafted the affidavit, the warrant application, and the warrant, or when he conducted the

Accordingly, the judgment of the Court of Appeals is affirmed.

It is so ordered.

■ DISSENT: JUSTICE KENNEDY, with whom the CHIEF JUSTICE joins, dissenting.

I agree with the Court that the Fourth Amendment was violated in this case. The Fourth Amendment states that "no Warrants shall issue, but upon probable cause, supported by Oath or affirmation, and particularly describing the place to be search, and the persons or things to be seized." The warrant issued in this case did not particularly describe the things to be seized, and so did not comply with the Fourth Amendment. I disagree with the Court on whether the officer who obtained the warrant and led the search team is entitled to qualified immunity for his role in the search. In my view, the officer should receive qualified immunity.

The present case involves a straightforward mistake of fact. Although the Court does not acknowledge it directly, it is obvious from the record below that the officer simply made a clerical error when he filled out the proposed warrant and offered it to the Magistrate Judge. The officer used the proper description of the property to be seized when he completed the affidavit. He also used the proper description in the accompanying application. When he typed up the description a third time for the proposed warrant, however, the officer accidentally entered a description of the place to be searched in the part of the warrant form that called for a description of the property to be seized. No one noticed the error before the search was executed. Although the record is not entirely clear on this point, the mistake apparently remained undiscovered until the day after the search when respondents' attorney reviewed the warrant for defects. The officer, being unaware of his mistake, did not rely on it in any way. It is uncontested that the officer trained the search team and executed the warrant based on his mistaken belief that the warrant contained the proper description of the items to be seized.

The question is whether the officer's mistaken belief that the warrant contained the proper language was a reasonable belief. In my view, it was. A law enforcement officer charged with leading a team to execute a search warrant for illegal weapons must fulfill a number of serious responsibilities. The officer must establish probable cause to believe the crime has been committed and that evidence is likely to be found at the place to be search; must articulate specific items that can be seized, and a specific place to be searched; must obtain the warrant from a magistrate judge; and must instruct a search team to execute the warrant within the time allowed by the warrant. The officer must also oversee the execution of the warrant in

search. This is not the situation, therefore, in which we have recognized that "officers in the dangerous and difficult process of making arrests and executing search warrants" require "some latitude." *Maryland* v. *Garrison,* 480 U.S. 79, 87, 107 S. Ct. 1013 (1987).

Nor are we according "the correctness of paper forms" a higher status than "substantive rights." As we have explained, the Fourth Amendment's particularity requirement assures the subject of the search that a magistrate has duly authorized the officer to conduct a search of limited scope. This substantive right is not protected when the officer fails to take the time to glance at the authorizing document and detect a glaring defect that Justice Kennedy agrees is of constitutional magnitude.

a way that protects officer safety, directs a thorough and professional search for the evidence, and avoids unnecessary destruction of property. These difficult and important tasks demand the officer's full attention in the heat of an ongoing and often dangerous criminal investigation.

An officer who complies fully with all of these duties can be excused for not being aware that he had made a clerical error in the course of filling out the proposed warrant. See *Maryland v. Garrison,* 480 U.S. 79, 87, 107 S. Ct 1013 (1987) (recognizing "the need to allow some latitude for honest mistakes that are made by officers in the dangerous and difficult process of making arrests and executing search warrants"). An officer who drafts an affidavit, types up an application and proposed warrant, and then obtains a judge's approval naturally assumes that he has filled out the warrant form correctly. Even if the officer checks over the warrant, he may very well miss a mistake. We all tend toward myopia when looking for our own errors. Every lawyer and every judge can recite examples of documents that they wrote, checked, and double checked, but that still contained glaring errors. Law enforcement officers are no different. It would be better if the officer recognizes the error, of course. It would be better still if he does not make the mistake in the first place. In the context of an otherwise proper search, however, and officer's failure to recognize his clerical error on a warrant form can be a reasonable mistake.

■ JUSTICE THOMAS with whom JUSTICE SCALIA joins, and with whom THE CHIEF JUSTICE joins as to Part III, dissenting.

The Fourth Amendment provides: "The right of the people to be secure in their persons, houses, and papers, and effects, against unreasonable searches and seizures, shall not be violated, and no Warrants shall issue, but upon probable cause, supported by Oath or affirmation, and the persons or things to be seized." The precise relationship between the Amendment's Warrant Clause and Unreasonableness Clause is unclear. But neither Clause explicitly requires a warrant. While "it is of course textually possible to consider [a warrant requirement] implicit within the requirement of reasonableness," California v. Acevedo, 500 U.S. 565, 582, 111. Ct. 1982 (1991) (Scalia, J., concurring in judgment), the text of the Fourth Amendment certainly does not mandate this result. Nor does the Amendment's history, which is clear as to the Amendment's principal target (general warrants), but not as clear with respect to when warrants were required, if ever. Indeed, because of the very different nature and scope of federal authority and ability to conduct searches and arrests at the founding, it is possible that neither the history of the Fourth Amendment nor the common law provides much guidance.

As a result, the Court has vacillated between imposing a categorical warrant requirement and applying a general reasonableness standard. That is, our cases stand for the illuminating proposition that warrantless searches are *per se* unreasonable, except, of course, when they are not.

Today the Court holds that the warrant in this case was "so obvious deficient" that the ensuing search must be regarded as a warrantless search and thus presumptively unreasonable. However, the text of the Fourth Amendment, its history, and the sheer number of exceptions to Court's categorical warrant requirement seriously undermine the bases upon which the Court today rests its holding. Instead of adding to this confusing jurisprudence, as the Court has done, I would turn to first principles in order to determine the relationship between the Warrant Clause and the Unreasonableness Clause. But even within the Court's current framework, a search conducted pursuant to a "warrantless search." Consequently, despite the defective warrant, I would still ask whether this search was unreasonable and would conclude that it was not. Furthermore, even if the Court were correct that this search violated the Constitution (and in particular, respondents' Fourth Amendment rights), given the confused state of our Fourth Amendment jurisprudence and the reasonableness of petitioner's actions, I cannot agree with the Court's conclusion that petitioner is not entitled to qualified immunity. For these reasons, I respectfully dissent.

I

"[A]ny Fourth Amendment case may present two separate questions: whether the search was conducted pursuant to a warrant issued in accordance with the second Clause, and, if not, whether it was nevertheless 'reasonable' within the meaning of the first." *United States v. Leon*, 468 U.S. 897, 961, 104 S. Ct. 3405 (1984) (Stevens, J. Dissenting). By categorizing the search here to be a "warrantless" one, the Court declines to perform a reasonableness inquiry and ignore the fact that this search is quite different from searches that the Court has considered to be "warrantless" in the past. Our cases involving "warrantless" searches do not generally involve situations in which an officer has obtained a warrant that is later determined to be facially defective, but rather involve situations in which the officers neither sought nor obtained a warrant. By simply treating this case as if no warrant had even been sought or issued, the Court glosses over what should be the key inquiry: whether it is always appropriate to treat a search made pursuant to a warrant that fails to describe particularly the things to be seized as presumptively unreasonable.

In the instant case, the items to be seized were clearly specified in the warrant application and set forth in the affidavit, both of which were given to the Judge (Magistrate). The Magistrate reviewed all of the documents and signed the warrant application. It is clear that respondents here received the protection of the Warrant Clause, as described in *Johnson* and *McDonald*. Under these circumstances, I would not hold that any ensuing search constitutes a presumptively unreasonable warrantless search. Instead, I would determine whether , despite the invalid warrant, the resulting search was reasonable and hence constitutional.

II

Because the search was not unreasonable, I would conclude that it was constitutional. Prior to execution of the warrant, petitioner briefed the search team and provided a copy of the search warrant application, the supporting affidavit, and the warrant for the officers to review. Petitioner orally reviewed the terms of the warrant with the officers, including the specific items for which the officers were authorized to search. Petitioner and his search team then conducted the search entirely within the scope of the warrant application and warrant that is, within the scope of what the

Magistrate had authorized. Finding no illegal weapons or explosives, the search team seized nothing.

The only remaining question is whether petitioner's failure to notice the defect was objectively unreasonable. The Court today points to no cases directing an officer to proofread a warrant after it has been passed on by a neutral magistrate, where the officer is already fully aware of the scope of the intended search and the magistrate gives no reason to believe that he has authorized anything other than the requested search. Nor does the Court point to any case suggesting that where the same officer both prepares and executes the invalid warrant, he can never rely on the magistrate's assurance that the warrant is proper. Indeed, in *Massachusetts v. Sheppard*, 468 U.S. 981, 104 S. Ct. 3424 (1984), The Court suggested that although an officer who is not involved in the warrant application process would normally read the issued warrant to determine the object of the search, an executing officer who is also the affiant might not need to do so. *Id.*, 468 U.S. at 989, n. 6, 104 S. Ct. 3424.

Although the Court contends that it does not impose a proofreading requirement upon officers executing warrants, I see no other way to read its decision, particularly where, as here, petitioner could have done nothing more to ensure the reasonableness of his actions than to proofread the warrant. After receiving several allegations that respondents possessed illegal firearms and explosives, petitioner prepared an application for a warrant to search respondents' ranch, along with a supporting affidavit detailing the history of allegations against respondents, petitioner's investigation into these allegations, and petitioner's verification of the sources of the allegations. Petitioner properly filled out the warrant application, which described both the place to be search and the things to be seized, and obtained the Magistrate's signature on both the warrant application and the warrant itself. Prior to execution of the warrant, petitioner briefed the search team to ensure that each officer understood the limits of the search. Petitioner and his search team then executed the warrant within those limits. And when the error in the search warrant was discovered, petitioner promptly faxed the missing information to respondents. In my view, petitioner's actions were objectively reasonable, and thus he should be entitled to qualified immunity.

D. ALTERNATIVE REMEDIES

Add after note 1 on page 608:

For another variation on the sovereign immunity theme, see *Inyo County v. Paiute–Shoshone Indians of the Bishop Community of the Bishop Colony*, 538 U.S. 701, 123 S.Ct. 1887 (2003). In dicta, the Court indicated that Indian tribes, like States, are not "persons" subject to suits under 42 U.S.C. § 1983. Moreover, the tribe sought to interpose 42 U.S.C. § 1983 as a claimant to argue it was immune from the execution of a search. The Court determined that, in the situation presented, the Tribe did not qualify as a person within the jurisdiction of the United States under § 1983. The Tribe could not sue under § 1983 to vindicate the sovereign right it claimed. Section 1983 was designed to secure private rights against government encroachment, not to advance a sovereign's prerogative to withhold evidence relevant to a criminal investigation.

Add at the end of note 3 on page 608:

Would this explain the difference in the Court's approach to the facts in *Massachusetts v. Sheppard*, 468 U.S. 981, 104 S.Ct. 3424 (1984) [described in note 1 on page 598 *supra*] as compared to the Court's approach to the facts in *Groh v. Ramirez*, 540 U.S. 551, 124 S.Ct. 1284 (2004) [added in this supplement to note 1 on page 598]?

G. DERIVATIVE EVIDENCE: PRINCIPLES AND LIMITATIONS

Add after first paragraph of note 3 on page 666:

If officers fail to give *Miranda* warnings to a suspect in a situation in which they are required (custodial interrogation), but the suspect nevertheless makes a voluntary statement that leads to the discovery of physical evidence, must the physical evidence be suppressed?:

United States v. Patane

542 U.S. 630, 124 S.Ct. 2620 (2004).

■ OPINION: JUSTICE THOMAS announced the judgment of the Court and delivered an opinion, in which THE CHIEF JUSTICE and JUSTICE SCALIA join.

In this case we must decide whether a failure to give a suspect the warnings prescribed by *Miranda v. Arizona*, 384 U.S. 436, 86 S. Ct. 1602 (1966), requires suppression of the physical fruits of the suspect's unwarned but voluntary statements. The Court has previously addressed this question but has not reached a definitive conclusion. See *Massachusetts v. White*, 439 U.S. 280, 99 S. Ct. 712 (1978) *(per curiam)* (dividing evenly on the question); see also *Patterson v. United States*, 485 U.S. 922, 108 S. Ct. 1093 (1988) (White, J., dissenting from denial of certiorari). Although we believe that the Court's decisions in *Oregon v. Elstad*, 470 U.S. 298, 105 S. Ct. 1285 (1985), and *Michigan v. Tucker*, 417 U.S. 433, 94 S. Ct. 2357 (1974), are instructive, the Courts of Appeals have split on the question after our decision in *Dickerson v. United States*, 530 U.S. 428, 120 S. Ct. 2326 (2000). See, *e.g.*, *United States v. Villalba-Alvarado*, 345 F.3d 1007 (8th Cir. 2003) (holding admissible the physical fruits of a *Miranda* violation); *United States v. Sterling*, 283 F.3d 216 (4th Cir. 2002) (same); *United States v. DeSumma*, 272 F.3d 176 (CA3 2001) (same); *United States v. Faulkingham*, 295 F.3d 85 (1st Cir. 2002) (holding admissible the physical fruits of a negligent *Miranda* violation). Because the *Miranda* rule protects against violations of the Self–Incrimination Clause, which, in turn, is not implicated by the introduction at trial of physical evidence resulting from voluntary statements, we answer the question presented in the negative.

I

In June 2001, respondent, Samuel Francis Patane, was arrested for harassing his ex-girlfriend, Linda O'Donnell. He was released on bond, subject to a temporary restraining order that prohibited him from contacting O'Donnell. Respondent apparently violated the restraining order by attempting to telephone O'Donnell. On June 6, 2001, Officer Tracy Fox of the Colorado Springs Police Department began to investigate the matter. On the same day, a county probation officer informed an agent of the Bureau of Alcohol, Tobacco, and Firearms (ATF), that respondent, a convicted felon, illegally possessed a .40 Glock pistol. The ATF relayed this information to Detective Josh Benner, who worked closely with the ATF. Together, Detective Benner and Officer Fox proceeded to respondent's residence.

After reaching the residence and inquiring into respondent's attempts to contact O'Donnell, Officer Fox arrested respondent for violating the restraining order. Detective Benner attempted to advise respondent of his *Miranda* rights but got no further than the right to remain silent. At that point, respondent interrupted, asserting that he knew his rights, and neither officer attempted to complete the warning.[1] App. 40.

Detective Benner then asked respondent about the Glock. Respondent was initially reluctant to discuss the matter, stating: "I am not sure I should tell you anything about the Glock because I don't want you to take it away from me." Detective Benner persisted, and respondent told him that the pistol was in his bedroom. Respondent then gave Detective Benner permission to retrieve the pistol. Detective Benner found the pistol and seized it.

A grand jury indicted respondent for possession of a firearm by a convicted felon, in violation of 18 U.S.C. § 922(g)(1). The District Court granted respondent's motion to suppress the firearm, reasoning that the officers lacked probable cause to arrest respondent for violating the restraining order. It therefore declined to rule on respondent's alternative argument that the gun should be suppressed as the fruit of an unwarned statement.

The Court of Appeals reversed the District Court's ruling with respect to probable cause but affirmed the suppression order on respondent's alternative theory. The court rejected the Government's argument that this Court's decisions in *Elstad, supra,* and Tucker, supra, foreclosed application of the fruit of the poisonous tree doctrine of *Wong Sun* v. *United States,* 371 U.S. 471, 83 S. Ct. 407 (1963), to the present context (cite omitted). These holdings were, the Court of Appeals reasoned, based on the view that *Miranda* announced a prophylactic rule, a position that it found to be incompatible with this Court's decision in *Dickerson* (cite omitted) ("*Miranda* announced a constitutional rule that Congress may not supersede legislatively"). The Court of Appeals thus equated *Dickerson*'s announcement that *Miranda* is a constitutional rule with the proposition that a failure to warn pursuant to *Miranda* is itself a violation of the Constitution (and, more particularly, of the suspect's Fifth Amendment rights). Based on its understanding of *Dickerson,* the Court of Appeals rejected the

---

1. The Government concedes that respondent's answers to subsequent on-the-scene questioning are inadmissible at trial under *Miranda* v. *Arizona,* 384 U.S. 436, 86 S. Ct. 1602 (1966), despite the partial warning and respondent's assertions that he knew his rights.

post-*Dickerson* views of the Third and Fourth Circuits that the fruits doctrine does not apply to *Miranda* violations (cites omitted) It also disagreed with the First Circuit's conclusion that suppression is not generally required in the case of negligent failures to warn (cites omitted) . . . explaining that "deterrence is necessary not merely to deter intentional wrongdoing, but also to ensure that officers diligently (non-negligently) protect—and properly are trained to protect—the constitutional rights of citizens," (cite omitted). We granted certiorari (cite omitted).

As we explain below, the *Miranda* rule is a prophylactic employed to protect against violations of the Self–Incrimination Clause. The Self–Incrimination Clause, however, is not implicated by the admission into evidence of the physical fruit of a voluntary statement. Accordingly, there is no justification for extending the *Miranda* rule to this context. And just as the Self–Incrimination Clause primarily focuses on the criminal trial, so too does the *Miranda* rule. The *Miranda* rule is not a code of police conduct, and police do not violate the Constitution (or even the *Miranda* rule, for that matter) by mere failures to warn. For this reason, the exclusionary rule articulated in cases such as *Wong Sun* does not apply. Accordingly, we reverse the judgment of the Court of Appeals and remand the case for further proceedings consistent with this opinion.

II

The Self–Incrimination Clause provides: "No person . . . shall be compelled in any criminal case to be a witness against himself." U.S. Const., Amdt. 5. We need not decide here the precise boundaries of the Clause's protection. For present purposes, it suffices to note that the core protection afforded by the Self–Incrimination Clause is a prohibition on compelling a criminal defendant to testify against himself at trial (cites omitted).

To be sure, the Court has recognized and applied several prophylactic rules designed to protect the core privilege against self-incrimination (cite omitted). . . .

Similarly, in *Miranda*, the Court concluded that the possibility of coercion inherent in custodial interrogations unacceptably raises the risk that a suspect's privilege against self-incrimination might be violated. See *Dickerson*, 530 U.S., at 434–435, 120 S. Ct. 2326; *Miranda*, 384 U.S., at 467, 86 S. Ct. 1602. To protect against this danger, the *Miranda* rule creates a presumption of coercion, in the absence of specific warnings, that is generally irrebuttable for purposes of the prosecution's case in chief.

But because these prophylactic rules (including the *Miranda* rule) necessarily sweep beyond the actual protections of the Self–Incrimination Clause, (cites omitted). . . .

It is for these reasons that statements taken without *Miranda* warnings (though not actually compelled) can be used to impeach a defendant's testimony at trial, (cites omitted). More generally, the *Miranda* rule "does not require that the statements [taken without complying with the rule] and their fruits be discarded as inherently tainted," *Elstad*, 470 U.S., at 307, 105 S. Ct. 1285. Such a blanket suppression rule could not be justified by reference to the "Fifth Amendment goal of assuring trustworthy evidence" or by any deterrence rationale, (cites omitted) and would therefore fail our close-fit requirement.

Furthermore, the Self–Incrimination Clause contains its own exclusionary rule. It provides that "no person ... shall be compelled in any criminal case to be a witness against himself." Amdt. 5. Unlike the Fourth Amendment's bar on unreasonable searches, the Self–Incrimination Clause is self-executing. We have repeatedly explained "that those subjected to coercive police interrogations have an *automatic* protection from the use of their involuntary statements (or evidence derived from their statements) in any subsequent criminal trial." *Chavez*, 538 U.S., at 769, 123 S. Ct. 1994 (plurality opinion) (citing, for example, *Elstad, supra,* at 307–308, 105 S. Ct. 1285). This explicit textual protection supports a strong presumption against expanding the *Miranda* rule any further. Cf. *Graham* v. *Connor*, 490 U.S. 386, 109 S. Ct. 1865 (1989).

Finally, nothing in *Dickerson*, including its characterization of *Miranda* as announcing a constitutional rule, 530 U.S., at 444, 120 S. Ct. 2326, changes any of these observations. Indeed, in *Dickerson*, the Court specifically noted that the Court's "subsequent cases have reduced the impact of the *Miranda* rule on legitimate law enforcement while reaffirming [*Miranda*]'s core ruling that unwarned statements may not be used as evidence in the prosecution's case in chief." *Id.,* at 443–444, 120 S. Ct. 2326. This description of *Miranda*, especially the emphasis on the use of "unwarned statements ... in the prosecution's case in chief," makes clear our continued focus on the protections of the Self–Incrimination Clause. The Court's reliance on our *Miranda* precedents, including both *Tucker* and *Elstad*, see, *e.g., Dickerson, supra,* at 438, 441, 147 L. Ed. 2d 405, 120 S. Ct. 2326, further demonstrates the continuing validity of those decisions. In short, nothing in *Dickerson* calls into question our continued insistence that the closest possible fit be maintained between the Self–Incrimination Clause and any rule designed to protect it.

III

Our cases also make clear the related point that a mere failure to give *Miranda* warnings does not, by itself, violate a suspect's constitutional rights or even the *Miranda* rule. So much was evident in many of our pre-*Dickerson* cases, and we have adhered to this view since *Dickerson* (cites omitted). . . .

It follows that police do not violate a suspect's constitutional rights (or the *Miranda* rule) by negligent or even deliberate failures to provide the suspect with the full panoply of warnings prescribed by *Miranda*. Potential violations occur, if at all, only upon the admission of unwarned statements into evidence at trial. And, at that point, "the exclusion of unwarned statements ... is a complete and sufficient remedy" for any perceived *Miranda* violation (cite omitted).

Thus, unlike unreasonable searches under the Fourth Amendment or actual violations of the Due Process Clause or the Self–Incrimination Clause, there is, with respect to mere failures to warn, nothing to deter. There is therefore no reason to apply the "fruit of the poisonous tree" doctrine of *Wong Sun,* (cite omitted) It is not for this Court to impose its preferred police practices on either federal law enforcement officials or their state counterparts.

IV

In the present case, the Court of Appeals, relying on *Dickerson*, wholly adopted the position that the taking of unwarned statements violates a suspect's constitutional rights (cite omitted). And, of course, if this were so, a strong deterrence-based argument could be made for suppression of the fruits (cites omitted).

But *Dickerson*'s characterization of *Miranda* as a constitutional rule does not lessen the need to maintain the closest possible fit between the Self–Incrimination Clause and any judge-made rule designed to protect it. And there is no such fit here. Introduction of the nontestimonial fruit of a voluntary statement, such as respondent's Glock, does not implicate the Self Incrimination Clause. The admission of such fruit presents no risk that a defendant's coerced statements (however defined) will be used against him at a criminal trial. In any case, "the exclusion of unwarned statements ... is a complete and sufficient remedy" for any perceived *Miranda* violation. *Chavez*, 538 U.S., at 790, 123 S. Ct. 1994 (Kennedy, J., concurring in part and dissenting in part). See also H. Friendly, Benchmarks 280–281 (1967). There is simply no need to extend (and therefore no justification for extending) the prophylactic rule of *Miranda* to this context.

Similarly, because police cannot violate the Self–Incrimination Clause by taking unwarned though voluntary statements, an exclusionary rule cannot be justified by reference to a deterrence effect on law enforcement, as the Court of Appeals believed (cite omitted), our decision not to apply *Wong Sun* to mere failures to give *Miranda* warnings was sound at the time *Tucker* and *Elstad* were decided, and we decline to apply *Wong Sun* to such failures now....

Accordingly, we reverse the judgment of the Court of Appeals and remand the case for further proceedings consistent with this opinion.

It is so ordered.

■ CONCUR: Justice Kennedy, with whom Justice O'Connor joins, concurring in the judgment

In *Oregon* v. *Elstad, New York* v. *Quarles*, and *Harris* v. *New York* (cites omitted), evidence obtained following an unwarned interrogation was held admissible. This result was based in large part on our recognition that the concerns underlying the *Miranda* v. *Arizona,* 384 U.S. 436, 86 S. Ct. 1602 (1966), rule must be accommodated to other objectives of the criminal justice system. I agree with the plurality that *Dickerson* v. *United States,* 530 U.S. 428, 120 S. Ct. 2326 (2000), did not undermine these precedents and, in fact, cited them in support. Here, it is sufficient to note that the Government presents an even stronger case for admitting the evidence obtained as the result of Patane's unwarned statement. Admission of nontestimonial physical fruits (the Glock in this case), even more so than the postwarning statements to the police in *Elstad* and *Michigan* v. *Tucker,* 417 U.S. 433, 94 S. Ct. 2357 (1974), does not run the risk of admitting into trial an accused's coerced incriminating statements against himself. In light of the important probative value of reliable physical evidence, it is doubtful that exclusion can be justified by a deterrence rationale sensitive to both law enforcement interests and a suspect's rights during an in-custody interrogation. Unlike the plurality, however, I find it unnecessary to decide whether the detective's failure to give Patane the full *Miranda* warnings should be characterized as a violation of the *Miranda* rule itself, or whether there is "anything to deter" so long as the unwarned statements are not later introduced at trial.

With these observations, I concur in the judgment of the Court.

■ DISSENT: Justice Souter, with whom Justice Stevens and Justice Ginsburg join, dissenting.

The majority repeatedly says that the Fifth Amendment does not address the admissibility of nontestimonial evidence, an overstatement that is beside the point. The issue actually presented today is whether courts should apply the fruit of the poisonous tree doctrine lest we create an incentive for the police to omit *Miranda* warnings, see *Miranda* v. *Arizona*, 384 U.S. 436, 86 S. Ct. 1602 (1966), before custodial interrogation.[1] In closing their eyes to the consequences of giving an evidentiary advantage to those who ignore *Miranda*, the majority adds an important inducement for interrogators to ignore the rule in that case.

Miranda rested on insight into the inherently coercive character of custodial interrogation and the inherently difficult exercise of assessing the voluntariness of any confession resulting from it. Unless the police give the prescribed warnings meant to counter the coercive atmosphere, a custodial confession is inadmissible, there being no need for the previous time-consuming and difficult enquiry into voluntariness. That inducement to forestall involuntary statements and troublesome issues of fact can only atrophy if we turn around and recognize an evidentiary benefit when an unwarned statement leads investigators to tangible evidence. There is, of course, a price for excluding evidence, but the Fifth Amendment is worth a price, and in the absence of a very good reason, the logic of *Miranda* should be followed: a *Miranda* violation raises a presumption of coercion, *Oregon* v. *Elstad*, 470 U.S. 298, 306–307, 105 S. Ct. 1285, and the Fifth Amendment privilege against compelled self-incrimination extends to the exclusion of derivative evidence, see *United States* v. *Hubbell*, 530 U.S. 27, 37–38, 120 S. Ct. 2037 (2000) (recognizing "the Fifth Amendment's protection against the prosecutor's use of incriminating information derived directly or indirectly from . . . [actually] compelled testimony"); *Kastigar* v. *United States*, 406 U.S. 441, 453, 92 S. Ct. 1653 (1972). That should be the end of this case.

The fact that the books contain some exceptions to the *Miranda* exclusionary rule carries no weight here. In *Harris* v. *New York*, 401 U.S.

---

1. In so saying, we are taking the legal issue as it comes to us, even though the facts give off the scent of a made-up case. If there was a *Miranda* failure, the most immediate reason was that Patane told the police to stop giving the warnings because he already knew his rights. There could easily be an analogy in this case to the bumbling mistake the police committed in *Oregon* v. *Elstad*, 470 U.S. 298, 105 S. Ct. 1285 (1985). See *Missouri* v. *Seibert*, ___ U.S. ___, 124 S. Ct. 2601 (2004) (plurality opinion).

222, 91 S. Ct. 643 (1971), it was respect for the integrity of the judicial process that justified the admission of unwarned statements as impeachment evidence. But Patane's suppression motion can hardly be described as seeking to "pervert" *Miranda* "into a license to use perjury" or otherwise handicap the "traditional truth-testing devices of the adversary process" (cite omitted). Nor is there any suggestion that the officers' failure to warn Patane was justified or mitigated by a public emergency or other exigent circumstance, as in *New York* v. *Quarles*, 467 U.S. 649, 104 S. Ct. 2626 (1984). And of course the premise of *Oregon* v. *Elstad, supra*, is not on point; although a failure to give *Miranda* warnings before one individual statement does not necessarily bar the admission of a subsequent statement given after adequate warnings, 470 U.S. 298, 105 S. Ct. 1285; cf. *Missouri* v. *Seibert* (cite omitted) (plurality opinion), that rule obviously does not apply to physical evidence seized once and for all. [2]

There is no way to read this case except as an unjustifiable invitation to law enforcement officers to flout *Miranda* when there may be physical evidence to be gained. The incentive is an odd one, coming from the Court on the same day it decides *Missouri* v. *Seibert*. I respectfully dissent.

■ JUSTICE BREYER, dissenting.

For reasons similar to those set forth in JUSTICE SOUTER's dissent and in my concurring opinion in *Missouri* v. *Seibert*, I would extend to this context the "fruit of the poisonous tree" approach, which I believe the Court has come close to adopting in *Seibert*. Under that approach, courts would exclude physical evidence derived from unwarned questioning unless the failure to provide *Miranda* warnings was in good faith (cites omitted). Because the courts below made no explicit finding as to good or bad faith, I would remand for such a determination.

Add at end of note 7 on pages 668–669:

Does *Elstad* apply when the Sixth Amendment has attached?

John J. Fellers v. United States

540 U.S. 519, 124 S.Ct. 1019 (2004).

■ OPINION: JUSTICE O'CONNOR delivered the opinion of the Court.

After a grand jury indicted petitioner John J. Fellers, police officers arrested him at his home. During the course of the arrest, petitioner made several inculpatory statements. He argued that the officers deliberately elicited these statements from him outside the presence of counsel, and that the admission at trial of the fruits of those statements therefore violated his Sixth Amendment right to counsel. Petitioner contends that in

---

2. To the extent that *Michigan* v. *Tucker*, 417 U.S. 433, 94 S. Ct. 2357 (1974) (admitting the testimony of a witness who was discovered because of an unwarned custodial interrogation), created another exception to *Miranda*, it is off the point here. In *Tucker*, we explicitly declined to lay down a broad rule about the fruits of unwarned statements. Instead, we "placed our holding on a narrower ground," relying principally on the fact that the interrogation occurred before *Miranda* was decided and was conducted in good faith according to constitutional standards governing at that time. 417 U.S., at 447–448, 94 S. Ct. 2357 (citing *Escobedo v. Illinois*, 378 U.S. 478, 84 S. Ct. 1758 (1964)).

rejecting this argument, the Court of Appeals for the Eighth Circuit improperly held that the Sixth Amendment right to counsel was "not applicable" because "the officers did not interrogate [petitioner] at his home." We granted the petition for a writ of certiorari, (cites omitted), and now reverse.

I

On February 24, 2000, after a grand jury indicted petitioner for conspiracy to distribute methamphetamine, Lincoln Police Sergeant Michael Garnett and Lancaster County Deputy Sheriff Jeff Bliemeister went to petitioner's home in Lincoln, Nebraska, to arrest him. The officers knocked on petitioner's door and, when petitioner answered, identified themselves and asked if they could come in. Petitioner invited the officers into his living room (cites omitted).

The officers advised petitioner they had come to discuss his involvement in methamphetamine distribution. They informed petitioner that they had a federal warrant for his arrest and that a grand jury had indicted him for conspiracy to distribute methamphetamine. The officers told petitioner that the indictment referred to his involvement with certain individuals, four of whom they named. Petitioner then told the officers that he knew the four people and had used methamphetamine during his association with them.

After spending about 15 minutes in petitioner's home, the officers transported petitioner to the Lancaster County jail. There, the officers advised petitioner for the first time of his rights under *Miranda* v. Arizona, and *Patterson* v. *Illinois,* (cites omitted) Petitioner and the two officers signed a *Miranda* waiver form, and petitioner then reiterated the inculpatory statements he had made earlier, admitted to having associated with other individuals implicated in the charged conspiracy, and admitted to having loaned money to one of them even though he suspected that she was involved in drug transactions.

Before trial, petitioner moved to suppress the inculpatory statements he made at his home and at the county jail. A Magistrate Judge conducted a hearing and recommended that the statements petitioner made at his home be suppressed because the officers had not informed petitioner of his *Miranda* rights. The Magistrate Judge found that petitioner made the statements in response to the officers' "implici[t] questions," noting that the officers had told petitioner that the purpose of their visit was to discuss his use and distribution of methamphetamine. The Magistrate Judge further recommended that portions of petitioner's jailhouse statement be suppressed as fruits of the prior failure to provide *Miranda* warnings.

The District Court suppressed the "unwarned" statements petitioner made at his house but admitted petitioner's jailhouse statements pursuant to *Oregon* v. *Elstad,* (cite omitted), concluding petitioner had knowingly and voluntarily waived his *Miranda* rights before making the statements.

Following a jury trial at which petitioner's jailhouse statements were admitted into evidence, petitioner was convicted of conspiring to possess with intent to distribute methamphetamine. Petitioner appealed, arguing

[handwritten margin notes:] Voluntary applies to Miranda

Does it apply to 6th Amendment right to counsel?

that his jailhouse statements should have been suppressed as fruits of the statements obtained at his home in violation of the Sixth Amendment. The Court of Appeals affirmed (cite omitted). With respect to petitioner's argument that the officers' failure to administer *Miranda* warnings at his home violated his Sixth Amendment right to counsel under *Patterson, supra,* the Court of Appeals stated: "*Patterson* is not applicable here . . . for the officers did not interrogate [petitioner] at his home." The Court of Appeals also concluded that the statements from the jail were properly admitted under the rule of *Elstad* (" 'Though *Miranda* requires that the unwarned admission must be suppressed, the admissibility of any subsequent statement should turn in these circumstances solely on whether it is knowingly and voluntarily made' " (quoting *Elstad, supra,* at 309, 84 L. Ed. 2d 222, 105 S. Ct. 1285)).

Judge Riley filed a concurring opinion. He concluded that during their conversation at petitioner's home, officers "deliberately elicited incriminating information" from petitioner (cite omitted). That "post-indictment conduct outside the presence of counsel," Judge Riley reasoned, violated petitioner's Sixth Amendment rights. Judge Riley nevertheless concurred in the judgment, concluding that the jailhouse statements were admissible under the rationale of *Elstad* in light of petitioner's knowing and voluntary waiver of his right to counsel.

II

The Sixth Amendment right to counsel is triggered "at or after the time that judicial proceedings have been initiated . . . 'whether by way of formal charge, preliminary hearing, indictment, information, or arraignment.' " *Brewer* v. *Williams,* 430 U.S. 387, 398, 97 S. Ct. 1232 (1977) (quoting *Kirby* v. *Illinois,* 406 U.S. 682, 689, 92 S. Ct. 1877 (1972)). We have held that an accused is denied "the basic protections" of the Sixth Amendment "when there [is] used against him at his trial evidence of his own incriminating words, which federal agents . . . deliberately elicited from him after he had been indicted and in the absence of his counsel." *Massiah* v. *United States,* 377 U.S. 201, 206, 84 S. Ct. 1199 (1964); cf. *Patterson* v. *Illinois, supra* (holding that the Sixth Amendment does not bar postindictment questioning in the absence of counsel if a defendant waives the right to counsel).

We have consistently applied the deliberate-elicitation standard in subsequent Sixth Amendment cases, see *United States v. Henry,* (cite omitted)("The question here is whether under the facts of this case a Government agent 'deliberately elicited' incriminating statements . . . within the meaning of *Massiah*"); *Brewer, supra,* at 399, 97 S. Ct. 1232 (finding a Sixth Amendment violation where a detective "deliberately and designedly set out to elicit information from [the suspect]"), and we have expressly distinguished this standard from the Fifth Amendment custodial-interrogation standard, see *Michigan* v. *Jackson,* 475 U.S. 625, 632, n. 5, 106 S. Ct. 1404 (1986) ("[T]he Sixth Amendment provides a right to counsel . . . even when there is no interrogation and no Fifth Amendment applicability"); *Rhode Island* v. *Innis,* 446 U.S. 291, 300, n. 4, 100 S. Ct. 1682 (1980) ("The definitions of 'interrogation' under the Fifth and Sixth Amendments, if indeed the term 'interrogation' is even apt in the Sixth Amendment context, are not necessarily interchangeable"); cf. *United States* v. *Wade,* 388 U.S. 218, 87 S. Ct. 1926 (1967) (holding that the Sixth Amendment provides the right to counsel at a postindictment lineup even though the Fifth Amendment is not implicated).

The Court of Appeals erred in holding that the absence of an "interrogation" foreclosed petitioner's claim that the jailhouse statements should have been suppressed as fruits of the statements taken from petitioner at his home. First, there is no question that the officers in this case "deliberately elicited" information from petitioner. Indeed, the officers, upon arriving at petitioner's house, informed him that their purpose in coming was to discuss his involvement in the distribution of methamphetamine and his association with certain charged co-conspirators (cite omitted). Because the ensuing discussion took place after petitioner had been indicted, outside the presence of counsel, and in the absence of any waiver of petitioner's Sixth Amendment rights, the Court of Appeals erred in holding that the officers' actions did not violate the Sixth Amendment standards established in *Massiah*, *supra*, and its progeny.

Second, because of its erroneous determination that petitioner was not questioned in violation of Sixth Amendment standards, the Court of Appeals improperly conducted its "fruits" analysis under the Fifth Amendment. Specifically, it applied *Elstad, supra*, to hold that the admissibility of the jailhouse statements turns solely on whether the statements were " 'knowingly and voluntarily made' " (cites omitted). The Court of Appeals did not reach the question whether the Sixth Amendment requires suppression of petitioner's jailhouse statements on the ground that they were the fruits of previous questioning conducted in violation of the Sixth Amendment deliberate-elicitation standard. We have not had occasion to decide whether the rationale of *Elstad* applies when a suspect makes incriminating statements after a knowing and voluntary waiver of his right to counsel notwithstanding earlier police questioning in violation of Sixth Amendment standards. We therefore remand to the Court of Appeals to address this issue in the first instance.

Accordingly, the judgment of the Court of Appeals is reversed, and the case is remanded for further proceedings consistent with this opinion.

* * *

Add after note 7 on page 669:

The Supreme Court revisited the validity of the "question first" tactics permitted by *Elstad* in the following case:

Missouri v. Seibert

542 U.S. 600, 124 S.Ct. 2601 (2004).

■ OPINION: JUSTICE SOUTER announced the judgment of the Court and delivered an opinion, in which JUSTICE STEVENS, JUSTICE GINSBURG, and JUSTICE BREYER join.

This case tests a police protocol for custodial interrogation that calls for giving no warnings of the rights to silence and counsel until interrogation has produced a confession. Although such a statement is generally inadmissible, since taken in violation of *Miranda* v. *Arizona*, 384 U.S. 436, 86 S. Ct. 1602 (1966), the interrogating officer follows it with *Miranda* warnings and then leads the suspect to cover the same ground a second time. The question here is the admissibility of the repeated statement. Because this midstream recitation of warnings after interrogation and unwarned confession could not effectively comply with *Miranda*'s constitutional requirement, we hold that a statement repeated after a warning in such circumstances is inadmissible.

I

Respondent Patrice Seibert's 12–year-old son Jonathan had cerebral palsy, and when he died in his sleep she feared charges of neglect because of bedsores on his body. In her presence, two of her teenage sons and two of their friends devised a plan to conceal the facts surrounding Jonathan's death by incinerating his body in the course of burning the family's mobile home, in which they planned to leave Donald Rector, a mentally ill teenager living with the family, to avoid any appearance that Jonathan had been unattended. Seibert's son Darian and a friend set the fire, and Donald died.

Five days later, the police awakened Seibert at 3 a.m. at a hospital where Darian was being treated for burns. In arresting her, Officer Kevin Clinton followed instructions from Rolla, Missouri, officer Richard Hanrahan that he refrain from giving *Miranda* warnings. After Seibert had been taken to the police station and left alone in an interview room for 15 to 20 minutes, Hanrahan questioned her without *Miranda* warnings for 30 to 40 minutes, squeezing her arm and repeating "Donald was also to die in his sleep." App. 59 (internal quotation marks omitted). After Seibert finally admitted she knew Donald was meant to die in the fire, she was given a 20–minute coffee and cigarette break. Officer Hanrahan then turned on a tape recorder, gave Seibert the *Miranda* warnings, and obtained a signed waiver of rights from her. He resumed the questioning with "Ok, 'trice, we've been talking for a little while about what happened on Wednesday the twelfth, haven't we?," App. 66, and confronted her with her prewarning statements:

Hanrahan: "Now, in discussion you told us, you told us that there was an understanding about Donald."

Seibert: "Yes."

Hanrahan: "Did that take place earlier that morning?"

Seibert: "Yes."

Hanrahan: "And what was the understanding about Donald?"

Seibert: "If they could get him out of the trailer, to take him out of the trailer."

Hanrahan: "And if they couldn't?"

Seibert: "I, I never even thought about it. I just figured they would."

Hanrahan: " 'Trice, didn't you tell me that he was supposed to die in his sleep?' "

Seibert: "If that would happen, 'cause he was on that new medicine, you know . . . ."

Hanrahan: "The Prozac? And it makes him sleepy. So he was supposed to die in his sleep?"

Seibert: "Yes." *Id.*, at 70.

After being charged with first-degree murder for her role in Donald's death, Seibert sought to exclude both her prewarning and postwarning statements. At the suppression hearing, Officer Hanrahan testified that he made a "conscious decision" to withhold *Miranda* warnings, thus resorting to an interrogation technique he had been taught: question first, then give the warnings, and then repeat the question "until I get the answer that she's already provided once." App. 31–34. He acknowledged that Seibert's ultimate statement was "largely a repeat of information . . . obtained" prior to the warning. *Id.*, at 30.

The trial court suppressed the prewarning statement but admitted the responses given after the *Miranda* recitation. A jury convicted Seibert of second-degree murder. On appeal, the Missouri Court of Appeals affirmed, treating this case as indistinguishable from *Oregon v. Elstad*, 470 U.S. 298, 105 S. Ct. 1285 (1985).

The Supreme Court of Missouri reversed, holding that "in the circumstances here, where the interrogation was nearly continuous, . . . the second statement, clearly the product of the invalid first statement, should have been suppressed" (cite omitted). The court distinguished *Elstad* on the ground that warnings had not intentionally been withheld there, (cite omitted), and reasoned that "Officer Hanrahan's intentional omission of a *Miranda* warning was intended to deprive Seibert of the opportunity knowingly and intelligently to waive her *Miranda* rights," (cite omitted). Since there were "no circumstances that would seem to dispel the effect of the *Miranda* violation," the court held that the postwarning confession was involuntary and therefore inadmissible. *Ibid.* To allow the police to achieve an "end run" around *Miranda*, the court explained, would encourage *Miranda* violations and diminish *Miranda*'s role in protecting the privilege against self-incrimination (cite omitted). One judge dissented, taking the view that *Elstad* applied even though the police intentionally withheld *Miranda* warnings before the initial statement, and believing that "Seibert's unwarned responses to Officer Hanrahan's questioning did not prevent her from waiving her rights and confessing." 93 S. W. 3d, at 708 (opinion of Benton, J.).

We granted certiorari to resolve a split in the Courts of Appeals. . . . We now affirm.

II

"In criminal trials, in the courts of the United States, wherever a question arises whether a confession is incompetent because not voluntary, the issue is controlled by that portion of the Fifth Amendment . . . commanding that no person 'shall be compelled in any criminal case to be a witness against himself.' " *Bram* v. *United States*, 168 U.S. 532, 542, 18 S. Ct. 183 (1897). A parallel rule governing the admissibility of confessions in state courts emerged from the Due Process Clause of the Fourteenth Amendment, see, *e.g.*, *Brown* v. *Mississippi*, 297 U.S. 278, 80 L. Ed. 682, 56 S. Ct. 461 (1936), which governed state cases until we concluded in *Malloy* v. *Hogan,* 378 U.S. 1, 8, 84 S. Ct. 1489 (1964), that "the Fourteenth Amendment secures against state invasion the same privilege that the Fifth Amendment guarantees against federal infringement—the right of a person to remain silent unless he chooses to speak in the unfettered exercise of his own will, and to suffer no penalty . . . for such silence." "In unifying the Fifth and Fourteenth Amendment voluntariness tests, *Malloy* 'made clear what had already become apparent—that the substantive and procedural safeguards surrounding admissibility of confessions in state cases had become exceedingly exacting, reflecting all the policies embedded in the privilege' against self-incrimination." *Miranda*, 384 U.S., at 464, 86 S. Ct. 1602 .

In *Miranda*, we explained that the "voluntariness doctrine in the state cases . . . encompasses all interrogation practices which are likely to exert such pressure upon an individual as to disable him from making a free and rational choice," (cite omitted). We appreciated the difficulty of judicial enquiry *post hoc* into the circumstances of a police interrogation, *Dickerson v. United States* (cite omitted), and recognized that "the coercion inherent in custodial interrogation blurs the line between voluntary and involuntary statements, and thus heightens the risk" that the privilege against self-incrimination will not be observed, (cite omitted). Hence our concern that the "traditional totality-of-the-circumstances" test posed an "unacceptably great" risk that involuntary custodial confessions would escape detection (cite omitted).

Accordingly, "to reduce the risk of a coerced confession and to implement the Self–Incrimination Clause," (cite omitted) this Court in *Miranda* concluded that "the accused must be adequately and effectively apprised of his rights and the exercise of those rights must be fully honored," (cite omitted).

Miranda conditioned the admissibility at trial of any custodial confession on warning a suspect of his rights: failure to give the prescribed warnings and obtain a waiver of rights before custodial questioning generally requires exclusion of any statements obtained. Conversely, giving the warnings and getting a waiver has generally produced a virtual ticket of admissibility; maintaining that a statement is involuntary even though given after warnings and voluntary waiver of rights requires unusual stamina, and litigation over voluntariness tends to end with the finding of a valid waiver. See *Berkemer* v. *McCarty*, 468 U.S. 420, 433, n. 20, 104 S. Ct. 3138 (1984) ("Cases in which a defendant can make a colorable argument that a self-incriminating statement was 'compelled' despite the fact that the law enforcement authorities adhered to the dictates of *Miranda* are rare"). To point out the obvious, this common consequence would not be common at all were it not that *Miranda* warnings are customarily given under circumstances allowing for a real choice between talking and remaining silent.

III

There are those, of course, who preferred the old way of doing things, giving no warnings and litigating the voluntariness of any statement in nearly every instance. In the aftermath of *Miranda*, Congress even passed a statute seeking to restore that old regime, 18 U.S.C. § 3501, although the Act lay dormant for years until finally invoked and challenged in *Dickerson* v. *United States*.... *Dickerson* reaffirmed *Miranda* and held that its constitutional character prevailed against the statute.

The technique of interrogating in successive, unwarned and warned phases raises a new challenge to *Miranda*. Although we have no statistics on the frequency of this practice, it is not confined to Rolla, Missouri. An officer of that police department testified that the strategy of withholding *Miranda* warnings until after interrogating and drawing out a confession was promoted not only by his own department, but by a national police training organization and other departments in which he had worked. App. 31–32. Consistently with the officer's testimony, the Police Law Institute, for example, instructs that "officers may conduct a two-stage interrogation.... At any point during the pre-*Miranda* interrogation, usually after arrestees have confessed, officers may then read the *Miranda* warnings and ask for a waiver. If the arrestees waive their *Miranda* rights, officers will be able to repeat any *subsequent* incriminating statements later in court." Police Law Institute, Illinois Police Law Manual 83 (Jan. 2001–Dec. 2003), http://www.illinoispolicelaw.org/training/lessons/ILPLMIR.pdf (as visited Dec. 31, 2003, and available in the Clerk of Court's case file) (hereinafter Police Law Manual) (emphasis in original).[3] The upshot of all this advice is a question-first practice of some popularity, as one can see from the

---

3. Emphasizing the impeachment exception to the *Miranda* rule approved by this Court, *Harris* v. *New York*, 401 U.S. 222, 91 S. Ct. 643 (1971), some training programs advise officers to omit *Miranda* warnings altogether or to continue questioning after the suspect invokes his rights. See, *e.g.*, Police Law Manual 83 ("There is no need to give a *Miranda* warning before asking questions if ... the answers given ... will not be required by the prosecutor during the prosecution's case-in-chief"); California Commission on Peace Officer Standards and Training, Video Training Programs for California Law Enforcement, Miranda: Post–Invocation Questioning (broadcast July 11, 1996) ("We ... have been encouraging you to continue to question a suspect after they've invoked their *Miranda* rights"); D. Zulawski & D. Wicklander, Practical Aspects of Interview and Interrogation 50–51 (2d ed. 2002) (describing the practice of "beachheading" as useful for impeachment purpose (emphasis deleted)); see also Weisselberg, Saving *Miranda*, 84 Cornell L. Rev. 109, 110, 132–139 (1998) (collecting California training materials encouraging

questioning "outside *Miranda*"). This training is reflected in the reported cases involving deliberate questioning after invocation of *Miranda* rights (cites omitted). Scholars have noted the growing trend of such practices. See, *e.g.*, Leo, Questioning the Relevance of *Miranda* in the Twenty–First Century, 99 Mich. L. Rev. 1000, 1010 (2001); Weisselberg, In the Stationhouse After *Dickerson*, 99 Mich. L. Rev. 1121, 1123–1154 (2001).

It is not the case, of course, that law enforcement educators en masse are urging that *Miranda* be honored only in the breach (cites omitted).... Most police manuals do not advocate the question-first tactic, because they understand that *Oregon* v. *Elstad* (cite omitted), involved an officer's good-faith failure to warn. See, *e.g.*, Inbau, Reid, & Buckley 241 (*Elstad*'s "facts as well as [its] specific holding" instruct that "where an interrogator has failed to administer the *Miranda* warnings in the mistaken belief that, under the circumstances of the particular case, the warnings were not required, ... corrective measures ... salvage an interrogation opportunity").

reported cases describing its use, sometimes in obedience to departmental policy.

IV

When a confession so obtained is offered and challenged, attention must be paid to the conflicting objects of *Miranda* and question-first. *Miranda* addressed "interrogation practices ... likely ... to disable [an individual] from making a free and rational choice" about speaking, 384 U.S., at 464–465, 86 S. Ct. 1602, and held that a suspect must be "adequately and effectively" advised of the choice the Constitution guarantees, id., at 467, 86 S. Ct. 1602. The object of question-first is to render *Miranda* warnings ineffective by waiting for a particularly opportune time to give them, after the suspect has already confessed.

Just as "no talismanic incantation [is] required to satisfy [*Miranda's*] strictures," (cite omitted) it would be absurd to think that mere recitation of the litany suffices to satisfy *Miranda* in every conceivable circumstance. "The inquiry is simply whether the warnings reasonably 'convey to [a suspect] his rights as required by *Miranda.*'" *Duckworth* v. *Eagan*, 492 U.S. 195, 203, 109 S. Ct. 2875 (1989) (quoting *Prysock, supra,* at 361, 101 S. Ct. 2806). The threshold issue when interrogators question first and warn later is thus whether it would be reasonable to find that in these circumstances the warnings could function "effectively" as *Miranda* requires. Could the warnings effectively advise the suspect that he had a real choice about giving an admissible statement at that juncture? Could they reasonably convey that he could choose to stop talking even if he had talked earlier? For unless the warnings could place a suspect who has just been interrogated in practical justification for accepting the formal warnings as compliance with *Miranda*, or for treating the second stage of interrogation as distinct from the first, unwarned and inadmissible segment.[4]

---

4. Respondent Seibert argues that her second confession should be excluded from evidence under the doctrine known by the metaphor of the "fruit of the poisonous tree," developed in the Fourth Amendment context in *Wong Sun* v. *United States*, 371 U.S. 471, 83 S. Ct. 407 (1963): evidence otherwise admissible but discovered as a result of an earlier violation is excluded as tainted, lest the law encourage future violations. But the Court in *Elstad* rejected the *Wong Sun* fruits doctrine for analyzing the admissibility of a subsequent warned confession following "an initial failure ... to administer the warnings required by *Miranda.*" *Elstad*, 470 U.S., at 300, 105 S. Ct. 1285. In *Elstad*, "a simple failure to administer the warnings, unaccompanied by any actual coercion or other circumstances calculated to undermine the suspect's ability to exercise his free will" did not "so taint the investigatory process that a subsequent voluntary and informed waiver is ineffective for some indeterminate period.

Though *Miranda* requires that the unwarned admission must be suppressed, the admissibility of any subsequent statement should turn in these circumstances solely on whether it is knowingly and voluntarily made" (cite omitted). *Elstad* held that "a suspect who has once responded to unwarned yet uncoercive questioning is not thereby disabled from waiving his rights and confessing after he has been given the requisite *Miranda* warnings." (cite omitted). In a sequential confession case, clarity is served if the later confession is approached by asking whether in the circumstances the *Miranda* warnings given could reasonably be found effective. If yes, a court can take up the standard issues of voluntary waiver and voluntary statement; if no, the subsequent statement is inadmissible for want of adequate *Miranda* warnings, because the earlier and later statements are realistically seen as parts of a single, unwarned sequence of questioning.

There is no doubt about the answer that proponents of question-first give to this question about the effectiveness of warnings given only after successful interrogation, and we think their answer is correct. By any objective measure, applied to circumstances exemplified here, it is likely that if the interrogators employ the technique of withholding warnings until after interrogation succeeds in eliciting a confession, the warnings will be ineffective in preparing the suspect for successive interrogation, close in time and similar in content. After all, the reason that question-first is catching on is as obvious as its manifest purpose, which is to get a confession the suspect would not make if he understood his rights at the outset; the sensible underlying assumption is that with one confession in hand before the warnings, the interrogator can count on getting its duplicate, with trifling additional trouble. Upon hearing warnings only in the aftermath of interrogation and just after making a confession, a suspect would hardly think he had a genuine right to remain silent, let alone persist in so believing once the police began to lead him over the same ground again.[5] A more likely reaction on a suspect's part would be perplexity about the reason for discussing rights at that point, bewilderment being an unpromising frame of mind for knowledgeable decision. What is worse, telling a suspect that "anything you say can and will be used against you," without expressly excepting the statement just given, could lead to an entirely reasonable inference that what he has just said will be used, with subsequent silence being of no avail. Thus,."when *Miranda* warnings are inserted in the midst of coordinated and continuing interrogation, they are likely to mislead and 'deprive a defendant of knowledge essential to his ability to understand the nature of his rights and the consequences of abandoning them.' " *Moran* v. *Burbine*, 475 U.S. 412, 424, 106 S. Ct. 1135 (1986). By the same token, it would ordinarily be unrealistic to treat two spates of integrated and proximately conducted questioning as independent interrogations subject to independent evaluation simply because *Miranda* warnings formally punctuate them in the middle.

V

Missouri argues that a confession repeated at the end of an interrogation sequence envisioned in a question-first strategy is admissible on the authority of *Oregon* v. *Elstad*, 470 U.S. 298, 105 S. Ct. 1285 (1985), but the argument disfigures that case. In *Elstad*, the police went to the young suspect's house to take him into custody on a charge of burglary. Before the arrest, one officer spoke with the suspect's mother, while the other one joined the suspect in a "brief stop in the living room," where the officer said he "felt" the young man was involved in a burglary, (internal quotation marks omitted). The suspect acknowledged he had been at the scene. This Court noted that the pause in the living room "was not to interrogate

---

5. It bears emphasizing that the effectiveness *Miranda* assumes the warnings can have must potentially extend through the repeated interrogation, since a suspect has a right to stop at any time. It seems highly unlikely that a suspect could retain any such understanding when the interrogator leads him a second time through a line of questioning the suspect has already answered fully. The point is not that a later unknowing or involuntary confession cancels out an earlier, adequate warning; the point is that the warning is unlikely to be effective in the question-first sequence we have described.

the suspect but to notify his mother of the reason for his arrest,'', and described the incident as having ''none of the earmarks of coercion. ''The Court, indeed, took care to mention that the officer's initial failure to warn was an ''oversight'' that ''may have been the result of confusion as to whether the brief exchange qualified as 'custodial interrogation' or ... may simply have reflected ... reluctance to initiate an alarming police procedure before [an officer] had spoken with respondent's mother.'' At the outset of a later and systematic station house interrogation going well beyond the scope of the laconic prior admission, the suspect was given *Miranda* warnings and made a full confession. In holding the second statement admissible and voluntary, *Elstad* rejected the ''cat out of the bag'' theory that any short, earlier admission, obtained in arguably innocent neglect of *Miranda*, determined the character of the later, warned confession; on the facts of that case, the Court thought any causal connection between the first and second responses to the police was ''speculative and attenuated.''. Although the *Elstad* Court expressed no explicit conclusion about either officer's state of mind, it is fair to read *Elstad* as treating the living room conversation as a good-faith *Miranda* mistake, not only open to correction by careful warnings before systematic questioning in that particular case, but posing no threat to warn-first practice generally. See *Elstad*, (characterizing the officers' omission of *Miranda* warnings as ''a simple failure to administer the warnings, unaccompanied by any actual coercion or other circumstances calculated to undermine the suspect's ability to exercise his free will'');(Justice Brennan's concern in dissent that *Elstad* would invite question-first practice ''distorts the reasoning and holding of our decision, but, worse, invites trial courts and prosecutors to do the same'') (citations to *Elstad* omitted).

The contrast between *Elstad* and this case reveals ''a series of relevant facts that bear on whether *Miranda* warnings delivered midstream could be effective enough to accomplish their object: the completeness and detail of the questions and answers in the first round of interrogation, the overlapping content of the two statements, the timing and setting of the first and the second, the continuity of police personnel, and the degree to which the interrogator's questions treated the second round as continuous with the first.'' In *Elstad*, it was not unreasonable to see the occasion for questioning at the station house as presenting a markedly different experience from the short conversation at home; since a reasonable person in the suspect's shoes could have seen the station house questioning as a new and distinct experience, the *Miranda* warnings could have made sense as presenting a genuine choice whether to follow up on the earlier admission.

At the opposite extreme are the facts here, which by any objective measure reveal a police strategy adapted to undermine the *Miranda* warnings. [6]The unwarned interrogation was conducted in the station house, and the questioning was systematic, exhaustive, and managed with psychological skill. When the police were finished there was little, if anything, of incriminating potential left unsaid. The warned phase of questioning pro-

---

6. Because the intent of the officer will rarely be as candidly admitted as it was here (even as it is likely to determine the conduct of the interrogation), the focus is on facts apart from intent that show the question-first tactic at work

ceeded after a pause of only 15 to 20 minutes, in the same place as the unwarned segment. When the same officer who had conducted the first phase recited the *Miranda* warnings, he said nothing to counter the probable misimpression that the advice that anything Seibert said could be used against her also applied to the details of the inculpatory statement previously elicited. In particular, the police did not advise that her prior statement could not be used.[7] Nothing was said or done to dispel the oddity of warning about legal rights to silence and counsel right after the police had led her through a systematic interrogation, and any uncertainty on her part about a right to stop talking about matters previously discussed would only have been aggravated by the way Officer Hanrahan set the scene by saying "we've been talking for a little while about what happened on Wednesday the twelfth, haven't we?" App. 66. The impression that the further questioning was a mere continuation of the earlier questions and responses was fostered by references back to the confession already given. It would have been reasonable to regard the two sessions as parts of a continuum, in which it would have been unnatural to refuse to repeat at the second stage what had been said before. These circumstances must be seen as challenging the comprehensibility and efficacy of the *Miranda* warnings to the point that a reasonable person in the suspect's shoes would not have understood them to convey a message that she retained a choice about continuing to talk.[8]

VI

Strategists dedicated to draining the substance out of *Miranda* cannot accomplish by training instructions what *Dickerson* held Congress could not do by statute. Because the question-first tactic effectively threatens to thwart *Miranda*'s purpose of reducing the risk that a coerced confession would be admitted, and because the facts here do not reasonably support a conclusion that the warnings given could have served their purpose, Seibert's postwarning statements are inadmissible. The judgment of the Supreme Court of Missouri is affirmed.

It is so ordered.

■ CONCUR: JUSTICE BREYER, concurring (with whom Justice Kennedy joins).

In my view, the following simple rule should apply to the two-stage interrogation technique: Courts should exclude the "fruits" of the initial unwarned questioning unless the failure to warn was in good faith. Cf. *Oregon* v. *Elstad*, 470 U.S. 298, 309, 318, n. 5, 105 S. Ct. 1285 (1985); *United States* v. *Leon*, 468 U.S. 897, 104 S. Ct. 3405 (1984). I believe this is a sound and workable approach to the problem this case presents. Prosecutors and judges have long understood how to apply the "fruits" approach, which they use in other areas of law. See *Wong Sun* v. *United States*, 371

---

7. We do not hold that a formal addendum warning that a previous statement could not be used would be sufficient to change the character of the question-first procedure to the point of rendering an ensuing statement admissible, but its absence is clearly a factor that blunts the efficacy of the warnings and points to a continuing, not a new, interrogation.

8. Because we find that the warnings were inadequate, there is no need to assess the actual voluntariness of the statement.

U.S. 471, 83 S. Ct. 407 (1963). And in the workaday world of criminal law enforcement the administrative simplicity of the familiar has significant advantages over a more complex exclusionary rule. Cf. *post*, at 6–7 (O'Connor, J., dissenting). . . .

■ JUSTICE KENNEDY, concurring in the judgment.

The interrogation technique used in this case is designed to circumvent *Miranda v. Arizona*, 384 U.S. 436, 86 S. Ct. 1602 (1966). It undermines the *Miranda* warning and obscures its meaning. The plurality opinion is correct to conclude that statements obtained through the use of this technique are inadmissible. Although I agree with much in the careful and convincing opinion for the plurality, my approach does differ in some respects, requiring this separate statement.

The *Miranda* rule has become an important and accepted element of the criminal justice system. See *Dickerson* v. *United States,* 530 U.S. 428, 120 S. Ct. 2326 (2000). At the same time, not every violation of the rule requires suppression of the evidence obtained. Evidence is admissible when the central concerns of *Miranda* are not likely to be implicated and when other objectives of the criminal justice system are best served by its introduction. Thus, we have held that statements obtained in violation of the rule can be used for impeachment, so that the truth finding function of the trial is not distorted by the defense, see *Harris* v. *New York,* 401 U.S. 222, 91 S. Ct. 643 (1971); that there is an exception to protect countervailing concerns of public safety, see *New York* v. *Quarles,* 467 U.S. 649, 104 S. Ct. 2626 (1984); and that physical evidence obtained in reliance on statements taken in violation of the rule is admissible, see *United States* v. *Patane,* 542 U.S. 630, 124 S.Ct. 2620 (2004). These cases, in my view, are correct. They recognize that admission of evidence is proper when it would further important objectives without compromising *Miranda*'s central concerns. Under these precedents, the scope of the *Miranda* suppression remedy depends on a consideration of those legitimate interests and on whether admission of the evidence under the circumstances would frustrate *Miranda*'s central concerns and objectives. . . .

In my view, *Elstad* was correct in its reasoning and its result. *Elstad* reflects a balanced and pragmatic approach to enforcement of the *Miranda* warning. An officer may not realize that a suspect is in custody and warnings are required. The officer may not plan to question the suspect or may be waiting for a more appropriate time. Skilled investigators often interview suspects multiple times, and good police work may involve referring to prior statements to test their veracity or to refresh recollection. In light of these realities it would be extravagant to treat the presence of one statement that cannot be admitted under *Miranda* as sufficient reason to prohibit subsequent statements preceded by a proper warning. . . .

. . . the interrogating officer here relied on the defendant's prewarning statement to obtain the postwarning statement used against her at trial. The postwarning interview resembled a cross-examination. The officer confronted the defendant with her inadmissible prewarning statements and pushed her to acknowledge them. See App. 70 (" 'Trice, didn't you tell me that he was supposed to die in his sleep?' "). This shows the temptations for abuse inherent in the two-step technique. Reference to the prewarning statement was an implicit suggestion that the mere repetition of the earlier statement was not independently incriminating. The implicit suggestion was false.

The technique used in this case distorts the meaning of *Miranda* and furthers no legitimate countervailing interest. The *Miranda* rule would be frustrated were we to allow police to undermine its meaning and effect. The technique simply creates too high a risk that postwarning statements will be obtained when a suspect was deprived of "knowledge essential to his ability to understand the nature of his rights and the consequences of abandoning them." *Moran* v. *Burbine*, 475 U.S. 412, 423–424, 106 S. Ct. 1135 (1986). When an interrogator uses this deliberate, two-step strategy, predicated upon violating *Miranda* during an extended interview, post-warning statements that are related to the substance of prewarning statements must be excluded absent specific, curative steps.

The plurality concludes that whenever a two-stage interview occurs, admissibility of the postwarning statement should depend on "whether the *Miranda* warnings delivered midstream could have been effective enough to accomplish their object" given the specific facts of the case. This test envisions an objective inquiry from the perspective of the suspect, and applies in the case of both intentional and unintentional two-stage interrogations. In my view, this test cuts too broadly. *Miranda*'s clarity is one of its strengths, and a multifactor test that applies to every two-stage interrogation may serve to undermine that clarity. Cf. *Berkemer* v. *McCarty*, 468 U.S. 420, 430, 104 S. Ct. 3138 (1984). I would apply a narrower test applicable only in the infrequent case, such as we have here, in which the two-step interrogation technique was used in a calculated way to undermine the *Miranda* warning.

The admissibility of postwarning statements should continue to be governed by the principles of *Elstad* unless the deliberate two-step strategy was employed. If the deliberate two-step strategy has been used, postwarning statements that are related to the substance of prewarning statements must be excluded unless curative measures are taken before the postwarning statement is made. Curative measures should be designed to ensure that a reasonable person in the suspect's situation would understand the import and effect of the *Miranda* warning and of the *Miranda* waiver. For example, a substantial break in time and circumstances between the prewarning statement and the *Miranda* warning may suffice in most circumstances, as it allows the accused to distinguish the two contexts and appreciate that the interrogation has taken a new turn. Cf. *Westover* v. *United States*, decided with *Miranda* v. *Arizona*, 384 U.S. 436, 86 S. Ct. 1602 (1966). Alternatively, an additional warning that explains the likely inadmissibility of the prewarning custodial statement may be sufficient. No curative steps were taken in this case, however, so the postwarning statements are inadmissible and the conviction cannot stand.

For these reasons, I concur in the judgment of the Court.

■ DISSENT: JUSTICE O'CONNOR, with whom THE CHIEF JUSTICE, JUSTICE SCALIA, and JUSTICE THOMAS join, dissenting.

The plurality devours *Oregon v. Elstad,* 470 U.S. 298, 105 S. Ct. 1285 (1985), even as it accuses petitioner's argument of "disfiguring" that decision. I believe that we are bound by *Elstad* to reach a different result, and I would vacate the judgment of the Supreme Court of Missouri.

I

On two preliminary questions I am in full agreement with the plurality. First, the plurality appropriately follows *Elstad* in concluding that Seibert's statement cannot be held inadmissible under a "fruit of the poisonous tree" theory. Second, the plurality correctly declines to focus its analysis on the subjective intent of the interrogating officer.

A

This Court has made clear that there simply is no place for a robust deterrence doctrine with regard to violations of *Miranda v. Arizona,* 384 U.S. 436, 86 S. Ct. 1602 (1966). See *Dickerson* v. *United States,* 530 U.S. 428, 441, 20 S. Ct. 2326 (2000) ("Our decision in *[Elstad]*—refusing to apply the traditional 'fruits' doctrine developed in Fourth Amendment cases— . . . simply recognizes the fact that unreasonable searches under the Fourth Amendment are different from unwarned interrogation under the Fifth Amendment"); *Elstad, supra,* at 306, 84 L. Ed. 2d 222, 105 S. Ct. 1285 (unlike the Fourth Amendment exclusionary rule, the "*Miranda* exclusionary rule . . . serves the Fifth Amendment and sweeps more broadly than the Fifth Amendment itself"); see also *United States* v. *Patane,* ___ U.S. ___, 124 S. Ct. 2620 (June 28, 2004) (Kennedy, J., concurring in judgment) (refusal to suppress evidence obtained following an unwarned confession in *Elstad, New York v. Quarles,* 467 U.S. 649, 104 S. Ct. 2626 (1984), and *Harris* v. *New York,* 401 U.S. 222, 91 S. Ct. 643 (1971), was based on "our recognition that the concerns underlying the *Miranda* . . . rule and other objectives of the criminal justice system must be accommodated"). Consistent with that view, the Court today refuses to apply the traditional "fruits" analysis to the physical fruit of a claimed *Miranda* violation. *Patane.* The plurality correctly refuses to apply a similar analysis to testimonial fruits.

Although the analysis the plurality ultimately espouses examines the same facts and circumstances that a "fruits" analysis would consider (such as the lapse of time between the two interrogations and change of questioner or location), it does so for entirely different reasons. The fruits analysis would examine those factors because they are relevant to the balance of deterrence value versus the "drastic and socially costly course" of excluding reliable evidence. *Nix* v. *Williams,* 467 U.S. 431, 442–443, 104 S. Ct. 2501 (1984). The plurality, by contrast, looks to those factors to inform the *psychological* judgment regarding whether the suspect has been informed effectively of her right to remain silent. The analytical underpinnings of the two approaches are thus entirely distinct, and they should not be conflated just because they function similarly in practice. Cf. (concurring opinion) (emphasis in original).

B

The plurality's rejection of an intent-based test is also, in my view, correct. Freedom from compulsion lies at the heart of the Fifth Amendment, and requires us to assess whether a suspect's decision to speak truly was voluntary. Because voluntariness is a matter of the suspect's state of mind, we focus our analysis on the way in which suspects experience interrogation. See generally *Miranda*, 384 U.S., at 455, 86 S. Ct. 1602 (summarizing psychological tactics used by police that "undermine" the suspect's "will to resist," and noting that "the very fact of custodial interrogation . . . trades on the weakness of individuals"); (cite omitted) ("In-custody interrogation of persons suspected or accused of crime contains inherently compelling pressures which work to undermine the individual's will to resist and to compel him to speak where he would not otherwise do so freely").

Thoughts kept inside a police officer's head cannot affect that experience. See *Moran* v. *Burbine,* 475 U.S. 412, 106 S.Ct. 1135 (1986) ("Events occurring outside of the presence of the suspect and entirely unknown to him surely can have no bearing on the capacity to comprehend and knowingly relinquish a constitutional right"). In *Moran*, an attorney hired by the suspect's sister had been trying to contact the suspect and was told by the police, falsely, that they would not begin an interrogation that night (cite omitted). The suspect was not aware that an attorney had been hired for him (cite omitted). We rejected an analysis under which a different result would obtain for "the same defendant, armed with the same information and confronted with precisely the same police conduct" if something not known to the defendant—such as the fact that an attorney was attempting to contact him—had been different (cite omitted). The same principle applies here. A suspect who experienced the exact same interrogation as Seibert, save for a difference in the undivulged, subjective intent of the interrogating officer when he failed to give *Miranda* warnings, would not experience the interrogation any differently. "Whether intentional or inadvertent, the state of mind of the police is irrelevant to the question of the intelligence and voluntariness of respondent's election to abandon his rights. Although highly inappropriate, even deliberate deception of an attorney could not possibly affect a suspect's decision to waive his *Miranda* rights unless he were at least aware of the incident" (cite omitted). Cf. *Stansbury* v. *California,* 511 U.S. 318, 324–325, 114 S. Ct. 1526 (1994) *(per curiam)* (police officer's subjective intent is irrelevant to whether suspect is in custody for *Miranda* purposes; "one cannot expect the person under interrogation to probe the officer's innermost thoughts").

Because the isolated fact of Officer Hanrahan's intent could not have had any bearing on Seibert's "capacity to comprehend and knowingly relinquish" her right to remain silent, *Moran*, (cite omitted), it could not by itself affect the voluntariness of her confession. Moreover, recognizing an exception to *Elstad* for intentional violations would require focusing constitutional analysis on a police officer's subjective intent, an unattractive proposition that we all but uniformly avoid. In general, "we believe that 'sending state and federal courts on an expedition into the minds of police officers would produce a grave and fruitless misallocation of judicial resources.' " *United States* v. *Leon,* 468 U.S. 897, 922, n. 23, 104 S. Ct. 3405 (1984) (quoting *Massachusetts* v. *Painten,* 389 U.S. 560, 565, 88 S. Ct. 660 (1968) *(per curiam)* (White, J., dissenting)). This case presents the uncommonly straightforward circumstance of an officer openly admitting that the violation was intentional. But the inquiry will be complicated in other situations probably more likely to occur. For example, different officers involved in an interrogation might claim different states of mind regarding the failure to give *Miranda* warnings. Even in the simple case of a single officer who claims that a failure to give *Miranda* warnings was inadvertent, the likelihood of error will be high. See W. LaFave, Search and Seizure § 1.4(e), p. 124 (3d ed. 1996) ("There is no reason to believe that courts can with any degree of success determine in which instances the police had an ulterior motive").

These evidentiary difficulties have led us to reject an intent-based test in several criminal procedure contexts. For example, in *New York* v. *Quarles,* 467 U.S. 649, 104 S. Ct. 2626 (1984), one of the factors that led us to reject an inquiry into the subjective intent of the police officer in crafting a test for the "public safety" exception to *Miranda* was that officers' motives will be "largely unverifiable" (cite omitted). Similarly, our opinion in *Whren* v. *United States,* 517 U.S. 806, 813–814, 116 S. Ct. 1769 (1996), made clear that "the evidentiary difficulty of establishing subjective intent" was one of the reasons (albeit not the principal one) for refusing to consider intent in Fourth Amendment challenges generally.

For these reasons, I believe that the approach espoused by Justice Kennedy is ill advised. Justice Kennedy would extend *Miranda*'s exclusionary rule to any case in which the use of the "two-step interrogation technique" was "deliberate" or "calculated."(opinion concurring in judgment). This approach untethers the analysis from facts knowable to, and therefore having any potential directly to affect, the suspect. Far from promoting "clarity," *ibid.*, the approach will add a third step to the suppression inquiry. In virtually every two-stage interrogation case, in addition to addressing the standard *Miranda* and voluntariness questions, courts will be forced to conduct the kind of difficult, state-of-mind inquiry that we normally take pains to avoid.

II

The plurality's adherence to *Elstad,* and mine to the plurality, end there. Our decision in *Elstad* rejected two lines of argument advanced in favor of suppression. The first was based on the "fruit of the poisonous tree" doctrine, discussed above. The second was the argument that the "lingering compulsion" inherent in a defendant's having let the "cat out of the bag" required suppression (cite omitted). The Court of Appeals of Oregon, in accepting the latter argument, had endorsed a theory indistinguishable from the one today's plurality adopts: "The coercive impact of the unconstitutionally obtained statement remains, because in a defendant's mind it has sealed his fate. It is this impact that must be dissipated in order to make a subsequent confession admissible" (cite omitted).

We rejected this theory outright. We did so not because we refused to recognize the "psychological impact of the suspect's conviction that he has let the cat out of the bag," but because we refused to "endow" those "psychological effects" with "constitutional implications." (cite omitted).To do so, we said, would "effectively immunize a suspect who responds to pre-*Miranda* warning questions from the consequences of his subsequent informed waiver," an immunity that "comes at a high cost to legitimate law enforcement activity, while adding little desirable protection to the individual's interest in not being *compelled* to testify against himself" (cite omitted). . . .

I would analyze the two-step interrogation procedure under the voluntariness standards central to the Fifth Amendment and reiterated in *Elstad*. *Elstad* commands that if Seibert's first statement is shown to have been involuntary, the court must examine whether the taint dissipated through the passing of time or a change in circumstances: "When a prior statement is actually coerced, the time that passes between confessions, the change in place of interrogations, and the change in identity of the interrogators all bear on whether that coercion has carried over into the second confession." (cite omitted). In addition, Seibert's second statement should be suppressed if she showed that it was involuntary despite the *Miranda* warnings. *Elstad* (cite omitted). ("The relevant inquiry is whether, in fact, the second statement was also voluntarily made. As in any such inquiry, the finder of fact must examine the surrounding circumstances and the entire course of police conduct with respect to the suspect in evaluating the voluntariness of his statements"). Although I would leave this analysis for the Missouri courts to conduct on remand, I note that, unlike the officers in *Elstad*, Officer Hanrahan referred to Seibert's unwarned statement during the second part of the interrogation when she made a statement at odds with her unwarned confession. App. 70 (" 'Trice, didn't you tell me that he was supposed to die in his sleep?' "); cf. *Elstad* (cite omitted) (officers did not "exploit the unwarned admission to pressure respondent into waiving his right to remain silent"). Such a tactic may bear on the voluntariness inquiry . . . (cites omitted).

Because I believe that the plurality gives insufficient deference to *Elstad* and that Justice Kennedy places improper weight on subjective intent, I respectfully dissent.

* * *

CHAPTER 9

RIGHTS OF INDIGENTS

A. APPELLATE ASSISTANCE: THE EQUAL PROTECTION & DUE PROCESS APPROACHES

Page 780. Add to the end of Note 1 the following:

The "line drawing" approach was followed in Halbert v. Michigan, ___ U.S. ___, 125 S.Ct. 2582 (2005). Michigan adopted, by a state constitutional amendment, a system in which there was no appeal of right from a conviction based on guilty pleas or no contest pleas. A convict could ask for the right to appeal but there was no right to counsel at this stage. The Supreme Court invalidated the Michigan practice holding (over three dissenters) that the relevant line was not to be drawn between discretionary appeals and appeals as a matter of right. The correct line was between first appeals and all those that follow. The Court reasoned that the first level appeal was one designed to correct error in the specific proceedings below as opposed to discretionary second level appeals the granting of which was to be guided by the importance of the legal questions at issue. Moreover, the decision in *Ross* was based in part on the indigent defendant's ability to use the briefs and record created by counsel in the first appeal. No such materials would be available under the Michigan procedure.

B. TRIAL COUNSEL: THE SIXTH AMENDMENT APPROACH

Add at end of note 1 on page 792:

In *Alabama v. Shelton*, 535 U.S. 654, 122 S.Ct. 1764 (2002), the defendant was convicted of third-degree assault. The court imposed a 30 day jail sentence, but then immediately suspended it and placed Shelton on probation for two years. Was he entitled to the Sixth Amendment right to appointed counsel under the *Argersinger* and *Scott* opinions?

The Court, in a 5–4 opinion, held that he was entitled to state-appointed counsel.

Justice Ginsberg, writing for the majority, rejected the notions that this would impede a state's ability to impose probation and that it would cause states to incur additional expenses. Instead, the potential for imprisonment upon a probation violation required counsel to be provided.

Justice Scalia, writing for the dissent (joined by Chief Justice Rehnquist, and Justices Kennedy and Thomas) disagreed, urging that counsel be required only upon actual imprisonment.

CHAPTER 10

THE PRELIMINARY HEARING

Add to end of notes on page 826 after Counter of Riverside v. McLaughlin:

4. Congress may not eliminate the need for a prompt preliminary hearing or grand jury presentment by classifying those held as enemy combatants. The detained individual must be given an opportunity rebut the Government's factual allegations before a neutral fact-finder. *Hamdi v. Rumsfeld,* 542 U.S. 507, 124 S.Ct. 2633 (2004).

CHAPTER 13

PRE-TRIAL MOTIONS

A. DISMISSAL FOR DOUBLE JEOPARDY & RELATED PRINCIPLES

Add to Note 2 at top of page 925:

In Smith v. Massachusetts, ___ U.S. ___, 125 S.Ct. 1129 (2005), the Court found double jeopardy when the trial judge granted a motion of acquittal on one of three counts. The motion was granted at the end of the prosecutor's case. The defense presented one witness. Before closing (and on the same day as the acquittal motion was granted) the prosecutor found precedent which caused the trial judge to reverse her ruling and send the stricken count to the jury. A five member majority found that the acquittal was final and sending it to the jury constituted double jeopardy. The Court observed that Massachusetts could avoid the re-occurrence of this result by statute or rule which barred mid trial rulings from becoming final or simply precluding mid trial acquittals. For the dissenters, Justice Ginsburg wrote:

> Smith was subjected to a single, unbroken trial proceeding in which he was denied no opportunity to air his defense before presentation of the case to the jury. I would not deny prosecutors in such circumstances, based on a trial judge's temporary error, one full and fair opportunity to present the State's case.

Add as note 3 at the top of page 925:

3. In *Smith v. Doe*, 538 U.S. 84, 123 S.Ct. 1140 (2003), the Court upheld the constitutionality of the Alaska Sex Offender Registration Law against claims that it violated double jeopardy.

CHAPTER 17

TRIAL BY JURY

B.   SELECTION OF THE JURY

1.   CHALLENGES

Add at the end of Note 8 on page 1221, a new Note 8A.

Note

At the end of its most recent term, the Supreme Court addressed *Batson* issues in two cases. In one, the Court rules that a defendant need not show it is more likely than not that a prosecutor challenges were based on impermissible group bias, in order to require the prosecutor to offer explanations for the exercise of challenges. The Court reiterated that the party objecting to an opponent's exercise of a peremptory challenge bears the burden of proving "purposeful discrimination." But the objector does not have to show that challenges were more likely than noit based on bias in order to secure a hearing requiring explanations from the prosecutor. This opinion Johnson v. United States, ___ U.S. ___, 125 S.Ct. 1571 (2005) drew a single dissent and announced a procedural rule of broad application–a typical sort of high court decision.

On the same day, the Court issued a 33–page opinion which examined, in great detail, a prosecutor's explanations for striking 10 of the 11 qualified black jurors and found them wanting. So, it concluded the state trial judge was unreasonable to accept them. *Miller-El v. Dretke,* ___ U.S. ___, 125 S.Ct. 2317 (2005). It is rare for any reviewing court to reject explicitly the facts found by trial judges and even rarer for this to occur in the United States Supreme Court. Such opinions establish no general rules and establish no real precedent. They are limited to their facts. Three dissenters wrote an even longer dissent parsing the record to support a differing conclusion.

The path to resolution of the case prompted the following concurrence.

Justice Breyer, concurring.

In *Batson* v. *Kentucky*, the Court adopted a burden-shifting rule designed to ferret out the unconstitutional use of race in jury selection. In his separate opinion, Justice Thurgood Marshall predicted that the Court's rule would not achieve its goal. The only way to"end the racial discrimination that peremptories inject into the jury-selection process," he concluded, was to "eliminat[e] peremptory challenges entirely." Today's case reinforces Justice Marshall's concerns.

I

To begin with, this case illustrates the practical problems of proof that Justice Marshall described. As the Court's opinion makes clear, Miller–El marshaled extensive evidence of racial bias. But despite the strength of his claim, Miller–El's challenge has resulted in 17 years of largely unsuccessful and protracted litigation— including 8different judicial proceedings and 8 different judicial opinions, and involving 23 judges, of whom 6 found the *Batson* standard violated and 16 the contrary.

The complexity of this process reflects the difficulty of finding a legal test that will objectively measure the inherently subjective reasons that underlie use of a peremptory challenge. Batson seeks to square this circle by (1)requiring defendants to establish a prima facie case of discrimination, (2) asking prosecutors then to offer a race-neutral explanation for their use of the peremptory, and then (3) requiring defendants to prove that the neutral reason offered is pretextual. See ante, at 5. But Batson embodies defects intrinsic to the task.

At Batson's first step, litigants remain free to misuseperemptory challenges as long as the strikes fall below the prima facie threshold level. See 476 U. S., at 105 (Marshall, J., concurring). At Batson's second step, prosecutors need only tender a neutral reason, not a "persuasive, or even plausible" one. Purkett v. Elem, 514 U.S. 765, 768, 115 S.Ct. 1769 (1995) (per curiam); (" 'mustaches and the beards look suspicious' "). And most importantly, at step three, Batson asks judges to engage in the awkward, sometime hopeless, task of second-guessing a prosecutor's instinctive judgment—the underlying basis for which may be invisible even to the prosecutor exercising the challenge. See 476 U. S., at 106 (Marshall, J., concurring) (noting that the unconscious internalization of racial stereotypes may lead litigants more easily to conclude "that a prospective black juror is 'sullen,' or 'distant,' "even though that characterization would not have sprung to mind had the prospective juror been white); see also Page, Batson's Blind–Spot: Unconscious Stereotyping and the Peremptory Challenge, 85 B. U. L. Rev. 155, 161 (2005) (" '[s]ubtle forms of bias are automatic, unconscious, and unintentional' " and " 'escape notice, even the notice of those enacting the bias' " (quoting Fiske, What's in a Category?: Responsibility, Intent, and the Avoidability of Bias Against Outgroups, in The Social Psychology of Good and Evil 127 (A. Miller ed. 2004))). In such circumstances, it may be impossible for trial courts to discern if a " 'seat-of-the-pants' " peremptory challenge reflects a " 'seat-of-the-pants' " racial stereotype.

Given the inevitably clumsy fit between any objectively measurable standard and the subjective decisionmaking at issue, I am not surprised to find studies and anecdotal reports suggesting that, despite Batson, the discriminatory use of peremptory challenges remains a problem. See, e.g., Baldus, Woodworth, Zuckerman, Weiner, & Broffitt, The Use of Peremptory Challenges in Capital Murder Trials: A Legal and Empirical Analysis, 3 U. Pa. J. Const. L. 3, 52–53, 73, n. 197 (2001) (in 317 capital trials in Philadelphia between 1981 and 1997, prosecutors struck 51% of black jurors and 26% of nonblack jurors; defense counsel struck 26% of black jurors and 54% of nonblack jurors; and race-based uses of prosecutorial peremptories declined by only 2% after Batson); Rose, The Peremptory Challenge Accused of Race or Gender Discrimination? Some Data from One County, 23 Law and Human Behavior 695, 698–699 (1999) (in one North Carolina county, 71% of excused black jurors were removed bythe prosecution; 81% of excused white jurors were removed by the defense); Tucker, In Moore's Trials, Excluded Jurors Fit Racial Pattern, Washington Post, Apr. 2, 2001, p. A1 (in D. C. murder case spanning four trials, prosecutors excused 41 blacks or other minorities and 6whites; defense counsel struck 29 whites and 13 black venire members); Mize, A Legal Discrimination; Juries Are Not Supposed to be Picked on the Basis of Race and Sex, But It Happens All the Time, Washington Post, Oct. 8, 2000, p. B8 (authored by judge on the D. C. Superior Court); see also Melilli, Batson in Practice: What We Have Learned About Batson and Peremptory Challenges, 71 Notre Dame L. Rev. 447, 462–464 (1996) (finding Batson challenges' success rates lower where peremptories were used to strike black, rather than white, potential jurors); Brand, The Supreme Court, Equal Protection and Jury Selection: Denying That Race Still Matters, 1994 Wis. L. Rev. 511, 583–589 (examining judicial decisions and concluding that few Batson challenges succeed); Note, Batson v. Kentucky and J. E. B. v. Alabama ex rel. T. B.: Is the Peremptory Challenge Still Preeminent?, 36 Boston College L. Rev. 161, 189, and n. 303 (1994) (same); Montoya, The Future of the Post–Batson Peremptory Challenge: Voir Dire by Questionnaire and the "Blind" Peremptory Challenge, 29 U. Mich. J. L. Reform 981, 1006, nn. 126–127, 1035 (1996) (reporting attorneys' views on the difficulty of proving Batson claims).

II

Practical problems of proof to the side, peremptory challenges seem increasingly anomalous in our judicial system. On the one hand, the Court has widened and deepened Batson's basic constitutional rule. It has applied Batson's antidiscrimination test to the use of peremptories by criminal defendants, Georgia v. McCollum, 505 U.S. 42, 112 S.Ct. 2348 (1992), by private litigants in civil cases, Edmonson v. Leesville Concrete Co., 500 U.S. 614, 111 S.Ct. 2077 (1991), and by prosecutors where the defendant and the excluded juror are of different races, Powers v. Ohio, 499 U.S. 400, 111 S.Ct. 1364 (1991). It has recognized that the Constitution protects not just defendants, but the jurors themselves. Id., at 409. And it has held that equal protection principles prohibit excusing jurors on account of gender. See J. E. B. v. Alabama ex rel. T. B., 511 U.S. 127, 114 S.Ct. 1419 (1994). Some lower courts have extended Batson's rule to religious affiliation as well. See, e.g., United States v. Brown, 352 F.3d 654, 668–669 (CA2 2003); State v. Hodge, 248 Conn. 207, 244–246, 726 A.2d 531, 553 (1999); United States v. Stafford, 136 F.3d 1109, 1114 (CA7 1998) (suggesting same); see also Davis v. Minnesota, 511 U.S. 1115, 1117, 114 S.Ct. 2120 (1994) (THOMAS, J., dissenting from denial of certiorari). But see Casarez v. State, 913 S.W.2d 468, 496 (Tex. Crim. App. 1994) (en banc) (declining to extend Batson to religious affiliation); State v. Davis, 504 N.W.2d 767, 771 (Minn. 1993) (same).

On the other hand, the use of race-and gender-based stereotypes in the jury-selection process seems better organized and more systematized than ever before. See, e.g., Post, A Loaded Box of Stereotypes: Despite 'Batson,' Race, Gender Play Big Roles in Jury Selection., Nat. L. J., Apr. 25, 2005, pp. 1, 18 (discussing common reliance on race and gender in jury selection). For example, one jury-selection guide counsels attorneys to perform a "demographic analysis" that assigns numerical points to characteristics such as age, occupation, and marital status—in addition to race as well as gender. See V. Starr & A. McCormick, Jury Selection 193–200 (3d ed. 2001). Thus, in a hypothetical dispute between a white landlord and an African-American tenant, the authors suggest awarding two points to an African–American venire member while subtracting one point from her white counterpart. Id., at 197–199.

For example, a bar journal article counsels lawyers to "rate" potential jurors "demographically (age, gender, marital status, etc.) and mark who would be under stereotypical circumstances [their] natural enemies and allies." Drake, The Art of Litigating: Deselecting Jurors Like the Pros, 34 Md. Bar J. 18, 22 (Mar.–Apr. 2001) (emphasis in original).

For example, materials from a legal convention, while noting that "nationality" is less important than "once was thought," and emphasizing that "the answers a prospective juror gives to questions are much more valuable," still point out that "[s]tereotypically" those of "Italian, French, and Spanish" origin "are thought to be pro-plaintiff as well as other minorities, such as Mexican and Jewish[;][p]ersons of German, Scandinavian, Swedish, Finnish, Dutch, Nordic, British, Scottish, Oriental, and Russian origin are thought to be better for the defense"; African–Americans "have always been considered good for the plaintiff," and "[m]ore politically conservative minorities will be more likely to lean toward defendants." Blue,

Mirroring, Proxemics, Nonverbal Communication and Other Psychological Tools, Advocacy Track—Psychology of Trial, Association of Trial Lawyers of America Annual Convention Reference Materials, 1 Ann. 2001 ATLA–CLE 153, available at WESTLAW, ATLA–CLE database (June 8, 2005).

For example, a trial consulting firm advertises a new jury-selection technology: "Whether you are trying a civil case or a criminal case, SmartJURY™ has likely determined the exact demographics (age, race, gender, education, occupation, marital status, number of children, religion, and income) of the type of jurors you should select and the type you should strike." SmartJURY Product Information, http://www.cts-america.com/smartjury_pi.asp (as visited June 8, 2005, and available in Clerk of Court's case file).

These examples reflect a professional effort to fulfill the lawyer's obligation to help his or her client. Cf. J. E. B., supra, at 148–149 (O'CONNOR, J., concurring) (observing that jurors' race and gender may inform their perspective). Nevertheless, the outcome in terms of jury selection is the same as it would be were the motive less benign. And as long as that is so, the law's antidiscrimination command and a peremptory jury-selection system that permits or encourages the use of stereotypes work at cross-purposes.

Finally, a jury system without peremptories is no longer unthinkable. Members of the legal profession have begun serious consideration of that possibility. See, e.g., Alen v. Florida, 596 So.2d 1083, 1088–1089 (Fla. App. 1992) (Hubbart, J., concurring); Broderick, Why the Peremptory Challenge Should Be Abolished, 65 Temp. L. Rev. 369 (1992) (authored by Senior Judge on the U. S. District Court for the Eastern District of Pennsylvania); Hoffman, Peremptory Challenges Should be Abolished: A Trial Judge's Perspective, 64 U. Chi. L. Rev. 809 (1997) (authored by a Colorado state-court judge); Altschuler, The Supreme Court and the Jury: Voir Dire, Peremptory Challenges, and the Review of Jury Verdicts, 56 U. Chi. L. Rev. 153, 199–211 (1989); Amar, Reinventing Juries: Ten Suggested Reforms, 28 U. C. D. L. Rev. 1169, 1182–1183 (1995); Melilli, 71 Notre Dame L. Rev., at 502–503; Page, 85 B. U. L. Rev., at 245–246. And England, a common-law jurisdiction that has eliminated peremptory challenges, continues to administer fair trials based largely on random jury selection. See Criminal Justice Act, 1988, ch. 33, § 118(1), 22 Halsbury's Statutes 357 (4th ed. 2003 reissue) (U. K.); see also 2 Jury Service in Victoria, Final Report, ch. 5, p. 165 (Dec. 1997) (1993 study of English barristers showed majority support for system without peremptory challenges).

III

I recognize that peremptory challenges have a long historical pedigree. They may help to reassure a party of the fairness of the jury. But long ago, Blackstone recognized the peremptory challenge as an "arbitrary and capricious species of [a] challenge." 4 W. Blackstone, Commentaries on the Laws of England 346 (1769). If used to express stereotypical judgments about race, gender, religion, or national origin, peremptory challenges betray the jury's democratic origins and undermine its representative function. See 1 A. de Tocqueville, Democracy in America 287 (H. Reeve transl. 1900) ("[T]he institution of the jury raises the people . . . to the bench of judicial authority [and] invests [them] with the direction of society"); A. Amar, The Bill of Rights 94–96 (1998) (describing the Founders' vision of juries as venues for democratic participation); see also Stevens, Foreword, Symposium: The Jury at a Crossroad: The American Experience, 78 Chi.-Kent L. Rev. 907, 907–908 (2003) (citizens should not be denied the opportunity to serve as jurors unless an impartial judge states a reason for the denial, as with a strike for cause). The "scientific" use of peremptory challenges may also contribute to public cynicism about the fairness of the jury system and its role in American government. See, e.g., S. O'Connor,

Juries: They May Be Broke, But We Can Fix Them, Chautauqua Institution Lecture, July 6, 1995. And, of course, the right to a jury free of discriminatory taint is constitutionally protected—the right to use peremptory challenges is not. See Stilson v. United States, 250 U.S. 583, 586, 40 S.Ct. 28 (1919); see also Ross v. Oklahoma, 487 U.S. 81, 88, 108 S.Ct. 2273 (1988) (defendant's loss of a peremptory challenge does not violate his right to an impartial jury).

Justice Goldberg, dissenting in Swain v. Alabama, 380 U.S. 202, 85 S.Ct. 824 (1965), wrote, "Were it necessary to make an absolute choice between the right of a defendant to have a jury chosen in conformity with the requirements of the Fourteenth Amendment and the right to challenge peremptorily, the Constitution compels a choice of the former." Id., at 244; see also Batson, 476 U. S., at 107 (Marshall, J., concurring) (same); Edmonson, 500 U. S., at 630 (KENNEDY, J.) ("[I]f race stereotypes are the price for acceptance of a jury panel as fair, the price is too high to meet the standard of the Constitution"). This case suggests the need to confront that choice. In light of the considerations I have mentioned, I believe it necessary to reconsider Batson's test and the peremptory challenge system as a whole. With that qualification, I join the Court's opinion.

CHAPTER 18

QUALITY OF REPRESENTATION BY COUNSEL

B. THE DILEMMA OF DEFENSE COUNSEL

2. CASE ILLUSTRATIONS OF DEFENSE COUNSEL DILEMMAS

Add at the end of Note 2 on page 1285 (New Main Case)

In re Lawrence

Supreme Court of Oregon, 2004.
337 Or. 450, 98 P.3d 366.

* * *

In this lawyer disciplinary proceeding, the Oregon State Bar (Bar) charged the accused with violating various disciplinary rules of the Code of Professional Responsibility.

* * *

The accused was admitted to practice in 1989. She is an experienced criminal defense lawyer. In 1998, and at all times relevant to this proceeding, the accused worked "of counsel" for her husband's six-person law firm. At that time, the firm's lawyers included, among others, Kelly, who was a first-year associate. Lawyers at the firm often acted as court-appointed counsel for indigent defendants in criminal cases. The accused was the self-described "law guru" of the firm and routinely reviewed the files of the cases that the firm's associates handled to identify and draft motions that needed to be filed.

In 1996, Oregon voters approved . . . a constitutional amendment that gave crime victims various rights in criminal prosecutions. By 1998, the accused had developed a theory that . . . granted to victims of domestic assault the right to require a trial court to dismiss the criminal charges against their assailants. She sent a memorandum to the other lawyers in the firm to keep an eye out for cases in which she could test her theory. . . . She went on to write, "The way to set these cases up is for the victim to write/call [the deputy district attorney who is handling the case] and demand dismissal, and then tell [the deputy district attorney] who won't dismiss case that they want to address the judge."

In April 1998, the firm was appointed to represent Warren Battle in a domestic assault case. According to police reports, Warren Battle had grabbed his wife, Patricia Battle, pulled her out of a chair, and pushed her toward the bedroom. In so doing, he tore her clothes and left bruises, scratches, and red marks on her body. Those events took place in front of Patricia Battles' children. The firm assigned that case to Kelly, who had been working for the firm for about six weeks at that time. Shortly thereafter, Kelly met with both Warren and Patricia Battle. Patricia Battle was not represented by counsel, and Kelly informed her of her rights under ORS 135.970 (requiring, among other things, that defense counsel inform the victim that she need not talk to him if she did not desire to do so). Patricia Battle told Kelly that she earlier had succeeded in having the court waive a "no-contact" condition that had been part of Warren Battle's release agreement and that she also had tried, unsuccessfully, to persuade the district attorney to dismiss the charges against her husband. At that time, she had assumed that the matter was out of her hands. . . .

Kelly recognized that the Battles' circumstances fit the paradigm that the accused had identified in her memorandum to the firm and, accordingly, explained to the Battles the concept that the accused had developed. Kelly also explained to the Battles that the accused handled motions for the firm. Kelly told the Battles that he would talk to the accused about the case and then left the meeting. He went to the accused's office, where he proceeded to describe the situation and to show her a letter and a proposed affidavit that he had drafted for Patricia Battle's signature.

* * *

When Kelly presented the affidavit to the accused, it contained only one substantive paragraph, stating in effect that Patricia Battle wished to assert what she claimed was her right under Article I, section 42, of the Oregon Constitution (1996) to have the case against her husband dismissed. The accused added two paragraphs to the affidavit, one stating that Patricia Battle had contacted the district attorney's office and communicated her wishes that the case be dismissed, and one stating that the district attorney had not responded. The letter was directed to the district attorney and asked him to schedule a hearing to dismiss the criminal charges. The accused apparently did not change the accompanying letter.

Kelly typed the documents while Patricia Battle was in the office; Patricia Battle then signed them. Both the letter and the affidavit were printed on plain white paper and bore no indication that they had been prepared by the accused's law firm. As noted, Patricia Battle later testified that, at the time that she met with Kelly, she knew nothing about Article I, section 42 (1996). Neither Kelly nor the accused ever advised Patricia Battle that she should seek independent counsel. The affidavit eventually was filed with the court, and the letter was sent to the district attorney.

The next day, the accused reviewed the Battle file, did some legal research, and drafted a brief entitled "Amicus Brief in Support of Crime Victim's Right to Compel Dismissal of Charges." After she talked to Kelly about the information that he had obtained from Patricia Battle, the accused signed the brief and, she testified, gave it to Kelly for filing and service. . . .

In any event, the accused's office sent the brief to the court (and served it on the district attorney) without any attachment; the affidavit was filed separately. No one filed a motion to dismiss the charges against Battle, but the court scheduled a hearing in the matter for May 1998. Neither the trial court judge nor the court clerk knew how the hearing on the motion to dismiss came to be placed on the calendar.

The accused and Kelly met with the Battles in the accused's office on the morning of the hearing, to prepare Patricia Battle for the hearing. Present at the meeting were the accused, Kelly, the Battles, and Patricia Battle's sister, Scott. According to Scott, the accused was "in charge of the meeting." The accused told Patricia Battle that she would be helping her with what to say to get the charges dismissed, as well as how to say it. She explained how the hearing would proceed and what Patricia Battle should tell the court. Specifically, she told Patricia Battle that she should say that her rights had been violated. The accused also stated at that meeting that she did not want Patricia Battle to be sworn in as a witness at the hearing, because she did not want any sworn statements on the record that later could be used in the criminal case against Warren Battle. The accused did not tell Patricia Battle that her interests might be in conflict with her husband's or that she should seek her own counsel. It appears that, during the meeting, Patricia Battle did not fully understand that the accused represented only Warren Battle. Scott, for her part, affirmatively formed the impression that the accused represented Patricia Battle.

Following the meeting, the accused, Kelly, the Battles, and Scott appeared before Judge Harris at the hearing concerning the request to dismiss the charges. The accused appeared as Warren Battle's lawyer. Judge Harris asked the accused if she was representing Patricia Battle, and she answered no. During the hearing, Judge Harris asked that Patricia Battle be sworn to make a statement. The accused objected. According to the accused, she did so because the request was "procedurally inappropriate, "insofar as the motion was Patricia Battle's own and Patricia Battle was appearing before the court, therefore, to represent herself pro se, not as a witness.

During the course of the hearing, Judge Harris became concerned that members of the accused's firm had been giving legal advice to Patricia Battle, the victim, while representing her husband, the defendant. Among other things, the accused prefaced a question to Patricia Battle during the hearing with the statement, "You told me in my office * * * some of the things that you did to make contact with various persons in the district attorney's office * * *." In addition, Judge Harris had observed that the affidavit was notarized by a person in the accused's office and appeared to have been professionally prepared, but no lawyer's name appeared on the document. Accordingly, before ruling on the motion, he called the lawyers into chambers and expressed his concerns. He later testified before the trial panel that he told the accused that he thought that there was an ethical conflict and that he was concerned about it and wanted to "explore and invite response." In the course of the in-chambers meeting, Judge Harris pointedly asked the accused if she had been giving advice to Patricia Battle.

The accused did not then (or at any other time) respond directly to Judge Harris's question. Instead, she told Judge Harris that she was allowed to communicate with the victim and that it was appropriate to involve herself as she had. The accused did not disclose the specifics of any communications that she or any other lawyer at the firm had had with Patricia Battle. She did not tell Judge Harris that Kelly had met with the Battles and had advised Patricia Battle that she might have a constitutional right to have the charges against her husband dismissed; she did not mention that the firm had prepared the affidavit and the letter and that she had made substantive additions to the affidavit; she did not inform Judge Harris that she had told Patricia Battle that she would try to prevent her from being sworn as a witness; and she did not disclose—although one of her questions to Patricia Battle in open court certainly suggested it—that she had met with the Battles earlier that day. Instead, she spoke generally of her right to facilitate a victim's effort to have the charges against an assailant dismissed and then returned to her legal arguments in support of the "amicus" brief. Upon returning to the hearing, Judge Harris denied Patricia Battle's request to have the charges against her husband dismissed.

A few days later, the accused sent a letter to Judge Harris to address his apparent concern that "an alleged action" by her or her law firm represented a conflict of interest, a conflict that she herself claimed not to see. She stated that, as she saw it, the interests of the defendant and the victim were not in conflict, because each wanted the criminal charges dismissed. Although she acknowledged Judge Harris's concerns, she still did not provide him with any factual details about her firm's contact with Patricia Battle or what she had done on Patricia Battle's behalf. Instead, she analogized her situation to that of a lawyer representing a defendant who approaches a victim about preparing documents memorializing a civil compromise. She did not mention Kelly in her letter at all.

Judge Harris responded to that letter in a letter of his own in which he stated, "Based on your analysis of the applicable statute and DR's, I am satisfied that my impression and belief at the time of our conversation, was incorrect." Judge Harris went on to "apologize for the error."

In June 1998, a Yamhill County deputy district attorney filed a complaint with the Disciplinary Counsel's Office concerning the accused's conduct. Subsequently, the Disciplinary Counsel's Office asked the accused to explain whether her "advice to Patricia Battle and preparation of an Amicus Brief on [Battle's] behalf violated DR 7–104(A)(2)." . . .

The Bar filed its formal complaint against the accused in October 2000; the charges were heard in November 2001. . . . The trial panel did not issue its opinion until June 4, 2003, more than 18 months after the trial and more than five years after the events that led to this proceeding. As noted, the trial panel concluded that the accused had committed all the charged violations of the disciplinary rules and suspended the accused from the practice of law for six months.

II. ALLEGED VIOLATIONS

A. Advising Unrepresented Person

* * *

DR 7–104(A) provides in part:

> "During the course of the lawyer's representation of a client, a lawyer shall not:
>
> " * * *%
>
> "(2) Give advice to a person who is not represented by a lawyer, other than the advice to secure counsel, if the interests of such person are or have a reasonable possibility of being in conflict with the interests of the lawyer's client."

* * *

The accused steadfastly has maintained that Patricia Battle's interests were not in actual conflict with those of the accused's client because both desired the same outcome, viz., dismissal of the criminal charges against Warren Battle. However, the rule against giving advice to an unrepresented person applies both in cases in which the interests of the two parties actually conflict and in which there is the reasonable possibility of the interests conflicting. The question, then, is whether there was a reasonable possibility of Patricia Battle's interests being adverse to those of her husband, notwithstanding the fact that they had a common desire, at least for some period of time, in having the criminal case against Warren Battle dismissed.

* * *

We think that the objective personal interests of an alleged batterer and the batterer's victim are inherently adverse and, therefore, that there is a "likely" conflict of interest when a lawyer gives advice to both the abuser and the victim. For example, an unrepresented victim who is financially or otherwise dependent on the abuser may think that he or she has few options available other than to have the abuser return to the home to support or help the victim and any children involved. The victim, therefore, may be motivated to recant for reasons other than that the abuse did not happen. Such a scenario could place the victim in a position of having to lie, thereby placing the victim in danger of being charged with perjury or filing a false police report, among other things. In addition, a lawyer who has only the victim's interests in mind well may be able to show the victim that other resources are available to assist him or her and that it would be in his or her and (and any children's) best interest to have the abuser prosecuted.

In fact, the accused's conduct at the hearing demonstrates that she thought that there was a possibility of a conflict of interest. The accused objected to Patricia Battle being sworn in during the hearing on the motion to dismiss the charges against Warren Battle. The accused made that objection, as she earlier had informed Patricia Battle that she would, because she was concerned that anything that Patricia Battle said under oath at the hearing could be used later against Warren Battle at his criminal trial. In addition, it is significant that the accused knew from the police reports in Warren Battle's client file that Patricia Battle had been injured in the altercation that had led to Warren Battle's arrest, that children had been present at the time of the incident, and that Warren

Battle had a criminal record and was a registered sex offender. Those facts suggest to us (and, we think, also must have suggested to the accused, notwithstanding her protestations to the contrary) that the Battles' objective personal interests were adverse and, therefore, that a likely conflict of interest existed between them. Based on the foregoing, we hold that the interests of Patricia Battle were or had the reasonable possibility of being in conflict with those of the accused's client, Warren Battle.

We next turn to the question whether the accused gave Patricia Battle advice other than the advice to secure counsel. . . . Here, the record shows by clear and convincing evidence that the accused had developed a novel interpretation of a new constitutional provision, Article I, section 42, of the Oregon Constitution (1996); that the accused, through Kelly, informed Patricia Battle (who never before had heard of Article I, section 42 (1996)) that, under her theory, Patricia Battle had a constitutional right to have the charges against her assailant dismissed; that the accused suggested to Patricia Battle, through Kelly, that Patricia Battle pursue a specific course of conduct to accomplish that end; that the accused assisted Kelly in drafting an affidavit for Patricia Battle's signature that explained that Patricia Battle wished to avail herself of her alleged constitutional right; and that the accused prepared Patricia Battle for the hearing before Judge Harris, telling her what to say and how to say it. Based on the foregoing, we conclude that the accused gave Patricia Battle, an unrepresented person, ''advice,'' as that word is used in DR 7–104(A)(2).

* * *

To summarize, we hold that the accused committed one violation of DR 7–104(A)(2).

1.   EFFECTIVE ASSISTANCE

Add at the bottom of Page 1313, a New Note

9.   A major theme of the ineffectiveness cases has been whether *per se* rules ought to be adopted. Arguably, the Court did so in Rompilla v. Beard, ___ U.S. ___, 125 S.Ct. 2456 (2005), a capital case in which defense counsel failed to examine a file pertaining to a prior conviction. While defense counsel were vigorous in their defense, it did appear that the file might well have opened a different and promising line of defense. The issue was whether the defense counsel had been reasonable in stopping their investigation at the point they did. Consider the following excerpts from the 5–4 decision and note that the facts are stated in the dissent.

''Justice Souter . . .''

A standard of reasonableness applied as if one stood in counsel's shoes spawns few hard-edged rules, and the merits of a number of counsel's choices in this case are subject to fair debate. This is not a case in which defense counsel simply ignored their obligation to find mitigating evidence, and their workload as busy public defenders did not keep them from making a number of efforts, including interviews with Rompilla and some members of his family, and examinations of reports by three mental health experts who gave opinions at the guilt phase. None of the sources proved particularly helpful.

Rompilla's own contributions to any mitigation case were minimal. Counsel found him uninterested in helping, as on their visit to his prison to go over a proposed mitigation strategy, when Rompilla told them he was "bored being here listening" and returned to his cell. To questions about childhood and schooling, his answers indicated they had been normal,, save for quitting school in the ninth grade. There were times when Rompilla was even actively obstructive by sending counsel off on false leads.

The lawyers also spoke with five members of Rompilla's family (his former wife, two brothers, a sister-in-law, and his son), and counsel testified that they developed a good relationship with the family in the course of their representation. The state postconviction court found that counsel spoke to the relatives in a "detailed manner," attempting to unearth mitigating information, although the weight of this finding is qualified by the lawyers' concession that "the overwhelming response from the family was that they didn't really feel as though they knew him all that well since he had spent the majority of his adult years and some of his childhood years in custody," Defense counsel also said that because the family was "coming from the position that [Rompilla] was innocent . . . they weren't looking for reasons for why he might have done this."

The third and final source tapped for mitigating material was the cadre of three mental health witnesses who were asked to look into Rompilla's mental state as of the time of the offense and his competency to stand trial. but their reports revealed "nothing useful" to Rompilla's case, and the lawyers consequently did not go to any other historical source that might have cast light on Rompilla's mental condition.

When new counsel entered the case to raise Rompilla's postconviction claims, however, they identified a number of likely avenues the trial lawyers could fruitfully have followed in building a mitigation case. School records are one example, which trial counsel never examined in spite of the professed unfamiliarity of the several family members with Rompilla's childhood, and despite counsel's knowledge that Rompilla left school after the ninth grade. Others examples are records of Rompilla's juvenile and adult incarcerations, which counsel did not consult, although they were aware of their client's criminal record. And while counsel knew from police reports provided in pretrial discovery that Rompilla had been drinking heavily at the time of his offense, and although one of the mental health experts reported that Rompilla's troubles with alcohol merited further investigation, counsel did not look for evidence of a history of dependence on alcohol that might have extenuating significance.

Before us, trial counsel and the Commonwealth respond to these unexplored possibilities by emphasizing this Court's recognition that the duty to investigate does not force defense lawyers to scour the globe on the off-chance something will turn up; reasonably diligent counsel may draw a line when they have good reason to think further investigation would be a waste. See *Wiggins v. Smith*, (further investigation excusable where counsel has evidence suggesting it would be fruitless); *Strickland v. Washington*, (counsel could "reasonably surmise . . . that character and psychological evidence would be of little help"); *Burger v. Kemp, (1987)* (limited investigation reasonable because all witnesses brought to counsel's attention provided predominantly harmful information). The Commonwealth argues that the information trial counsel gathered from Rompilla and the other sources gave them sound reason to think it would have been pointless to spend time and money on the additional investigation espoused by postconviction counsel, and we can say that there is room for debate about trial counsel's obligation to follow at least some of those potential lines of enquiry. There is no need to say more, however, for a further point is clear and dispositive: the lawyers were deficient in failing to examine the court file on Rompilla's prior conviction.

* * *

There is an obvious reason that the failure to examine Rompilla's prior conviction file fell below the level of reasonable performance. Counsel knew that the Commonwealth intended to seek the death penalty by proving Rompilla had a significant history of felony convictions indicating the use or threat of violence, an aggravator under state law. Counsel further knew that the Commonwealth would attempt to establish this history by proving Rompilla's prior conviction for rape and assault, and would emphasize his violent character by introducing a transcript of the rape victim's testimony given in that earlier trial. There is no question that defense counsel were on notice, since they acknowledge that a "plea letter," written by one of them four days prior to trial, mentioned the prosecutor's plans. *Ibid.* It is also undisputed that the prior conviction file was a public document, readily available for the asking at the very courthouse where Rompilla was to be tried.

With every effort to view the facts as a defense lawyer would have done at the time, it is difficult to see how counsel could have failed to realize that without examining the readily available file they were seriously compromising their opportunity to respond to a case for aggravation. The prosecution was going to use the dramatic facts of a similar prior offense, and Rompilla's counsel had a duty to make all reasonable efforts to learn what they could about the offense. Reasonable efforts certainly included obtaining the Commonwealth's own readily available file on the prior conviction to learn what the Commonwealth knew about the crime, to discover any mitigating evidence the Commonwealth would downplay and to anticipate the details of the aggravating evidence the Commonwealth would emphasize. n4 Without making reasonable efforts to review the file, defense counsel could have had no hope of knowing whether the prosecution was quoting selectively from the transcript, or whether there were circumstances extenuating the behavior described by the victim. The obligation to get the file was particularly pressing here owing to the similarity of the violent prior offense to the crime charged and Rompilla's sentencing strategy stressing residual doubt. Without making efforts to learn the details and rebut the relevance of the earlier crime, a convincing argument for residual doubt was certainly beyond any hope.

* * *

At argument the most that Pennsylvania (and the United States as *amicus*) could say was that defense counsel's efforts to find mitigating evidence by other means excused them from looking at the prior conviction file. And that, of course, is the position taken by the state postconviction courts. Without specifically discussing the prior case file, they too found that defense counsel's efforts were enough to free them from any obligation to enquire further.

We think this conclusion of the state court fails to answer the considerations we have set out, to the point of being an objectively unreasonable conclusion. It flouts prudence to deny that a defense lawyer should try to look at a file he knows the prosecution will cull for aggravating evidence, let alone when the file is sitting in the trial courthouse, open for the asking. No reasonable lawyer would forgo examination of the file thinking he could do as well by asking the defendant or family relations whether they recalled anything helpful or damaging in the prior victim's testimony. Nor would a reasonable lawyer compare possible searches for school reports, juvenile records, and evidence of drinking habits to the opportunity to take a look at a file disclosing what the prosecutor knows and even plans to read from in his case. Questioning a few more family members and searching for old records can promise less than looking for a needle in a haystack, when a lawyer truly has reason to doubt there is any needle there. . . . But looking at a file the prosecution says it will use is a sure bet: whatever may be in that file is going to tell defense counsel something about what the prosecution can produce.

The dissent thinks this analysis creates a "rigid, *per se*" rule that requires defense counsel to do a complete review of the file on any prior conviction introduced (opinion of KENNEDY, J.), but that is a mistake. Counsel fell short here because they failed to make reasonable efforts to review the prior conviction file, despite knowing that the prosecution intended to introduce Rompilla's prior conviction not merely by entering a notice of conviction into evidence but by quoting damaging testimony of the rape victim in that case. The unreasonableness of attempting no more than they did was heightened by the easy availability of the file at the trial courthouse, and the great risk that testimony about a similar violent crime would hamstring counsel's chosen defense of residual doubt. It is owing to these circumstances that the state courts were objectively unreasonable in concluding that counsel could reasonably decline to make any effort to review the file. Other situations, where a defense lawyer is not charged with knowledge that the prosecutor intends to use a prior conviction in this way, might well warrant a different assessment.

* * *

If the defense lawyers had looked in the file on Rompilla's prior conviction, it is uncontested they would have found a range of mitigation leads that no other source had opened up. In the same file with the transcript of the prior trial were the records of Rompilla's imprisonment on the earlier conviction, which defense counsel testified she had never seen ... The prison files pictured Rompilla's childhood and mental health very differently from anything defense counsel had seen or heard. An evaluation by a corrections counselor states that Rompilla was "reared in the slum environment of Allentown, Pa. vicinity. He early came to the attention of juvenile authorities, quit school at 16, [and] started a series of incarcerations in and out Penna. often of assaultive nature and commonly related to over-indulgence in alcoholic beverages." The same file discloses test results that the defense's mental health experts would have viewed as pointing to schizophrenia and other disorders, and test scores showing a third grade level of cognition after nine years of schooling.

* * *

The accumulated entries would have destroyed the benign conception of Rompilla's upbringing and mental capacity defense counsel had formed from talking with Rompilla himself and some of his family members, and from the reports of the mental health experts. With this information, counsel would have become skeptical of the impression given by the five family members and would unquestionably have gone further to build a mitigation case. Further effort would presumably have unearthed much of the material postconviction counsel found, including testimony from several members of Rompilla's family, whom trial counsel did not interview. Judge Sloviter summarized this evidence:

"Rompilla's parents were both severe alcoholics who drank constantly. His mother drank during her pregnancy with Rompilla, and he and his brothers eventually developed serious drinking problems. His father, who had a vicious temper, frequently beat Rompilla's mother, leaving her bruised and black-eyed, and bragged about his cheating on her. His parents fought violently, and on at least one occasion his mother stabbed his father. He was abused by his father who beat him when he was young with his hands, fists, leather straps, belts and sticks. All of the children lived in terror. There were no expressions of parental love, affection or approval. Instead, he was subjected to yelling and verbal abuse. His father locked Rompilla and his brother Richard in a small wire mesh dog pen that was filthy and excrement filled. He had an isolated background, and was not allowed to visit other children or to speak to anyone on the phone. They had no indoor plumbing in the house, he slept in the attic with no heat, and the children were not given clothes and attended school in rags."

The jury never heard any of this and neither did the mental health experts who examined Rompilla before trial. While they found "nothing helpful to [Rompilla's] case," *Rompilla,* their postconviction counterparts, alerted by information from school, medical, and prison records that trial counsel never saw, found plenty of "'red flags'" pointing up a need to test further. (Sloviter, J., dissenting). When they tested, they found that Rompilla "suffers from organic brain damage, an extreme mental disturbance significantly impairing several of his cognitive functions.". They also said that "Rompilla's problems relate back to his childhood, and were likely caused by fetal alcohol syndrome [and that] Rompilla's capacity to appreciate the criminality of his conduct or to conform his conduct to the law was substantially impaired at the time of the offense.". . . .

These findings in turn would probably have prompted a look at school and juvenile records, all of them easy to get, showing, for example, that when Rompilla was 16 his mother "was missing from home frequently for a period of one or several weeks at a time." . . . The same report noted that his mother "has been reported . . . frequently under the influence of alcoholic beverages, with the result that the children have always been poorly kept and on the filthy side which was also the condition of the home at all times." *Ibid.* School records showed Rompilla's IQ was in the mentally retarded range. . . .

This evidence adds up to a mitigation case that bears no relation to the few naked pleas for mercy actually put before the jury, and although we suppose it is possible that a jury could have heard it all and still have decided on the death penalty, that is not the test.

Pennsylvania must either retry the case on penalty or stipulate to a life sentence.

It is so ordered.

JUSTICE O'CONNOR, concurring.

I write separately to put to rest one concern. The dissent worries that the Court's opinion "imposes on defense counsel a rigid requirement to review all documents in what it calls the 'case file' of any prior conviction that the prosecution might rely on at trial." . But the Court's opinion imposes no such rule. Rather, today's decision simply applies our longstanding case-by-case approach to determining whether an attorney's performance was unconstitutionally deficient under *Strickland v. Washington* . . . In particular, there were three circumstances which made the attorneys' failure to examine Rompilla's prior conviction file unreasonable.

First, Rompilla's attorneys knew that their client's prior conviction would be at the very heart of the *prosecution's* case. The prior conviction went not to a collateral matter, but rather to one of the aggravating circumstances making Rompilla eligible for the death penalty. The prosecutors intended not merely to mention the fact of prior conviction, but to read testimony about the details of the crime. That crime, besides being quite violent in its own right, was very similar to the murder for which Rompilla was on trial, and Rompilla had committed the murder at issue a mere three months after his release from prison on the earlier conviction. In other words, the prosecutor clearly planned to use details of the prior crime as powerful evidence that Rompilla was a dangerous man for whom the death penalty would be both appropriate punishment and a necessary means of incapacitation. This was evidence the defense should have been prepared to meet: A reasonable defense lawyer would have attached a high importance to obtaining the record of the prior trial, in order to anticipate and find ways of deflecting the prosecutor's aggravation argument.

Second, the prosecutor's planned use of the prior conviction threatened to eviscerate one of the *defense's* primary mitigation arguments. Rompilla was convicted on the basis of strong circumstantial evidence. His lawyers structured the entire mitigation argument around the hope of convincing the jury that residual doubt about Rompilla's guilt made it inappropriate to impose the death penalty. In announcing an intention to introduce testimony about Rompilla's similar prior offense, the prosecutor put Rompilla's attorneys on notice that the prospective defense on mitigation likely would be ineffective and counterproductive. The similarities between the two crimes, combined with the timing and the already strong circumstantial evidence, raised a strong likelihood that the jury would reject Rompilla's residual doubt argument. Rompilla's attorneys' reliance on this transparently weak argument risked damaging their credibility. Such a scenario called for further investigation, to determine whether circumstances of the prior case gave any hope of saving the residual doubt argument, or whether the best strategy instead would be to jettison that argument so as to focus on other, more promising issues.

Third, the attorneys' decision not to obtain Rompilla's prior conviction file was not the result of an informed tactical decision about how the lawyers' time would best be spent. Although Rompilla's attorneys had ample warning that the details of Rompilla's prior conviction would be critical to their case, their failure to obtain that file would not necessarily have been deficient if it had resulted from the lawyers' careful exercise of judgment about how best to marshal their time and serve their client. But Rompilla's attorneys did not ignore the prior case file in order to spend their time on other crucial leads. They did not determine that the file was so inaccessible or so large that examining it would necessarily divert them from other trial-preparation tasks they thought more promising. They did not learn at the 11th hour about the prosecution's intent to use the prior conviction, when it was too late for them to change plans. Rather, their failure to obtain the crucial file "was the result of inattention, not reasoned strategic judgment." *Wiggins v. Smith,* 539 U.S. 510, 534, 123 S.Ct. 2527, 156 L.Ed.2d 471 (2003).

Because the Court's opinion is consistent with the " 'case-by-case examination of the evidence' " called for under our cases . . .

JUSTICE KENNEDY, with whom THE CHIEF JUSTICE, JUSTICE SCALIA, and JUSTICE THOMAS join, dissenting.

Today the Court brands two committed criminal defense attorneys as ineffective—"outside the wide range of professionally competent counsel," *Strickland v. Washington, (1984)*—because they did not look in an old case file and stumble upon something they had not set out to find. By implication the Court also labels incompetent the work done by the three mental health professionals who examined Ronald Rompilla. To reach this result, the majority imposes on defense counsel a rigid requirement to review all documents in what it calls the "case file" of any prior conviction that the prosecution might rely on at trial. The Court's holding, a mistake under any standard of review, is all the more troubling because this case arises under the Antiterrorism and Effective Death Penalty Act of 1996. In order to grant Rompilla habeas relief the Court must say, and indeed does say, that the Pennsylvania Supreme Court was objectively unreasonable in failing to anticipate today's new case file rule.

* * *

Rompilla's attorneys recognized from the outset that building an effective mitigation case was crucial to helping their client avoid the death penalty. Rompilla stood accused of a brutal crime. In January 1988, James Scanlon was murdered while he was closing the Cozy Corner Cafe, a bar he owned in Allentown, Pennsylvania. Scanlon's body was discovered later the next morning, lying in a pool of blood. Scanlon had been stabbed multiple times, including 16 wounds around the neck and head. Scanlon also had been beaten with a blunt object, and his face had been gashed, possibly with shards from broken liquor and beer bottles found at the scene of the crime. After Scanlon was stabbed to death his body had been set on fire.

Substantial evidence linked Rompilla to the crime ... He was at the Cozy Corner Cafe near closing time on the night of the murder and was observed going to the bathroom approximately 10 times during a 1–hour period. A window in that bathroom, the police later determined, was the probable point of entry used by Scanlon's assailant. A pair of Rompilla's sneakers seized by the police matched a bloody footprint found near the victim's body, and blood on the sneakers matched the victim's blood type. Rompilla's fingerprint was found on one of the two knives used to commit the murder. Sometime after leaving the bar on the night of the murder, Rompilla checked into a nearby motel under a false name. Although he told the police he left the bar with only two dollars, Rompilla had paid cash for the room and flashed a large amount of money to the desk clerks. The victim's wallet was discovered in the bushes just outside of Rompilla's motel room. When the police questioned Rompilla about the murder, his version of events was inconsistent with the testimony of other witnesses.

Rompilla was represented at trial by Fredrick Charles, the chief public defender for Lehigh County at the time, and Maria Dantos, an assistant public defender. Charles and Dantos were assisted by John Whispell, an investigator in the public defender's office. Rompilla's defense team sought to develop mitigating evidence from various sources. First, they questioned Rompilla extensively about his upbringing and background. ... To make these conversations more productive they provided Rompilla with a list of the mitigating circumstances recognized by Pennsylvania law. ... Second, Charles and Dantos arranged for Rompilla to be examined by three experienced mental health professionals, experts described by Charles as "the best forensic psychiatrist around here, [another] tremendous psychiatrist and a fabulous forensic psychologist." Finally, Rompilla's attorneys questioned his family extensively in search of any information that might help spare Rompilla the death penalty. Dantos, in particular, developed a "very close" relationship with Rompilla's family, which was a "constant source of information." Indeed, after trial Rompilla's wife sent Dantos a letter expressing her gratitude. The letter referred to Charles and Dantos as "superb human beings" who "fought and felt everything [Rompilla's] family did."

The Court acknowledges the steps taken by Rompilla's attorneys in preparation for sentencing but finds fault nonetheless. "The lawyers were deficient," the Court says, "in failing to examine the court file on Rompilla's prior conviction."

* * *

A *per se* rule requiring counsel in every case to review the records of prior convictions used by the State as aggravation evidence is a radical departure from *Strickland* and its progeny. We have warned in the past against the creation of "specific guidelines" or "checklists for judicial evaluation of attorney performance." See also *Wiggins v. Smith, (2003)*; *Roe v. Flores–Ortega, (2000)*. "No particular set of detailed rules for counsel's conduct can satisfactorily take account of the variety of circumstances faced by defense counsel or the range of legitimate decisions regarding how best to represent a criminal defendant. Any such set of rules would interfere with the constitutionally protected independence of counsel and restrict the wide latitude counsel must have in making tactical decisions. Indeed, the existence of detailed guidelines for representation could distract from the overriding mission of vigorous advocacy of the defendant's cause."

* * *

While the Court disclaims any intention to create a bright-line rule, this affords little comfort. The Court's opinion makes clear it has imposed on counsel a broad obligation to review prior conviction case files where those priors are used in aggravation—and to review every document in those files if not every single page of every document, regardless of the prosecution's proposed use for the prior conviction. . . . The Court also protests that the exceptional weight Rompilla's attorneys at sentencing placed on residual doubt required them to review the prior conviction file, (O'CONNOR, J., concurring). In fact, residual doubt was not central to Rompilla's mitigation case. Rompilla's family members did testify at sentencing that they thought he was innocent, but Dantos tried to draw attention away from this point and instead use the family's testimony to humanize Rompilla and ask for mercy.

* * *

Even with the benefit of hindsight the Court struggles to explain how the file would have proved helpful, offering only the vague speculation that Rompilla's attorneys might have discovered "circumstances that extenuated the behavior described by the [rape] victim." What the Court means by "circumstances" is a mystery. If the Court is referring to details on Rompilla's mental fitness or upbringing, surely Rompilla's attorneys were more likely to discover such information through the sources they consulted: Rompilla; his family; and the three mental health experts that examined him.

Perhaps the circumstances to which the majority refers are the details of Rompilla's 1974 crimes. Charles and Dantos, however, had enough information about the prior convictions to determine that reviewing the case file was not the most effective use of their time. Rompilla had been convicted of breaking into the residence of Josephine Macrenna, who lived in an apartment above the bar she owned. After Macrenna gave him the bar's receipts for the night, Rompilla demanded that she disrobe. When she initially resisted, Rompilla slashed her left breast with a knife. Rompilla then held Macrenna at knifepoint while he raped her for over an hour. Charles and Dantos were aware of these circumstances of the prior conviction and the brutality of the crime. It did not take a review of the case file to know that quibbling with the Commonwealth's version of events was a dubious trial strategy. At sentencing Dantos fought vigorously to prevent the Commonwealth from introducing the details of the 1974 crimes, *id.*, at 16–40, but once the transcript was admitted there was nothing that could be done. Rompilla was unlikely to endear himself to the jury by arguing that his prior conviction for burglary, theft, and rape really was not as bad as the Commonwealth was making it out to be. Recognizing this, Rompilla's attorneys instead devoted their limited time and resources to developing a mitigation case. That those efforts turned up little useful evidence does not make the *ex ante* strategic calculation of Rompilla's attorneys constitutionally deficient.

One of the primary reasons this Court has rejected a checklist approach to effective assistance of counsel is that each new requirement risks distracting attorneys from the real objective of providing vigorous advocacy as dictated by the facts and circumstances in the particular case. The Court's rigid requirement that counsel always review the case files of convictions the prosecution seeks to use at trial will be just such a distraction. Capital defendants often have a history of crime. For example, as of 2003, 64 percent of inmates on death row had prior felony convictions. . . . If the prosecution relies on these convictions as aggravators, the

Court has now obligated defense attorneys to review the boxes of documents that come with them.

In imposing this new rule, the Court states that counsel in this case could review the "entire file" with "ease." There is simply no support in the record for this assumption. Case files often comprise numerous boxes. The file may contain, among other things, witness statements, forensic evidence, arrest reports, grand jury transcripts, testimony and exhibits relating to any pretrial suppression hearings, trial transcripts, trial exhibits, post-trial motions and presentence reports. Full review of even a single prior conviction case file could be time consuming, and many of the documents in a file are duplicative or irrelevant. The Court, recognizing the flaw in its analysis, suggests that cases involving "warehouses of records" "will call for greater subtlety.". Yet for all we know, this is such a case. As to the time component, the Court tells us nothing as to the number of hours counsel had available to prepare for sentencing or why the decisions they made in allocating their time were so flawed as to constitute deficient performance under *Strickland.*

Today's decision will not increase the resources committed to capital defense. (At the time of Rompilla's trial, the Lehigh County Public Defender's Office had two investigators for 2,000 cases.... If defense attorneys dutifully comply with the Court's new rule, they will have to divert resources from other tasks. The net effect of today's holding in many cases—instances where trial counsel reasonably can conclude that reviewing old case files is not an effective use of time—will be to diminish the quality of representation. We have "consistently declined to impose mechanical rules on counsel—even when those rules might lead to better representation," *Roe v. Flores–Ortega,* I see no occasion to depart from this approach in order to impose a requirement that might well lead to worse representation).

It is quite possible defense attorneys, recognizing the absurdity of a one-size-fits-all approach to effective advocacy, will simply ignore the Court's new requirement and continue to exercise their best judgment about how to allocate time and resources in preparation for trial. While this decision would be understandable—and might even be required by state ethical rules, cf. Pa. Rules of Professional Conduct, Preamble, and Rule 1.1 (2005)—it leaves open the possibility that a defendant will seek to overturn his conviction based on something in a prior conviction case file that went unreviewed. This elevation of needle-in-a-haystack claims to the status of constitutional violations will benefit undeserving defendants and saddle States with the considerable costs of retrial and/or resentencing.

Today's decision is wrong under any standard, but the Court's error is compounded by the fact that this case arises on federal habeas.... Rompilla must show that the Pennsylvania Supreme Court decision was not just "incorrect or erroneous," but "objectively unreasonable." *Lockyer v. Andrade,* (citing *Williams v. Taylor, (2000)).* He cannot do so.

The Court pays lipservice to the *Williams* standard, but it proceeds to adopt a rigid, *per se* obligation that binds counsel in every case and finds little support in our precedents. Indeed, *Strickland,* the case the Court purports to apply, is directly to the contrary: "Most important, in adjudicating a claim of actual [*54] ineffectiveness of counsel, a court should keep in mind that the principles we have stated do not establish mechanical rules."

* * *

The Court's theory of prejudice rests on serendipity. Nothing in the old case file diminishes the aggravating nature of the prior conviction. The only way Rompilla's attorneys could have minimized the aggravating force of the earlier rape conviction was through Dantos' forceful, but ultimately unsuccessful, fight to exclude the transcript at sentencing. The Court, recognizing this problem, instead finds prejudice through chance. If Rompilla's attorneys had reviewed the case file of his prior rape and burglary conviction, the Court says, they would have stumbled across "a range of mitigation leads."

The range of leads to which the Court refers is in fact a handful of notations within a single 10–page document. The document, an "Initial Transfer Petition," appears to have been prepared by the Pennsylvania Department of Corrections after Rompilla's conviction to facilitate his initial assignment to one of the Commonwealth's maximum-security prisons.

Rompilla cannot demonstrate prejudice because nothing in the record indicates that Rompilla's trial attorneys would have discovered the transfer petition, or the clues contained in it, if they had reviewed the old file. The majority faults Rompilla's attorneys for failing to "learn what the Commonwealth knew about the crime," "discover any mitigating evidence the Commonwealth would downplay," and "anticipate the details of the aggravating evidence the Commonwealth would emphasize." Yet if Rompilla's attorneys had reviewed the case file with these purposes in mind, they almost surely would have attributed no significance to the transfer petition following only a cursory review. The petition, after all, was prepared by the Bureau of Correction after Rompilla's conviction for the purpose of determining Rompilla's initial prison assignment. It contained no details regarding the circumstances of the conviction. Reviewing the prior conviction file for information to counter the Commonwealth, counsel would have looked first at the transcript of the trial testimony, and perhaps then to probative exhibits or forensic evidence. There would have been no reason for counsel to read, or even to skim, this obscure document.

The Court claims that the transfer petition would have been discovered because it was in the "same file" with the transcript, but this characterization is misleading and the conclusion the Court draws from it is accordingly fallacious. The record indicates only that the transfer petition was a part of the same case file, but Rompilla provides no indication of the size of the file, which for all we know originally comprised several boxes of documents. By the time of Rompilla's state postconviction hearing, moreover, the transfer petition was not stored in any "file" at all—it had been transferred to microfilm.

* * *

The majority thus finds itself in a bind. If counsel's alleged deficiency lies in the failure to review the file for the purposes the majority has identified, then there is no prejudice: for there is no reasonable probability that review of the file for those purposes would have led counsel to accord the transfer petition enough attention to discover the leads the majority cites. Prejudice could only be demonstrated if the deficiency in counsel's performance were to be described not as the failure to perform a purposive review of the file, but instead as the failure to accord intense scrutiny to every single page of every single document in that file, regardless of the purpose motivating the review ... Surely, however, the Court would not require defense counsel to look at every document, no matter how tangential, included in the prior conviction file on the off chance that some notation therein might provide a lead, which in turn might result in the discovery of useful information. The Constitution does not mandate that defense attorneys perform busy work. This rigid requirement would divert counsel's limited time and energy away from more important tasks. In this way, it would ultimately disserve the rationale underlying the Court's new rule, which is to ensure that defense counsel counter the State's aggravation case effectively.

If the Court does intend to impose on counsel a constitutional obligation to review every page of every document included in the case file of a prior conviction, then today's holding is even more misguided than I imagined.

* * *

Today, the Court succumbs to the very temptation that *Strickland* warned against. In the process, the majority imposes on defense attorneys a rigid requirement that finds no support in our cases or common sense.

10. In Florida v. Nixon, ___ U.S. ___, 125 S.Ct. 551 (2004), a unanimous Court held that a defense counsel may make, without the client's consent, a decision to admit guilt at trial in order to improve the chances of avoiding the death penalty.

* * *

Justice Ginsburg delivered the opinion of the Court.

This capital case concerns defense counsel's strategic decision to concede, at the guilt phase of the trial, the defendant's commission of murder, and to concentrate the defense on establishing, at the penalty phase, cause for sparing the defendant's life. Any concession of that order, the Florida Supreme Court held, made without the defendant's express consent—however gruesome the crime and despite the strength of the evidence of guilt—automatically ranks as prejudicial ineffective assistance of counsel necessitating a new trial. We reverse the Florida Supreme Court's judgment.

* * *

On Monday, August 13, 1984, near a dirt road in the environs of Tallahassee, Florida, a passing motorist discovered Jeanne Bickner's charred body. Bickner had been tied to a tree and set on fire while still alive.Her left leg and arm, and most of her hair and skin, had been burned away. The next day, police found Bickner's car, abandoned on a Tallahassee street corner, on fire. Id., at 2520. Police arrested 23-year-old Joe Elton Nixon later that morning, after Nixon's brother informed the sheriff's office that Nixon had confessed to the murder.

Questioned by the police, Nixon described in graphic detail how he had kidnaped Bickner, then killed her. He recounted that he had approached Bickner, a stranger, in a mall, and asked her to help him jump-start his car. Bickner offered Nixon a ride home in her 1973 MG sports car. Once on the road, Nixon directed Bickner to drive to a remote place; en route, he overpowered her and stopped the car. Nixon next put Bickner in the MG's trunk, drove into a wooded area, removed Bickner from the car, and tied her to a tree with jumper cables. Bickner pleaded with Nixon to release her, offering him money in exchange. Concerned that Bickner might identify him, Nixon decided to kill her. He set fire to Bickner's personal belongings and ignited her with burning objects. Nixon drove away in the MG, and later told his brother and girlfriend what he had done. He burned the MG on Tuesday, August 14, after reading in the newspaper that Bickner's body had been discovered.

The State gathered overwhelming evidence establishing that Nixon had committed the murder in the manner he described. A witness saw Nixon approach Bickner in the mall's parking lot on August 12, and observed Bickner taking jumper cables out of the trunk of her car and giving them to Nixon. Several witnesses told police they saw Nixon driving around in the MG in the hours and days following Bickner's death. Nixon's palm print was found on the trunk of the car. Nixon's girlfriend, Wanda Robinson, and his brother, John Nixon, both stated that Nixon told them he had killed someone and showed them two rings later identified as Bickner's. According to Nixon's brother, Nixon pawned the rings, and attempted to sell the car. At a local pawnshop, police recovered the rings and a receipt for them bearing Nixon's driver's license number; the pawnshop owner identified Nixon as the person who sold the rings to him.

. . . Assistant public defender Michael Corin, assigned to represent Nixon, filed a plea of not guilty, and deposed all of the State's potential witnesses. Corin concluded, given the strength of the evidence, that Nixon's guilt was not "subject to any reasonable dispute." Corin thereupon commenced plea negotiations, hoping to persuade the prosecution to drop the death penalty in exchange for Nixon's guilty pleas to all charges. Negotiations broke down when the prosecutors indicated their unwillingness to recommend a sentence other than death.

Faced with the inevitability of going to trial on a capital charge, Corin turned his attention to the penalty phase, believing that the only way to save Nixon's life would be to present extensive mitigation evidence centering on Nixon's mental instability. Experienced in capital defense, Corin feared that denying Nixon's commission of the kidnaping and murder during the guilt phase would compromise Corin's ability to persuade the jury, during the penalty phase, that Nixon's conduct was the product of his mental illness. Corin concluded that the best strategy would be to concede guilt, thereby preserving his credibility in urging leniency during the penalty phase.

Corin attempted to explain this strategy to Nixon at least three times. Although Corin had represented Nixon previously on unrelated charges and the two had a good relationship in Corin's estimation, Nixon was generally unresponsive during their discussions. He never verbally approved or protested Corin's proposed strategy. Overall, Nixon gave Corin very little, if any, assistance or direction in preparing the case, and refused to attend pretrial dispositions of various motions. Corin eventually exercised his professional judgment to pursue the concession strategy. As he explained: "There are many times lawyers make decisions because they have to make them because the client does nothing."

When Nixon's trial began on July 15, 1985, his unresponsiveness deepened into disruptive and violent behavior. On the second day of jury selection, Nixon pulled off his clothing, demanded a black judge and lawyer, refused to be escorted into the courtroom, and threatened to force the guards to shoot him. An extended on-the-record colloquy followed Nixon's bizarre behavior, during which Corin urged the trial judge to explain Nixon's rights to him and ascertain whether Nixon understood the significance of absenting himself from the trial. Corin also argued that restraining Nixon and compelling him to be present would prejudice him in the eyes of the jury. When the judge examined Nixon on the record in a holding cell, Nixon stated he had no interest in the trial and threatened to misbehave if forced to attend. The judge ruled that Nixon had intelligently and voluntarily waived his right to be present at trial.

The guilt phase of the trial thus began in Nixon's absence. In his opening statement, Corin acknowledged Nixon's guilt and urged the jury to focus on the penalty phase:

"In this case, there won't be any question, none whatsoever, that my client, Joe Elton Nixon, caused Jeannie Bickner's death. . . . [T]hat fact will be proved to your satisfaction beyond any doubt.

"This case is about the death of Joe Elton Nixon and whether it should occur within the next few years by electrocution or maybe its natural expiration after a lifetime of confinement.

. . .

"Now, in arriving at your verdict, in your penalty recommendation, for we will get that far, you are going to learn many facts ... about Joe Elton Nixon. Some of those facts are going to be good. That may not seem clear to you at this time. But, and sadly, most of the things you learn of Joe Elton Nixon are not going to be good. But, I'm suggesting to you that when you have seen all the testimony, heard all the testimony and the evidence that has been shown, there are going to be reasons why you should recommend that his life be spared."

During its case in chief, the State introduced the tape of Nixon's confession, expert testimony on the manner in which Bickner died, and witness testimony regarding Nixon's confessions to his relatives and his possession of Bickner's car and personal effects. Corin cross-examined these witnesses only when he felt their statements needed clarification, and he did not present a defense case. Corin did object to the introduction of crime scene photographs as unduly prejudicial, and actively contested several aspects of the jury instructions during the charge conference. In his closing argument, Corin again conceded Nixon's guilt, and reminded the jury of the importance of the penalty phase: "I will hope to ... argue to you and give you reasons not that Mr. Nixon's life be spared one final and terminal confinement forever, but that he not be sentenced to die." The jury found Nixon guilty on all counts.

At the start of the penalty phase, Corin argued to the jury that "Joe Elton Nixon is not normal organically, intellectually, emotionally or educationally or in any other way." Corin presented the testimony of eight witnesses. Relatives and friends described Nixon's childhood emotional troubles and his erratic behavior in the days preceding the murder. A psychiatrist and a psychologist addressed Nixon's antisocial personality, his history of emotional instability and psychiatric care, his low IQ, and the possibility that at some point he suffered brain damage. The State presented little evidence during the penalty phase, simply incorporating its guilt-phase evidence by reference, and introducing testimony, over Corin's objection, that Nixon had removed Bickner's underwear in order to terrorize her.

In his closing argument, Corin emphasized Nixon's youth, the psychiatric evidence, and the jury's discretion to consider any mitigating circumstances. Corin urged that, if not sentenced to death, "Joe Elton Nixon would [n]ever be released from confinement." The death penalty, Corin maintained, was appropriate only for "intact human being[s]," and "Joe Elton Nixon is not one of those. He's never been one of those. He never will be one of those." Corin concluded: "You know, we're not around here all that long. And it's rare when we have the opportunity to give or take life. And you have that opportunity to give life. And I'm going to ask you to do that. Thank you." After deliberating for approximately three hours, the jury recommended that Nixon be sentenced to death.

In accord with the jury's recommendation, the trial court imposed the death penalty. Notably, at the close of the penalty phase, the court commended Corin's performance during the trial, stating that "the tactic employed by trial counsel ... was an excellent analysis of [the] reality of his case." The evidence of guilt "would have persuaded any jury ... beyond all doubt," and "[f]or trial counsel to have inferred that Mr. Nixon was not guilty ... would have deprived [counsel] of any credibility during the penalty phase."

* * *

Observing that "no competent, substantial evidence ... establish[ed] that Nixon affirmatively and explicitly agreed to counsel's strategy," the Florida Supreme Court reversed and remanded for a new trial. Nixon v. State, 857 So.2d 172, 176 (Fla. 2003) (Nixon III) (emphasis in original)....

An attorney undoubtedly has a duty to consult with the client regarding "important decisions," including questions of overarching defense strategy. Strickland, 466 U.S., at 688, 104 S.Ct. 2052, 80 L.Ed.2d 674. That obligation, however, does not require counsel to obtain the defendant's consent to "every tactical decision." Taylor v. Illinois, 484 U.S. 400, 417–418, 108 S.Ct. 646, 98 L.Ed.2d 798 (1988) (an attorney has authority to manage most aspects of the defense without obtaining his client's approval). But certain decisions regarding the exercise or waiver of basic trial rights are of such moment that they cannot be made for the defendant by a surrogate. A defendant, this Court affirmed, has "the ultimate authority" to determine "whether to plead guilty, waive a jury, testify in his or her own behalf, or take an appeal." Jones v. Barnes, 463 U.S. 745, 751, 103 S.Ct. 3308, 77 L.Ed.2d 987 (1983). Concerning those decisions, an attorney must both consult with the defendant and obtain consent to the recommended course of action.

A guilty plea, we recognized in Boykin v. Alabama, is an event of signal significance in a criminal proceeding. By entering a guilty plea, a defendant waives constitutional rights that inhere in a criminal trial, including the right to trial by jury, the protection against self-incrimination, and the right to confront one's accusers. While a guilty plea may be tactically advantageous for the defendant, the plea is not simply a strategic choice; it is "itself a conviction," and the high stakes for the defendant require "the utmost solicitude," Accordingly, counsel lacks authority to consent to a guilty plea on a client's behalf, Brookhart v. Janis; moreover, a defendant's tacit acquiescence in the decision to plead is insufficient to render the plea valid

The Florida Supreme Court ... deemed Corin's statements to the jury "the functional equivalent of a guilty plea." We disagree with that assessment.

Despite Corin's concession, Nixon retained the rights accorded a defendant in a criminal trial.... The State was obliged to present during the guilt phase competent, admissible evidence establishing the essential elements of the crimes with which Nixon was charged. That aggressive evidence would thus be separated from the penalty phase, enabling the defense to concentrate that portion of the trial on mitigating factors. Further, the defense reserved the right to cross-examine witnesses for the prosecution and could endeavor, as Corin did, to exclude prejudicial evidence. In addition, in the event of errors in the trial or jury instructions, a concession of guilt would not hinder the defendant's right to appeal.

* * *

Corin was obliged to, and in fact several times did, explain his proposed trial strategy to Nixon. Given Nixon's constant resistance to answering inquiries put to him by counsel and court. Corin was not additionally required to gain express consent before conceding Nixon's guilt.

* * *

The Florida Supreme Court's erroneous equation of Corin's concession strategy to a guilty plea led it to apply the wrong standard in determining whether counsel's performance ranked as ineffective assistance. The court first presumed deficient performance, then applied the presumption of prejudice that United States v. Cronic, reserved for situations in which counsel has entirely failed to function as the client's advocate. The Florida court therefore did not hold Nixon to the standard prescribed in Strickland v. Washington, (1984), which would have required Nixon to show that counsel's concession strategy was unreasonable.

* * *

Cronic recognized a narrow exception to Strickland's holding that a defendant who asserts ineffective assistance of counsel must demonstrate not only that his attorney's performance was deficient, but also that the deficiency prejudiced the defense. Cronic instructed that a presumption of prejudice would be in order in "circumstances that are so likely to prejudice the accused that the cost of litigating their effect in a particular case is unjustified." The Court elaborated: "[I]f counsel entirely fails to subject the prosecution's case to meaningful adversarial testing, then there has been a denial of Sixth Amendment rights that makes the adversary process itself presumptively unreliable." see Bell v. Cone, (for Cronic's presumed prejudice standard to apply, counsel's "failure must be complete"). We illustrated just how infrequently the "surrounding circumstances [will] justify a presumption of ineffectiveness" in Cronic itself. In that case, we reversed a Court of Appeals ruling that ranked as prejudicially inadequate the performance of an inexperienced, under-prepared attorney in a complex mail fraud trial.

On the record thus far developed, Corin's concession of Nixon's guilt does not rank as a "fail[ure] to function in any meaningful sense as the Government's adversary." Although such a concession in a run-of-the-mine trial might present a closer question, the gravity of the potential sentence in a capital trial and the proceeding's two-phase structure vitally affect counsel's strategic calculus. Attorneys representing capital defendants face daunting challenges in developing trial strategies, not least because the defendant's guilt is often clear. Prosecutors are more likely to seek the death penalty, and to refuse to accept a plea to a life sentence, when the evidence is overwhelming and the crime heinous. See Goodpaster, The Trial for Life: Effective Assistance of Counsel in Death Penalty Cases, 58 N. Y. U. L. Rev. 299, 329 (1983). In such cases, "avoiding execution [may be] the best and only realistic result possible." ABA Guidelines for the Appointment and Performance of Defense Counsel in Death Penalty Cases § 10.9.1, Commentary (rev. ed. 2003).

* * *

Counsel therefore may reasonably decide to focus on the trial's penalty phase, at which time counsel's mission is to persuade the trier that his client's life should be spared. Unable to negotiate a guilty plea in exchange for a life sentence, defense counsel must strive at the guilt phase to avoid a counterproductive course. See Lyon, Defending the Death Penalty Case: What Makes Death Different?, 42 Mercer L. Rev. 695, 708 (1991) ("It is not good to put on a 'he didn't do it' defense and a 'he is sorry he did it' mitigation. This just does not work. The jury will give the death penalty to the client and, in essence, the attorney."); Sundby, The Capital Jury and Absolution: The Intersection of Trial Strategy, Remorse, and the Death Penalty, 83 Cornell L. Rev. 1557, 1589–1591 (1998) (interviews of jurors in capital trials indicate that juries approach the sentencing phase "cynically" where counsel's sentencing-phase presentation is logically inconsistent with the guilt-phase defense); id., at 1597 (in capital cases, a "run-of-the-mill strategy of challenging the prosecution's case for failing to prove guilt beyond a reasonable doubt" can have dire implications for the sentencing phase). In this light, counsel cannot be deemed ineffective for attempting to impress the jury with his candor and his unwillingness to engage in "a useless charade." See Cronic, 466 U.S., at 656–657, n. 19, 80 L. Ed. 657 104 S. Ct. 2039. Renowned advocate Clarence Darrow, we note, famously employed a similar strategy as counsel for the youthful, cold-blooded killers Richard Loeb and Nathan Leopold. Imploring the judge to spare the boys' lives, Darrow declared: "I do not know how much salvage there is in these two boys.... I will be honest with this court as I have tried to be from the beginning. I know that these boys are not fit to be at large." Attorney for the Damned: Clarence Darrow in the

Courtroom 84 (A. Weinberg ed. 1989); see Tr. of Oral Arg. 40–41 (Darrow's clients) "did not expressly consent to what he did. But he saved their lives."

To summarize, in a capital case, counsel must consider in conjunction both the guilt and penalty phases in determining how best to proceed. When counsel informs the defendant of the strategy counsel believes to be in the defendant's best interest and the defendant is unresponsive, counsel's strategic choice is not impeded by any blanket rule demanding the defendant's explicit consent. Instead, if counsel's strategy, given the evidence bearing on the defendant's guilt, satisfies the Strickland standard, that is the end of the matter; no tenable claim of ineffective assistance would remain.

* * *

For the reasons stated, the judgment of the Florida Supreme Court is reversed, and the case is remanded for further proceedings not inconsistent with this opinion.

It is so ordered.

The Chief Justice took no part in the decision of this case.

CHAPTER 19

PRESENTING THE CASE—PROBLEMS ENCOUNTERED

E. CROSS-EXAMINATION AND IMPEACHMENT

1. THE ORDINARY WITNESS

Page 1444, before Delaware v. Fensterer, add (New Main Case)

Crawford v. Washington

Supreme Court of the United States, 2004.
541 U.S. 36, 124 S.Ct. 1354.

■ JUSTICE SCALIA delivered the opinion of the Court.

Petitioner Michael Crawford stabbed a man who allegedly tried to rape his wife, Sylvia. At his trial, the State played for the jury Sylvia's tape-recorded statement to the police describing the stabbing, even though he had no opportunity for cross-examination. The Washington Supreme Court upheld petitioner's conviction after determining that Sylvia's statement was reliable. . . .

* * *

The State charged petitioner with assault and attempted murder. At trial, he claimed self-defense. Sylvia did not testify because of the state marital privilege, which generally bars a spouse from testifying without the other spouse's consent. In Washington, this privilege does not extend to a spouse's out-of-court statements admissible under a hearsay exception, so the State sought to introduce Sylvia's tape-recorded statements to the police as evidence that the stabbing was not in self-defense. Noting that Sylvia had admitted she led petitioner to Lee's apartment and thus had facilitated the assault, the State invoked the hearsay exception for statements against penal interest, Wash. Rule Evid. 804(b)(3) (2003).

* * *

II

Ohio v. Roberts says that an unavailable witness's out-of-court statement may be admitted so long as it has adequate indicia of reliability—*i.e.,* falls within a "firmly rooted hearsay exception" or bears "particularized guarantees of trustworthiness." Petitioner argues that this test strays from the original meaning of the Confrontation Clause and urges us to reconsider it.

137

The Constitution's text does not alone resolve this case. One could plausibly read "witnesses against" a defendant to mean those who actually testify at trial, cf. *Woodsides v. State,* 3 Miss. 655, 664–665 (1837), those whose statements are offered at trial, see 3 J. Wigmore, Evidence § 1397, p. 104 (2d ed.1923) (hereinafter Wigmore), or something in-between. We must therefore turn to the historical background of the Clause to understand its meaning.

* * *

III

History supports two inferences about the meaning of the Sixth Amendment.

First, the principal evil at which the Confrontation Clause was directed was the civil-law mode of criminal procedure, and particularly its use of *ex parte* examinations as evidence against the accused. It was these practices that the Crown deployed in notorious treason cases like Raleigh's; that the Marian statutes invited; that English law's assertion of a right to confrontation was meant to prohibit; and that the founding-era rhetoric decried. . . .

Accordingly, we once again reject the view that the Confrontation Clause applies of its own force only to in-court testimony, and that its application to out-of-court statements introduced at trial depends upon "the law of Evidence for the time being." 3 Wigmore § 1397, at 101; accord, *Dutton v. Evans,* 400 U.S. 74, 94, 91 S.Ct. 210, 27 L.Ed.2d 213 (1970) (Harlan, J., concurring in result). Leaving the regulation of out-of-court statements to the law of evidence would render the Confrontation Clause powerless to prevent even the most flagrant inquisitorial practices. . . .

* * *

The text of the Confrontation Clause reflects this focus. It applies to "witnesses" against the accused—in other words, those who "bear testimony." 1 N. Webster, An American Dictionary of the English Language (1828). "Testimony," in turn, is typically "[a] solemn declaration or affirmation made for the purpose of establishing or proving some fact." *Ibid.* An accuser who makes a formal statement to government officers bears testimony in a sense that a person who makes a casual remark to an acquaintance does not. The constitutional text, like the history underlying the common-law right of confrontation, thus reflects an especially acute concern with a specific type of out-of-court statement.

* * *

Statements taken by police officers in the course of interrogations are also testimonial under even a narrow standard. . . .

* * *

The historical record also supports a second proposition: that the Framers would not have allowed admission of testimonial statements of a witness who did not appear at trial unless he was unavailable to testify, and the defendant had had a prior opportunity for cross-examination. The text of the Sixth Amendment does not suggest any open-ended exceptions from the confrontation requirement to be developed by the courts. Rather, the "right ... to be confronted with the witnesses against him," Amdt. 6, is most naturally read as a reference to the right of confrontation at common law, admitting only those exceptions established at the time of the founding. See *Mattox v. United States,* 156 U.S. 237, 243, 15 S.Ct. 337, 39 L.Ed. 409 (1895)....

We do not read the historical sources to say that a prior opportunity to cross-examine was merely a sufficient, rather than a necessary, condition for admissibility of testimonial statements. They suggest that this requirement was dispositive, and not merely one of several ways to establish reliability. This is not to deny, as THE CHIEF JUSTICE notes, that "[t]here were always exceptions to the general rule of exclusion" of hearsay evidence. Several had become well established by 1791. See 3 Wigmore § 1397, at 101. But there is scant evidence that exceptions were invoked to admit *testimonial* statements against the accused in a *criminal* case. Most of the hearsay exceptions covered statements that by their nature were not testimonial—for example, business records or statements in furtherance of a conspiracy. We do not infer from these that the Framers thought exceptions would apply even to prior testimony. Cf. *Lilly v. Virginia,* 527 U.S. 116, 134, 119 S.Ct. 1887, 144 L.Ed.2d 117 (1999) (plurality opinion) ("[A]ccomplices' confessions that inculpate a criminal defendant are not within a firmly rooted exception to the hearsay rule").

* * *

Even our recent cases, in their outcomes, hew closely to the traditional line. *Ohio v. Roberts,* 448 U.S., at 67–70, 100 S.Ct. 2531, admitted testimony from a preliminary hearing at which the defendant had examined the witness. *Lilly v. Virginia, supra,* excluded testimonial statements that the defendant had had no opportunity to test by cross-examination....

V

Although the results of our decisions have generally been faithful to the original meaning of the Confrontation Clause, the same cannot be said of our rationales. *Roberts* conditions the admissibility of all hearsay evidence on whether it falls under a "firmly rooted hearsay exception" or bears "particularized guarantees of trustworthiness." 448 U.S., at 66, 100 S.Ct. 2531. This test departs from the historical principles identified above in two respects. First, it is too broad: It applies the same mode of analysis whether or not the hearsay consists of *ex parte* testimony. This often results in close constitutional scrutiny in cases that are far removed from the core concerns of the Clause. At the same time, however, the test is too narrow: It admits statements that *do* consist of *ex parte* testimony upon a mere finding of reliability. This malleable standard often fails to protect against paradigmatic confrontation violations.

* * *

Where testimonial statements are involved, we do not think the Framers meant to leave the Sixth Amendment's protection to the vagaries of the rules of evidence, much less to amorphous notions of "reliability." Certainly none of the authorities discussed above acknowledges any general reliability exception to the common-law rule. Admitting statements deemed reliable by a judge is fundamentally at odds with the right of confrontation. To be sure, the Clause's ultimate goal is to ensure reliability of evidence, but it is a procedural rather than a substantive guarantee. It commands, not that evidence be reliable, but that reliability be assessed in a particular manner: by testing in the crucible of cross-examination. The Clause thus reflects a judgment, not only about the desirability of reliable evidence (a point on which there could be little dissent), but about how reliability can best be determined. . . .

The *Roberts* test allows a jury to hear evidence, untested by the adversary process, based on a mere judicial determination of reliability. It thus replaces the constitutionally prescribed method of assessing reliability with a wholly foreign one. In this respect, it is very different from exceptions to the Confrontation Clause that make no claim to be a surrogate means of assessing reliability. . . .

* * *

Dispensing with confrontation because testimony is obviously reliable is akin to dispensing with jury trial because a defendant is obviously guilty. This is not what the Sixth Amendment prescribes.

B

The legacy of *Roberts* in other courts vindicates the Framers' wisdom in rejecting a general reliability exception. The framework is so unpredictable that it fails to provide meaningful protection from even core confrontation violations.

Reliability is an amorphous, if not entirely subjective, concept. There are countless factors bearing on whether a statement is reliable; the nine-factor balancing test applied by the Court of Appeals below is representative. See, *e.g., People v. Farrell*, 34 P.3d 401, 406–407 (Colo.2001) (eight-factor test). Whether a statement is deemed reliable depends heavily on which factors the judge considers and how much weight he accords each of them. Some courts wind up attaching the same significance to opposite facts. For example, the Colorado Supreme Court held a statement more reliable because its inculpation of the defendant was "detailed," *id.*, at 407, while the Fourth Circuit found a statement more reliable because the portion implicating another was "fleeting," *United States v. Photogrammetric Data Servs., Inc.*, 259 F.3d 229, 245 (C.A.4 2001). The Virginia Court of Appeals found a statement more reliable because the witness was in custody and charged with a crime (thus making the statement more obviously against her penal interest), see *Nowlin v. Commonwealth*, 40 Va.App. 327, 335–338, 579 S.E.2d 367, 371–372 (2003), while the Wisconsin Court of Appeals found a statement more reliable because the witness was *not* in custody and *not* a suspect, see *State v. Bintz*, 2002 WI App. 204, ¶ 13, 257 Wis.2d 177, 187, 650 N.W.2d 913, 918. Finally, the Colorado Supreme Court in one case found a statement more reliable because it was given "immediately after" the events at issue, *Farrell, supra*, at 407, while that same court, in another case, found a statement more reliable because two years had elapsed, *Stevens v. People,* 29 P.3d 305, 316 (Colo.2001).

The unpardonable vice of the *Roberts* test, however, is not its unpredictability, but its demonstrated capacity to admit core testimonial statements that the Confrontation Clause plainly meant to exclude. Despite the plurality's speculation in *Lilly,* 527 U.S., at 137, 119 S.Ct. 1887, that it was "highly unlikely" that accomplice confessions implicating the accused could survive *Roberts,* courts continue routinely to admit them. . . . One recent study found that, after *Lilly,* appellate courts admitted accomplice statements to the authorities in 25 out of 70 cases—more than one-third of the time. Kirst, Appellate Court Answers to the Confrontation Questions in *Lilly v. Virginia,* 53 Syracuse L.Rev. 87, 105 (2003). Courts have invoked *Roberts* to admit other sorts of plainly testimonial statements despite the absence of any opportunity to cross-examine.

To add insult to injury, some of the courts that admit untested testimonial statements find reliability in the very factors that *make* the statements testimonial. . . . One court relied on the fact that the witness's statement was made to police while in custody on pending charges—the theory being that this made the statement more clearly against penal interest and thus more reliable. Other courts routinely rely on the fact that a prior statement is given under oath in judicial proceedings. That inculpating statements are given in a testimonial setting is not an antidote to the confrontation problem, but rather the trigger that makes the Clause's demands most urgent. It is not enough to point out that most of the usual safeguards of the adversary process attend the statement, when the single safeguard missing is the one the Confrontation Clause demands.

Roberts' failings were on full display in the proceedings below. Sylvia Crawford made her statement while in police custody, herself a potential suspect in the case. Indeed, she had been told that whether she would be released "depend[ed] on how the investigation continues." App. 81. In response to often leading questions from police detectives, she implicated her husband in Lee's stabbing and at least arguably undermined his self-defense claim. Despite all this, the trial court admitted her statement, listing several reasons why it was reliable. In its opinion reversing, the Court of Appeals listed several *other* reasons why the statement was *not* reliable. Finally, the State Supreme Court relied exclusively on the interlocking character of the statement and disregarded every other factor the lower courts had considered. The case is thus a self-contained demonstration of *Roberts'* unpredictable and inconsistent application.

Each of the courts also made assumptions that cross-examination might well have undermined. The trial court, for example, stated that Sylvia Crawford's statement was reliable because she was an eyewitness with direct knowledge of the events. But Sylvia at one point told the police that she had "shut [her] eyes and . . . didn't really watch" part of the fight, and that she was "in shock." The trial court also buttressed its reliability finding by claiming that Sylvia was "being questioned by law enforcement, and, thus, the [questioner] is . . . neutral to her and not someone who would be inclined to advance her interests and shade her version of the truth unfavorably toward the defendant." The Framers would be astounded to learn that *ex parte* testimony could be admitted against a criminal defendant because it was elicited by "neutral" government officers. But even if the court's assessment of the officer's motives was accurate, it says nothing about Sylvia's perception of her situation. Only cross-examination could reveal that.

* * *

We readily concede that we could resolve this case by simply reweighing the "reliability factors" under *Roberts* and finding that Sylvia Crawford's statement falls short. But we view this as one of those rare cases in which the result below is so improbable that it reveals a fundamental failure on our part to interpret the Constitution in a way that secures its intended constraint on judicial discretion. Moreover, to reverse the Washington Supreme Court's decision after conducting our own reliability analysis would perpetuate, not avoid, what the Sixth Amendment condemns. The Constitution prescribes a procedure for determining the reliability of testimony in criminal trials, and we, no less than the state courts, lack authority to replace it with one of our own devising.

We have no doubt that the courts below were acting in utmost good faith when they found reliability. The Framers, however, would not have been content to indulge this assumption. They knew that judges, like other government officers, could not always be trusted to safeguard the rights of the people; the likes of the dread Lord Jeffreys were not yet too distant a memory. They were loath to leave too much discretion in judicial hands. Cf. U.S. Const., Amdt. 6 (criminal jury trial); Amdt. 7 (civil jury trial); By replacing categorical constitutional guarantees with open-ended balancing tests, we do violence to their design. Vague standards are manipulable, and, while that might be a small concern in run-of-the-mill assault prosecutions like this one, the Framers had an eye toward politically charged cases like Raleigh's—great state trials where the impartiality of even those at the highest levels of the judiciary might not be so clear. It is difficult to imagine *Roberts'* providing any meaningful protection in those circumstances.

* * *

Where nontestimonial hearsay is at issue, it is wholly consistent with the Framers' design to afford the States flexibility in their development of hearsay law—as does *Roberts,* and as would an approach that exempted such statements from Confrontation Clause scrutiny altogether. Where testimonial evidence is at issue, however, the Sixth Amendment demands what the common law required: unavailability and a prior opportunity for cross-examination. We leave for another day any effort to spell out a comprehensive definition of "testimonial." Whatever else the term covers, it applies at a minimum to prior testimony at a preliminary hearing, before a grand jury, or at a former trial; and to police interrogations. These are the modern practices with closest kinship to the abuses at which the Confrontation Clause was directed.

In this case, the State admitted Sylvia's testimonial statement against petitioner, despite the fact that he had no opportunity to cross-examine her. That alone is sufficient to make out a violation of the Sixth Amendment. *Roberts* notwithstanding, we decline to mine the record in search of indicia of reliability. Where testimonial statements are at issue, the only indicium of reliability sufficient to satisfy constitutional demands is the one the Constitution actually prescribes: confrontation.

The judgment of the Washington Supreme Court is reversed, and the case is remanded for further proceedings not inconsistent with this opinion.

It is so ordered.

■ CHIEF JUSTICE REHNQUIST, with whom JUSTICE O'CONNOR joins, concurring in the judgment.

I dissent from the Court's decision to overrule *Ohio v. Roberts,* 448 U.S. 56, 100 S.Ct. 2531, 65 L.Ed.2d 597 (1980). I believe that the Court's adoption of a new interpretation of the Confrontation Clause is not backed by sufficiently persuasive reasoning to overrule long-established precedent. Its decision casts a mantle of uncertainty over future criminal trials in both federal and state courts, and is by no means necessary to decide the present case.

The Court's distinction between testimonial and nontestimonial statements, contrary to its claim, is no better rooted in history than our current doctrine. Under the common law, although the courts were far from consistent, out-of-court statements made by someone other than the accused and not taken under oath, unlike *ex parte* depositions or affidavits, were generally not considered substantive evidence upon which a conviction could be based. See, *e.g., King v. Brasier,* 1 Leach 199, 200, 168 Eng. Rep. 202 (K.B.1779); see also J. Langbein, Origins of Adversary Criminal Trial 235–242 (2003); G. Gilbert, Evidence 152 (3d ed. 1769). Testimonial statements such as accusatory statements to police officers likely would have been disapproved of in the 18th century, not necessarily because they resembled *ex parte* affidavits or depositions as the Court reasons, but more likely than not because they were not made under oath. See *King v. Woodcock,* 1 Leach 500, 503, 168 Eng. Rep. 352, 353 (1789) (noting that a statement taken by a justice of the peace may not be admitted into evidence unless taken under oath). Without an oath, one usually did not get to the second step of whether confrontation was required.

* * *

Thus, while I agree that the Framers were mainly concerned about sworn affidavits and depositions, it does not follow that they were similarly concerned about the Court's broader category of testimonial statements. See 1 N. Webster, An American Dictionary of the English Language (1828) (defining ''Testimony'' as ''[a] solemn declaration or affirmation made for the purpose of establishing or proving some fact. *Such affirmation in judicial proceedings, may be verbal or written, but must be under oath* ''(emphasis added)). As far as I can tell, unsworn testimonial statements were treated no differently at common law than were nontestimonial statements, and it seems to me any classification of statements as testimonial beyond that of sworn affidavits and depositions will be somewhat arbitrary, merely a proxy for what the Framers might have intended had such evidence been liberally admitted as substantive evidence like it is today.

I therefore see no reason why the distinction the Court draws is preferable to our precedent. Starting with Chief Justice Marshall's interpretation as a Circuit Justice in 1807, 16 years after the ratification of the Sixth Amendment, *United States v. Burr,* 25 F.Cas. 187, 193 (No. 14,694) (CC Va. 1807), continuing with our cases in the late 19th century, *Mattox v. United States,* 156 U.S. 237, 243–244, 15 S.Ct. 337, 39 L.Ed. 409 (1895); *Kirby v. United States,* 174 U.S. 47, 54–57, 19 S.Ct. 574, 43 L.Ed. 890 (1899), and through today, *e.g., White v. Illinois,* 502 U.S. 346, 352–353, 112 S.Ct. 736, 116 L.Ed.2d 848 (1992), we have never drawn a distinction between testimonial and nontestimonial statements. And for that matter, neither has any other court of which I am aware. I see little value in trading our precedent for an imprecise approximation at this late date.

I am also not convinced that the Confrontation Clause categorically requires the exclusion of testimonial statements. Although many States had their own Confrontation Clauses, they were of recent vintage and were not interpreted with any regularity before 1791. State cases that recently followed the ratification of the Sixth Amendment were not uniform; the Court itself cites state cases from the early 19th century that took a more stringent view of the right to confrontation than does the Court, prohibiting former testimony even if the witness was subjected to cross-examination. See *ante,* at 1363 (citing *Finn v. Commonwealth,* 26 Va. 701, 708 (1827); *State v. Atkins,* 1 Tenn. 229 (1807) *(per curiam))*.

* * *

Between 1700 and 1800 the rules regarding the admissibility of out-of-court statements were still being developed. There were always exceptions to the general rule of exclusion, and it is not clear to me that the Framers categorically wanted to eliminate further ones. It is one thing to trace the right of confrontation back to the Roman Empire; it is quite another to conclude that such a right absolutely excludes a large category of evidence. It is an odd conclusion indeed to think that the Framers created a cut-and-dried rule with respect to the admissibility of testimonial statements when the law during their own time was not fully settled.

* * *

Exceptions to confrontation have always been derived from the experience that some out-of-court statements are just as reliable as cross-examined in-court testimony due to the circumstances under which they were made. We have recognized, for example, that co-conspirator statements simply "cannot be replicated, even if the declarant testifies to the same matters in court." *United States v. Inadi,* 475 U.S. 387, 395, 106 S.Ct. 1121, 89 L.Ed.2d 390 (1986). Because the statements are made while the declarant and the accused are partners in an illegal enterprise, the statements are unlikely to be false and their admission "actually furthers the 'Confrontation Clause's very mission' which is to 'advance the accuracy of the truth-determining process in criminal trials.'" *Id.,* at 396, 106 S.Ct. 1121 (quoting *Tennessee v. Street,* 471 U.S. 409, 415, 105 S.Ct. 2078, 85 L.Ed.2d 425 (1985) (some internal quotation marks omitted)). Similar reasons justify the introduction of spontaneous declarations, see *White,* 502 U.S., at 356, 112 S.Ct. 736, statements made in the course of procuring medical services, see *ibid.,* dying declarations, see *Kirby, supra,* at 61, 19 S.Ct. 574, and countless other hearsay exceptions. That a statement might be testimonial does nothing to undermine the wisdom of one of these exceptions.

* * *

In choosing the path it does, the Court of course overrules *Ohio v. Roberts,* 448 U.S. 56, 100 S.Ct. 2531, 65 L.Ed.2d 597 (1980), a case decided nearly a quarter of a century ago. *Stare decisis* is not an inexorable command in the area of constitutional law, see *Payne v. Tennessee,* 501 U.S. 808, 828, 111 S.Ct. 2597, 115 L.Ed.2d 720 (1991), but by and large, it "is the preferred course because it promotes the evenhanded, predictable, and consistent development of legal principles, fosters reliance on judicial decisions, and contributes to the actual and perceived integrity of the judicial process," *id.,* at 827, 111 S.Ct. 2597. And in making this appraisal, doubt that the new rule is indeed the "right" one should surely be weighed in the balance. Though there are no vested interests involved, unresolved questions for the future of everyday criminal trials throughout the country surely counsel the same sort of caution. The Court grandly declares that "[w]e leave for another day any effort to spell out a comprehensive definition of 'testimonial,' "*ante,* at 1374. But the thousands of federal prosecutors and the tens of thousands of state prosecutors need answers as to what beyond the specific kinds of "testimony" the Court lists, see *ibid.,* is covered by the new rule. They need them now, not months or years from now. Rules of criminal evidence are applied every day in courts throughout the country, and parties should not be left in the dark in this manner.

To its credit, the Court's analysis of "testimony" excludes at least some hearsay exceptions, such as business records and official records. To hold otherwise would require numerous additional witnesses without any apparent gain in the truth-seeking process. Likewise to the Court's credit is its implicit recognition that the mistaken application of its new rule by courts which guess wrong as to the scope of the rule is subject to harmless-error analysis.

But these are palliatives to what I believe is a mistaken change of course. It is a change of course not in the least necessary to reverse the judgment of the Supreme Court of Washington in this case. The result the Court reaches follows inexorably from *Roberts* and its progeny without any need for overruling that line of cases. . . .

What is "testimonial" under the *Crawford* case?

When are statements testimonial? The *Crawford* decision is rather cryptic on this point, leaving it to the lower courts to try to clarify this area of the law.

We leave for another day any effort to spell out a comprehensive definition of "testimonial." Whatever else the term covers, it applies at a minimum to prior testimony at a preliminary hearing, before a grand jury, or at a former trial; and to police interrogations. There are the modern practices with closest kinship to the abuses at which the Confrontation Clause was directed. *Crawford,* 541 U.S. at 68.

For a good discussion of what constitutes a "testimonial statement," under *Crawford*, see Robert P. Mosteller, "*Crawford v. Washington*: Encouraging and Ensuring the Confrontation of Witnesses," 39 U. Rich. L. Rev. 511, 566 et. seq. (2005).

When the United States Supreme Court decided *Crawford*, it abandoned the parallelism between the hearsay rule and the requirements of the confrontation clause. Now, courts must determine whether a statement is "testimonial" by looking to whether "a principal motive of either the person making the statement or the person or organization receiving it is to preserve for future use in legal proceedings."

One recurrent scenario that has challenged courts' ascertainment of motive is when a witness makes a 911 call.

Some courts have used a categorical approach, finding that if a statement qualifies as an "excited utterance," there could be no motive to falsify and thus no violation of the Confrontation Clause. *See Alaska v. Anderson*, 111 P.3d 350 (AL 2005).

Others have attempted a case by case analysis, placing the burden of proof on the party against whom the statement is offered. *Hammon v. State*, 829 N.E. 2d 444 (2005). For an example of a case in which a 911 call was found not to be testimonial, see *People v. Moscat*, 3 Misc. 3d 739, 777 N.Y.S. 2d 875 (2004)

Still others have held that even if a 911 call is admissible as an excited utterance, Crawford would bar the admission of the statement. See *United States v. Arnold*, 410 F.3d 895 (6th Cir. 2005).

Page 1505, add after "A Note on Consistency" (New Main Case)

New case replacing Stumpf v. Mitchell on p. 94 of the 2004 Supp.

In re Peter Sakarias on Habeas Corpus.

In re Tauno Waidla on Habeas Corpus.

Supreme Court of California
35 Cal.4th 140, 106 P.3d 931, 25 Cal.Rptr.3d 265

■ WERDEGAR, J.—In 1990, petitioners Peter Sakarias and Tauno Waidla were each, in separate trials, convicted of first degree murder with special circumstances and sentenced to death in the killing of Viivi Piirisild. We affirmed each of their convictions and sentences on automatic appeal, but issued orders to show cause in response to their petitions for writs of habeas corpus, on claims the prosecutor, in each trial, had presented factual theories inconsistent with those presented at the codefendant's trial.... On receipt of the returns and traverses, we consolidated the two causes for consideration and decision and appointed a referee to hear evidence and make factual findings. The referee has now issued his report, and the parties have filed briefs on the merits.

The evidence at petitioners' trials showed they both participated in the fatal attack on Viivi Piirisild, which was perpetrated with a hatchet and a knife. But both petitioners contend their joint prosecutor, Los Angeles County Deputy District Attorney Steven Ipsen, inconsistently and falsely portrayed their respective roles in the attack, attributing to each, in their respective trials, a series of three blows struck to the victim's head with the blade of the hatchet. . . . We agree with Sakarias that the prosecutor violated his due process rights by intentionally and without good faith justification arguing inconsistent and irreconcilable factual theories in the two trials, attributing to each petitioner in turn culpable acts that could have been committed by only one person. We also agree this violation prejudiced Sakarias, entitling him to relief. We do not decide whether the prosecutor's conduct was a due process violation as to Waidla, as we conclude any such violation was harmless in his case.

* * *

I.   Factual and Procedural Background

A.   Facts of the Crime

Waidla and Sakarias were both born in Estonia while that nation was part of the Soviet Union. They met as conscripts in the Soviet Army, from which they defected together, coming in 1987 to Los Angeles. There, they were taken under the wing of an Estonian–American couple, Avo and Viivi Piirisild, who offered to help them obtain jobs and education. For a period in 1987 to 1988, Waidla lived in the Piirisilds' guest house, performing remodeling work and other chores in exchange for his room and board.

Relations soon soured between petitioners and the Piirisilds. In May 1988, Waidla demanded the Piirisilds give him money or a sports car they had promised him for his work and threatened, otherwise, to report them for doing construction without a permit. When the Piirisilds told Waidla to leave their home, Waidla threatened to hurt or kill Avo. Later, Viivi received a postcard with a rattlesnake on it from Sakarias and Waidla, who were traveling together. Sakarias later told police he believed Viivi had been spreading harmful rumors about him and Waidla within the Estonian community, damaging their prospects for help from other Estonians around North America.

During early July 1988, petitioners broke into the Piirisilds' unoccupied cabin in Crestline. They stayed for several days, leaving only when they ran out of food and taking with them various items of the Piirisilds' property, including a hatchet. On July 12, angry, hungry, and in need of money, they went to the Piirisilds' North Hollywood home and broke in through the back door. They ate food from the kitchen and took some jewelry while waiting for Viivi to return home. Sakarias later told the police he and Waidla were planning to get money for food and to confront Viivi and frighten her into giving them the sports car; he also said that having contemplated killing themselves because of their poor situation, they decided to kill Viivi first so " 'she is not gonna see my funeral' "or, with her husband, " 'laugh on us for the rest of their lives.' "

When Viivi entered the house through the front door, petitioners immediately attacked her, using a knife and the hatchet they had taken from the Crestline cabin. They bludgeoned her with the blunt end of the hatchet, stabbed her with the knife, and chopped at her with the hatchet blade. Overall, the medical examiner found five blunt force impacts to Viivi's head (which fractured her skull and facial bones, knocked out her teeth, and broke her larynx), four stab wounds to her chest (two of which passed through vital organs), and three chopping wounds to her upper head. One of this last group of injuries, inflicted before death, was struck with "tremendous" force, penetrating Viivi's skull completely. The other two chopping wounds were inflicted with somewhat less force, after or around the time of death. The medical examiner attributed Viivi's death to the combination of wounds, several of which could have been fatal individually. After the attack in the entryway, petitioners dragged Viivi down the hall to a bedroom, where her body was found. According to the medical examiner's testimony at Waidla's trial, an abrasion on Viivi's lower back, caused by rubbing of her skin against another surface (which could have been incurred when she was dragged to the bedroom), was inflicted after her death.

Sakarias told police that during the initial attack he wielded the knife while Waidla used the hatchet. Sometime later, at Waidla's direction, he went to the bedroom and chopped Viivi's head twice with the hatchet. Waidla gave a statement admitting only a single bludgeoning blow, with the back of the hatchet at the outset of the attack, and denying any memory of how the rest of the attack proceeded. He recanted even that confession at his trial, testifying he had left Los Angeles three days before Viivi Piirisild was killed.

Petitioners sold the jewelry they took and used Viivi's credit cards for airline tickets, telephone calls, and other purchases. They were arrested more than a month later near the United States–Canada border in New York State.

B.   The Inconsistent Factual Theories

Petitioners were jointly charged with Viivi Piirisild's murder, but their cases were severed after Sakarias was found incompetent to stand trial. . . .

As reflected in the summary above, the evidence at petitioners' trials, taken as a whole, strongly suggests Waidla (who first wielded the hatchet, according to both petitioners' statements) struck the first, antemortem blow with the hatchet blade in the entryway, while Sakarias (who admitted doing so) inflicted the two postmortem or perimortem chopping wounds in the bedroom. (There was no evidence in either trial to suggest the perpetrators switched weapons during the initial attack.) But the prosecutor, Ipsen, did not argue at either trial the version of the attack best supported by all the evidence. Instead, at each defendant's trial he maintained the defendant on trial had inflicted *all* the chopping wounds.

In Waidla's trial, Ipsen introduced Waidla's admission that he, rather than Sakarias, had initially used the hatchet against Viivi Piirisild. (Sakarias's confession to police, in which he admitted striking two blows with the hatchet in the bedroom, was not introduced at Waidla's trial.) Although

Waidla only admitted hitting Viivi with the back of the hatchet, Ipsen argued the jury should find Waidla actually used the hatchet throughout, "choosing . . . the more devastating of the instruments," while Sakarias "accept[ed]" the knife, "the lesser implement." With the hatchet, Ipsen argued, Waidla first inflicted the blunt force injuries, then, "turning the hatchet blade so it was more effective . . . [he] was now able to chop through the top of her skull." Ipsen suggested Waidla simply did not want to acknowledge his role in the attack, "his repeated striking of Viivi Piirisild, and swinging with the sharp end of the hatchet . . . until she was dead." He emphasized the extended and repeated efforts both assailants made to ensure Viivi's death, "as Mr. Waidla indicated, himself with the hatchet, Mr. Sakarias who came up later with the knife." Waidla's use of the hatchet blade continued, Ipsen argued, even after Viivi was dead: " '[S]he's alive, she's alive, she's alive.' Sharp end, 'she's dead,' and then further blows indicating further blows were struck after she was dead, the non-hemorrhagic chop wounds to the head."

Having elicited, in the Waidla trial, the opinion of Dr. James Ribe, the medical examiner, that the abrasion on Viivi's lower back was incurred postmortem, Ipsen emphasized that the initial attack in the living room was fatal: "At the point that she was dragged into the back room, we know that Viivi Piirisild was already dead by the facts as the coroner testified. So, we know it was in that front room that the attack occurred, and that Viivi Piirisild was bludgeoned, chopped and stabbed until life left her body." Finally, in penalty argument, Ipsen urged a death sentence, in part because Waidla, after hitting Viivi repeatedly with the hatchet's blunt end, "chose to change the angle of the blade. . . . Although he felt her head and her flesh against the back of his hatchet numerous times, he knew his mission wasn't accomplished, and that's when he changed and switched and used the sharp edge of the hatchet to give that death blow."

In Sakarias's trial, the prosecutor asked the medical examiner, Dr. Ribe, about each stabbing, chopping, or blunt force injury shown in the autopsy photographs, in many instances asking whether the wounds were antemortem or postmortem, but he did not examine Dr. Ribe about the lower back abrasion at all. He thus avoided eliciting Dr. Ribe's opinion, expressed in Waidla's earlier trial, that the abrasion had occurred after death and could have been caused by dragging Viivi's body along the carpeted hallway to the bedroom.

Due to this omission, no evidence was before Sakarias's jury that Viivi Piirisild was dead by the time Sakarias, as he admitted, struck her with the hatchet in the bedroom. The prosecutor was thus able to, and did, argue that Sakarias had, in the bedroom, inflicted all three chopping injuries, including the first, antemortem one. Thus Ipsen, in his guilt phase argument, told the jury that Sakarias, in the bedroom, inflicted "three . . . sharp hatchet wounds to the top of Viivi's head with a tremendous force. . . .[P] . . . [P] We know that there are in fact three hatchet wounds; the first penetrating the top of the skull, and I know it was the first because it was a hemorrhagic wound, the one in the hairline, the one that chopped the top of her head completely off with the exception of some of the scalp that kept it completely on. [P] We know that when it's hemorrhagic it means that Viivi, whether conscious or not, still suffered that blow while alive, and we know that the last two in the forehead area being non-hemorrhagic were at a time when her body had ceased to live, or unfortunately actually possibly that the blood flow was not great enough to cause hemorrhage. [P] . . . [P] Again, Mr. Sakarias indicates he believes he hit her two times with the hatchet when he used the hatchet. Again, by the evidence, he was off by only one blow."

In the penalty phase argument at Sakarias's trial, the prosecutor again portrayed Sakarias as having inflicted the antemortem hatchet-blade wound, which he characterized as finally causing Viivi's death. Sakarias's participation in the crime could not be considered minor, Ipsen argued; he was "as involved in the murder of Viivi Piirisild as one could ask, swinging what I suggest were the blows that actually ended her life." Referring to Sakarias in the second person, Ipsen argued that if, after the attack in the living room, "you had called 911, realizing what you had done and attempted to save her life, . . . perhaps you would deserve the pity, the sympathy, perhaps the scales of justice would lean in your direction. [P] . . . [P] If, when you walked back to the back room with that hatchet and thought Viivi Piirisild is still alive, and you must have, otherwise you wouldn't have gone back there with that hatchet, and if you just simply didn't chop the top of her head off, as the evidence indicated you did in that back room, thus finally ending her life."

In addition to the prosecutorial arguments just recited, petitioners also complain of inconsistency in the prosecutor's penalty phase arguments relating to domination. (See *Pen. Code, § 190.3, factor (g)* ["substantial domination" by another may be considered in mitigation].) At Waidla's trial, Ipsen argued Waidla "is not one who is dominated by another, but instead the facts indicate that he was the dominate [*sic*] person between himself and Mr. Sakarias, that he was the planner, he was the one who knew of the Piirisild home and knew of the facts surrounding the burglary, the robbery of Mrs. Piirisild." At Sakarias's trial, in contrast, Ipsen argued Sakarias was "in no way" dominated by Waidla: "They were separate individuals joined by a common plan, a common hatred, common goals." Petitioners' actions in killing Viivi and escaping were those of "a partnership like a right hand and a left hand," with "absolutely no evidence of domination."

C.   The Habeas Corpus Proceedings

* * *

II.   Discussion

A.   Review of Referee's Findings

. . . Upon review, we find each of the referee's findings supported by substantial evidence and, like the parties, we accept them.

1.   *Ipsen's use of divergent factual theories was intentional*

Ipsen testified at the reference hearing, as he stated in his earlier declaration, that his presentation of inconsistent theories was "not intentional." He noted that in the interval between the trials he probably handled other cases and described himself as an "instinct[ive]" litigator who did not typically follow detailed notes or a script in his examination of witnesses. When he made his closing argument in the Sakarias case, he did not have in mind what he had argued to the Waidla jury: "the last thing I'm thinking about when I'm arguing in one trial is trying to remember what I argued in another trial."

The referee found Ipsen's claim of inadvertence "unconvincing": "Despite a lapse of eight months between trials, it is unlikely that a competent and committed prosecutor like Ipsen, handling the severed trials of two defendants jointly charged with capital murder, would simply forget at the second trial what specific factual theory of the gruesome murder he presented at the first. ... [T]he Waidla and Sakarias trials were Ipsen's first murder cases, his first death penalty cases. He was depressed about the death verdict in Waidla for approximately two weeks. It is improbable that his factual depiction of the killing in Waidla would have totally escaped his notice in Sakarias. Moreover, the assertion of inadvertence in presenting the inconsistent theories implies a level of carelessness that is simply not present in Ipsen's prosecution of Sakarias."

* * *

2. *Ipsen had strong reason to believe, while prosecuting Sakarias, that the victim was already dead when moved to the bedroom*

Although there were slight grounds for doubt, the referee found, "the great weight of the available evidence" supported the view that Viivi Piirisild died in the living room. The postmortem abrasion, in particular, was best explained as the result of Viivi's body being dragged across the carpet to the bedroom. While the abrasion could conceivably have had other causes, "[t]he dragging explained the size, nature, and location of the abrasion" and was also consistent with the condition of Viivi's clothing.

* * *

3. *Ipsen deliberately refrained from asking Dr. Ribe about the postmortem abrasion in Sakarias's trial*

The referee, observing that in Sakarias's trial Ipsen had introduced virtually all the same autopsy photographs as in Waidla's trial but had omitted exhibit 59K, which showed the abrasion on Viivi Piirisild's back, concluded Ipsen's omissions of this exhibit and of questioning regarding the abrasion were deliberate, designed to avoid the presentation of evidence "inconvenient" to his new and different theory of the attack, evidence "much easier to omit than to explain."

4. *Ipsen did not offer Sakarias's confession at Waidla's trial because he believed it would be inadmissible*

Ipsen testified he would have liked to introduce Sakarias's confession, which implicated Waidla equally, in Waidla's trial, but assumed it would be subject to a successful objection. "My understanding of the law at the time and still today, is that when I'm prosecuting Mr. Waidla and charging him with murder, I can't use the statement of his accomplice against him." At trial before a judge he knew to be highly experienced in criminal law, "If I had tried to get in evidence, which everyone knows is inadmissible and is wrong, I'd look like an idiot to say I'd like to offer the codefendant's statement."

The referee accepted Ipsen's testimony on this point, stating the confession would have been inadmissible under *People v. Aranda (1965)* and *Bruton v. United States (1968)*. The prosecutor's failure to offer the statement, the referee found, "did not relate to its inconsistency with the factual theory he intended to present at Waidla's trial."

* * *

B. The People's Bad Faith Use of Inconsistent Theories Deprived Sakarias of Due Process, Requiring Vacation of His Death Sentence

. . . The Attorney General contends the use of inconsistent arguments at separate trials "is permissible provided a prosecutor does not argue something that the prosecutor knows to be false." For reasons explained below, we conclude that fundamental fairness does not permit the People, without a good faith justification, to attribute to two defendants, in separate trials, a criminal act only one defendant could have committed. By doing so, the state necessarily urges conviction or an increase in culpability in one of the cases on a false factual basis, a result inconsistent with the goal of the criminal trial as a search for truth. At least where, as in Sakarias's case, the change in theories between the two trials is achieved partly through deliberate manipulation of the evidence put before the jury, the use of such inconsistent and irreconcilable theories impermissibly undermines the reliability of the convictions or sentences thereby obtained.

We also conclude, however, that where, as here, the available evidence points clearly to the truth of one theory and the falsity of the other, only the defendant against whom the false theory was used can show constitutionally significant prejudice. For that reason, we conclude that Sakarias, but not Waidla, is entitled to relief on his petition.

1. *The People may not convict two individuals of a crime only one could have committed or obtain harsher sentences against two individuals by unjustifiably attributing to each a culpable act only one could have committed*

Judicial disapproval of the state's use of inconsistent and irreconcilable theories in separate trials for the same crimes was first articulated in opinions by individual Supreme Court and lower federal court judges. (See *Jacobs v. Scott (1995) 513 U.S. 1067 [130 L. Ed. 2d 618, 115 S. Ct. 711]* (dis. opn. of Stevens, J., from denial of stay) [fundamentally unfair to execute a person "on the basis of a factual determination that the State has formally disavowed" in coperpetrator's later trial]; *Drake v. Kemp* (11th Cir. 1985) 762 F.2d 1449, 1479 (conc. opn. of Clark, J.) [prosecutor's "flip flopping of theories of the offense was inherently unfair"].) Drawing on these separate opinions, several federal courts have since held that a prosecutor's inconsistent argument in two defendants' separate trials attributing the same criminal or culpability-increasing act to each defendant denies the defendants fundamentally fair trials.

In *Thompson v. Calderon (9th Cir. 1997) 120 F.3d 1045 (Thompson)*, a majority of the en banc court held that inconsistent prosecutorial theories may present a due process violation. There, Leitch and Thompson were both charged with raping and killing Ginger Fleischli. At their joint preliminary hearing and at Leitch's trial, the prosecutor introduced and relied on evidence, including testimony by jailhouse informants recounting statements by Thompson, that indicated the two defendants had acted together, killing Fleischli because she was interfering with Leitch's efforts to reconcile with his ex-wife. (*Thompson*, (plur. opn. of Fletcher, J.).) At Thompson's trial (held before Leitch's), however, the same prosecutor had introduced and relied upon other evidence, to the effect that Thompson alone killed Fleischli to prevent her reporting that he had raped her. The prosecutor thus "asserted as the truth before Thompson's jury the story he subsequently labeled absurd and incredible in Leitch's trial."

The *Thompson* plurality concluded that "when no new significant evidence comes to light a prosecutor cannot, in order to convict two defendants at separate trials, offer inconsistent theories and facts regarding the same crime." Three of the 11 judges participating fully joined with Judge Fletcher in her opinion on this point. Two more, in a concurring opinion by Judge Tashima, agreed that prosecutorial use of wholly inconsistent theories violates due process, but believed that Thompson's entitlement to relief depended on whether he was prejudiced, which in turn required a determination "which of the two inconsistent theories pursued by the prosecutor represents the true facts and which is false."

In *Smith v. Groose (8th Cir. 2000) 205 F.3d 1045 (Smith)*, members of two criminal groups who had separately burglarized the same house during overlapping periods of the same day were tried separately for the murder of the occupants. At the trials of both Cunningham, a member of the first group of burglars, and Smith, a member of the second, Lytle, also a member of the second group, testified the occupants were killed by Cunningham's group. In one prior statement to police, Lytle had attributed the killings to a member of his own group, Bowman, while in another he said, consistently with his trial testimony, that Cunningham's group had killed the occupants. At Smith's trial, the prosecutor used Lytle's prior statement implicating Bowman in the killings, arguing to the jury that Smith, Bowman's accomplice in burglary, was guilty of felony murder. Later, at Cunningham's trial, the prosecutor relied on Lytle's testimony, introduced his prior consistent statement to police, did not introduce his prior inconsistent statement, and objected to defense efforts to impeach him. (*Id. at pp. 1047–1048, 1050*.) "In short, what the State claimed to be true in Smith's case it rejected in Cunningham's case, and vice versa." (*Id. at p. 1050*.)

The *Smith* court concluded, "the use of inherently . . . contradictory theories violates the principles of due process" (Smith, supra, 205 F.3d at *p. 1052*), for "[t]he State's duty to its citizens does not allow it to pursue as many convictions as possible without regard to fairness and the search for truth" (*id. at p. 1051*; see also *United States v. Butner (W.D.Mo. 2000) 2000 WL 1842410, *15–17* [following *Smith*]).

Recently, the Sixth Circuit Court of Appeals reached the same conclusion in *Stumpf v. Mitchell (6th Cir. 2004) 367 F.3d 594*, certiorari granted *sub nomine. Mitchell v. Stumpf (2005)* ___ U.S. ___ *[160 L. Ed. 2d 610, 25 S. Ct. 824]* (*Stumpf*). [EDITOR'S NOTE: The Supreme Court vacated the decision without ruling directly on the question of inconsistent arguments.] Stumpf and his accomplice, Wesley, robbed and killed a couple, the Stouts, in their home. That Stumpf shot Mr. Stout was undisputed, but whether he also shot Mrs. Stout or Wesley did so with Stumpf's handgun was unclear. At Stumpf's plea hearing, the prosecutor argued that since both victims were shot with the same weapon, the evidence showed Stumpf must have killed both victims " 'in order not to leave anyone available to identify him.' "(*Id. at p. 613*.) But at Wesley's later trial, the prosecutor introduced a jail informant's testimony that Wesley had confessed to picking up Stumpf's handgun and shooting Mrs. Stout. On that basis, the prosecutor argued Stumpf had left the room after shooting Mr. Stout, whereupon Wesley, " 'whose own gun was jammed, picked that chrome colored Raven up and as Mrs. Stout sat helplessly on her bed, shot her four times in order to leave no witnesses to the crime.' "(*Ibid.*; *id. at pp. 596–598*.)

The appellate court concluded, "the use of inconsistent, irreconcilable theories to convict two defendants for the same crime is a due process violation." The vice rests in the fact that of two inconsistent and irreconcilable theories, one must be false: "Because inconsistent theories render convictions unreliable, they constitute a violation of the due process rights of any defendant in whose trial they are used." In *Stumpf*, the state had clearly used such irreconcilable theories, for "[a]t each proceeding, the prosecutor argued that the defendant had been the one to pull the trigger, resulting in the fatal shots to [Mrs.] Stout."

These courts and judges have found a prosecutor's 180–degree change in theory "deeply troubling" in part because by taking a formal position inconsistent with the guilt or culpability of at least one convicted defendant, the government, through the prosecutor, has cast doubt on the factual basis for the conviction. "If the prosecutor's statements at the Hogan trial were correct, then Jacobs is innocent of capital murder." "The conclusion seems inescapable that the prosecutor obtained Henry Drake's conviction through the use of testimony he did not believe.... " "The prosecutor ... at Leitch's trial essentially ridiculed the theory he had used to obtain a conviction and death sentence at Thompson's trial." As both of two irreconcilable theories of guilt cannot be true, "inconsistent theories render convictions unreliable."

Because it undermines the reliability of the convictions or sentences, the prosecution's use of inconsistent and irreconcilable theories has also been criticized as inconsistent with the principles of public prosecution and the integrity of the criminal trial system. A criminal prosecutor's function "is not merely to prosecute crimes, but also to make certain that the truth is honored to the fullest extent possible during the course of the criminal prosecution and trial." (*United States v. Kattar (1st Cir. 1988) 840 F.2d 118, 127*.) His or her goal must be "not simply to obtain a conviction, but to obtain a fair conviction." (*Brown v. Borg (9th Cir. 1991) 951 F.2d 1011, 1015*, italics omitted.) "Although the prosecutor must prosecute with earnestness and vigor and 'may strike hard blows, he is not at liberty to strike foul ones.' "(*Smith, supra, 205 F.3d at p. 1049*, quoting *Berger v. United States (1935) 295 U.S. 78, 88 [79 L. Ed. 1314, 55 S. Ct. 629]*; see also ABA Model Code Prof. Responsibility, EC 7–13 ["The responsibility of a public prosecutor differs from that of the usual advocate; his duty is to seek justice, not merely to convict"].)

* * *

We have previously indicated that an inconsistent prosecutorial argument "made in bad faith" could be misconduct, and conversely that such argument was not improper if "based on the record and made in good faith" (*People v. Farmer (1989) 47 Cal.3d 888, 923 [254 Cal. Rptr. 508, 765 P.2d 940]* (*Farmer*)), though we did not have occasion in that case to deal more definitively with the problem. With the issue more squarely before us here, we hold that the People's use of irreconcilable theories of guilt or culpability, unjustified by a good faith justification for the inconsistency, is fundamentally unfair, for it necessarily creates the potential for—and, where prejudicial, actually achieves—a false conviction or increased punishment on a false factual basis for one of the accuseds. "The criminal trial should be viewed not as an adversarial sporting contest, but as a quest for truth." (*United States v. Kattar, supra, 840 F.2d at p. 127.*)

By intentionally and in bad faith seeking a conviction or death sentence for two defendants on the basis of culpable acts for which only one could be responsible, the People violate "the due process requirement that the government prosecute fairly in a search for truth. . . ." (*Smith, supra, 205 F.3d at p. 1053.*) In such circumstances, the People's conduct gives rise to a due process claim (under both the *United States* and *California Constitution*s) similar to a claim of factual innocence. Just as it would be impermissible for the state to punish a person factually innocent of the charged crime, so too does it violate due process to base criminal punishment on unjustified attribution of the same criminal or culpability-increasing acts to two different persons when only one could have committed them. In that situation, we *know* that *someone* is factually innocent of the culpable acts attributed to both. (See *Prosecutorial Inconsistency, supra, 89 Cal. L.Rev. at p. 1425* ["When the prosecution advances a position in the trial of one defendant and then adopts an inconsistent position in the trial of another on the same facts, the prosecution is relying on a known falsity"].)

2. *The People unjustifiably used inconsistent and irreconcilable theories to obtain a death sentence against Sakarias*

Prosecutor Ipsen attributed first to Waidla alone and later to Sakarias alone, in their respective trials, a series of blows to the victim's head with the hatchet blade. These two theories are irreconcilable; that Waidla alone inflicted each of these wounds, as the prosecutor maintained at his trial, and that Sakarias alone also did so, as the prosecutor maintained at his trial, is not possible. One or the other theory (or both, if each man inflicted some but not all of the wounds) must be false.

(6) The acts attributed to both Waidla and Sakarias in turn were not necessary to establish their guilt of first degree murder (*Pen. Code, § 189*) or the truth of the charged robbery-and burglary-murder special circumstances (*id., § 190.2, subd. (a)(17)*). But the prosecutor attributed the three hatchet-edge blows to each defendant in turn in order to establish an aggravating circumstance of the crime (*id., § 190.3*) on the basis of which the jury was urged to sentence each defendant to death. At least where the punishment involved is death, due process is as offended by the People's inconsistent and irreconcilable attribution of culpability-increasing acts as by the inconsistent and irreconcilable attribution of crimes.

* * *

Because Ipsen used different attributions of the chopping wounds to argue each petitioner should receive the death penalty, his factual theories were significantly inconsistent and irreconcilable. The present case is thus critically distinguishable from those in which the prosecutor's theories were held fundamentally consistent because any variation did not concern a fact used to convict the defendant or increase his or her punishment. (See *Nguyen v. Lindsey (9th Cir. 2000) 232 F.3d 1236, 1240–1241* [variation in prosecutorial argument as to which of two gangs fired the first shot in a gun battle that killed a bystander not significant where prosecutor at both trials pursued the same "underlying theory" that all participants in the gang battle were equally responsible for the death].) Unlike those cases, here Ipsen's underlying theory of why petitioners each deserved the death penalty was not the same in the two cases; in Waidla's case, it included Waidla's supposed striking of all three blows with the hatchet blade, while in Sakarias's case it included Sakarias's striking the same three blows.

We turn to the question of justification....

... We agree a significant change in the available evidence might, under some circumstances, warrant the use of an inconsistent prosecutorial theory in a subsequent trial. Here, one difference in evidence between the two trials was the introduction at Waidla's trial, but not at Sakarias's, of Dr. Ribe's testimony that the abrasion on the victim's back was nonhemorrhagic and therefore appeared to have been inflicted after death. But Ipsen's deliberate strategic choice in Sakarias's trial not to examine Dr. Ribe regarding the abrasion on the victim's lower back, as he had done a few months earlier at Waidla's trial, plainly cannot establish Ipsen's good faith or otherwise justify the use of irreconcilable theories. To the contrary, such manipulation of the evidence for the purpose of pursuing inconsistent theories establishes the prosecutor's *bad* faith....

The referee found, on substantial evidence, that Ipsen omitted questioning about the back abrasion in order to avoid presenting evidence "inconvenient" to his new theory that Sakarias had inflicted all three chopping wounds to the victim's head. Such intentional manipulation of the evidence was instrumental to, and cannot justify, the prosecutor's use of irreconcilable theories....

The dissenting opinion finds no indication of bad faith in Ipsen's conduct because, where the information available to the prosecutor is of public record or has been disclosed to the defense.... We agree no due process violation arises simply from a prosecutor's failure to introduce evidence favorable to the defense. But where, as here, a prosecutor who seeks convictions or death sentences against two individuals through inconsistent and irreconcilable factual theories deliberately omits in one trial evidence used in the other, so as to make possible the argument of the inconsistent theories, the prosecutor's manipulation of evidence does show that the inconsistent theories were not pursued in good faith. . . . Whether that conduct was prejudicial must still be determined.

* * *

3. *The People's use of inconsistent and irreconcilable theories was prejudicial as to Sakarias*

* * *

We need not decide here what result obtains when the likely truth of the prosecutor's inconsistent theories *cannot* be determined, for the case at bench is not one of ambiguous or inconclusive evidence. As the referee found, the great weight of available evidence indicates that Viivi Piirisild was dead or near death when dragged into the bedroom and thus that Waidla, rather than Sakarias, struck the antemortem, hemorrhagic hatchet-blade blow. True, *some* evidence—blood spatters in the bedroom— suggests the possibility of an antemortem blow being struck in that room. But that evidence is overwhelmed by other evidence that Viivi's hemorrhagic wounds, including the hemorrhagic chopping wound Ipsen characterized as the "death blow," were inflicted during petitioners' initial attack on her in the living room, including the large pool of blood in the living room, the minimum quantity of blood on the bedroom walls and ceiling, the lack of blood on the bedroom floor, Sakarias's statement that petitioners felled Viivi in the living room before eventually dragging her into the bedroom, and the nonhemorrhagic character of the abrasion on Viivi's back. As both petitioners' statements have Waidla using the hatchet during that initial attack and Sakarias the knife, and as no evidence at all suggests the two exchanged weapons during the initial attack, the inescapable inference from all the available evidence is that Waidla inflicted the hemorrhagic chopping wound to Viivi's head.

To the extent the false attribution of the antemortem hatchet-blade blow to Sakarias was potentially material to the penalty decision, it deprived Sakarias of a fair penalty trial and entitles him to relief. . . .

Aside from attributing the hemorrhagic chopping wound to Sakarias, the prosecutor introduced and relied upon other significant aggravating circumstances. Sakarias undisputedly played a direct role in the brutal, unprovoked killing of Viivi Piirisild. The uncontroverted evidence showed that Sakarias stabbed Viivi four times in the chest, including two potentially fatal wounds passing through vital organs, and that he later took the hatchet, went to the bedroom, and struck her at least twice in the head with the hatchet blade. Sakarias had a loaded handgun when arrested and later was found in possession of shanks in the county jail (for use, he said, against gang members who had robbed him). He also made statements during trial indicating a lack of remorse for killing Viivi and suggesting that he and Waidla had intended to kill Avo Piirisild as well.

Other considerations, however, make it impossible for us to conclude *beyond a reasonable doubt* that the prosecutorial argument that Sakarias struck all the hatchet-blade blows, including the first, antemortem one, played no role in the penalty decision. The first hatchet-blade wound was especially severe and was described in gruesome detail by the medical examiner on direct examination by the prosecutor. The path of the blade was parallel to the top of the head, straight up and down as if the victim was lying on the floor. The blade entered on the upper forehead, penetrated through the scalp and the skull bone, then hit the inside of the skull. Dr. Ribe believed the blade then "bounced" off the bone and continued to the rear and right of the victim's head, leaving another incision. The blow's force not only penetrated the front of the skull but fractured the back as well, pushing it backward. As a result, a portion of the upper skull and scalp were partially detached from the rest of the head, forming a flap that could be easily folded back. Because of the strength of an adult human's skull, Dr. Ribe believed a "tremendous amount of force," as much as an average man could exert swinging the hatchet "very hard," was needed to cause this wound.

In the guilt phase argument, the prosecutor discussed in detail Sakarias's attack on Viivi Piirisild with the hatchet, stating he went into the bedroom "to strike a few more blows, to make sure that Viivi was dead in case the stabbing and the bludgeoning weren't enough. [P] We know that there were three, in this series of blows, sharp hatchet wounds to the top of Viivi's head with a tremendous force. ... [P] And it was with this strength that Peter Sakarias swung this hatchet to penetrate this skull, to reach that most vital organ ... [P] ... [P] We know that there are in fact three hatchet wounds; the first penetrating the top of the skull, and I know it was the first because it was a hemorrhagic wound, the one in the hairline, the one that chopped the top of her head completely off with the exception of some of the scalp that kept it completely on. [P] ... [P] We know that this last series of chop wounds ... was consistent with the last three blows she received." In the penalty argument, the prosecutor twice again asserted that Sakarias had inflicted all the chopping wounds, "swinging what I suggest were the blows that actually ended her life." Sakarias, according to Ipsen, "simply ... chop[ped] the top of her head off, as the evidence indicated you did in that back room, thus finally ending her life."

As to mitigation, Sakarias was young (21 years old) at the time of the offense, had no record of violence, and had suffered persecution in the Soviet Army. He was diagnosed with schizo-affective disorder, characterized by paranoia and bipolar affect; the jury was informed that he had been found incompetent to stand trial in May 1990 and spent almost a year in a state hospital. The defense also played tapes of Sakarias's mother, father, and friends, recorded in Estonia, describing his childhood and youth. (*Sakarias, supra*, 22 Cal.4th at pp. 614–616.)

Some aspect or aspects of the case evidently gave one or more jurors considerable pause in the sentencing decision, as the penalty jury deliberated for more than 10 hours over three days and, at one point, declared itself unable to reach a unanimous verdict, before finally returning a verdict of death.

In light of the prominence the prosecutor gave the antemortem chopping wound, treating it as the final, fatal wound, and the likely impact the medical examiner's description of that wound and the force necessary to inflict it would have had, that the prosecutor's attribution of that blow to Sakarias had an effect on the penalty verdict is reasonably likely. Though Sakarias's undisputed conduct in stabbing Viivi Piirisild and stealing her property played, no doubt, a major role in the jury's decision, we cannot conclude beyond a reasonable doubt that the jury's decision would have been the same had it not also been told that Sakarias finally ended Viivi's life by swinging a hatchet with all his strength, nearly cutting off the top of her head. The prosecutor's intentional and unjustified argument, inconsistent with the factual theory and evidence he had presented at Waidla's trial, that Sakarias struck the antemortem hatchet-blade blow was therefore prejudicial to Sakarias as to penalty.

4. *The People's use of inconsistent and irreconcilable theories was harmless as to Waidla*

Our conclusion is necessarily different as to Waidla. As discussed earlier, and as the referee found, the great weight of the evidence available—the statements of both petitioners, the physical crime scene evidence, and the medical examiner's expert testimony—tended to show that Waidla wielded the hatchet in the initial attack, that the first chopping wound was inflicted before Viivi Piirisild's death, and that Viivi died in her living room from the initial attack before being dragged to the back bedroom. Ipsen's argument in Waidla's trial that Waidla struck the first, antemortem blow with the hatchet blade, therefore, was likely true.

Waidla points to Sakarias's statement that he struck Viivi with the hatchet in the bedroom. But Sakarias confessed to hitting Viivi with the hatchet only *twice*, which left open the possibility—a probability under the other evidence—that the first of the three chopping wounds was inflicted by Waidla during the initial attack. To be sure, in his arguments to the Waidla jury Ipsen suggested that Waidla had inflicted *all* the chop wounds, including the two postmortem or perimortem wounds that Ipsen had strong reason to believe were actually attributable to Sakarias. But this apparently false argument, inconsistent with the arguments made in Sakarias's trial, was not prejudicial to Waidla as to penalty, even under the reasonable likelihood standard of *United States v. Agurs, supra, 427 U.S. at page 103.* To the extent he focused on particular blows, the impact of the prosecutor's arguments derived from the hemorrhagic hatchet-blade wound, the chop "through the top of her skull" or "death blow," rather than from the fact that "further blows were struck after she was dead."

Waidla admitted that after burglarizing the home of Viivi Piirisild, an older woman who had been his benefactor, he hit her with the back of a hatchet he had stolen from her vacation cabin. The medical examiner opined that these blunt force wounds, which fractured several bones and knocked out Viivi's teeth, contributed to her death. The evidence, moreover, was strong that Waidla, during this attack, turned the hatchet around and struck Viivi with the sharp blade with such force as to penetrate her skull and cut a flap of skull and scalp from the top of her head. Even balanced against Waidla's youth, lack of a violent criminal record, and personal history of brutalization in the Soviet Army (*Waidla, supra, 22 Cal.4th at pp. 706, 712*), the circumstances of the crime offered a compelling case in aggravation. More to the point, the case would not have been made significantly less compelling by a prosecutorial concession that Sakarias may have inflicted the two later chop wounds, after Viivi had expired. As the Attorney General remarks, "Under the circumstances, it would have made no difference to the jury whether Waidla inflicted the nonhemorrhagic chopping wounds or handed the weapon to Sakarias so he could inflict them, particularly since the wounds were likely postmortem." We conclude beyond a reasonable doubt that the prosecutor's attribution of these two wounds to Waidla, though likely false, did not affect Waidla's penalty and does not entitle him to relief.

* * *

The order to show cause as to Waidla's petition is discharged.

Sakarias's petition for a writ of habeas corpus is granted insofar as it claims prosecutorial inconsistency material to the penalty verdict, and the judgment of the Los Angeles County Superior Court in *People v. Peter Sakarias*, No. A711340, therefore is vacated insofar as it imposes a sentence of death. . . .

CONCUR BY: BAXTER

DISSENT BY: BAXTER

DISSENT:

■ BAXTER, J., Concurring and Dissenting.—I concur in the judgment except insofar as it orders vacation of petitioner Sakarias's death judgment. As to Sakarias, I respectfully dissent.

* * *

. . . [T]he majority say Sakarias's due process rights were prejudicially violated as to penalty when, in their separate trials, Prosecutor Ipsen, acting in "bad faith," sought to enhance each petitioner's culpability by attributing the same *single* antemortem hatchet-chopping wound to each killer. Ipsen's bad faith is demonstrated, the majority assert, because (1) the available evidence pointed strongly to Waidla, not Sakarias, as the perpetrator of this act, and (2) Ipsen "manipulated" the evidence at Sakarias's trial by failing to elicit certain medical testimony he had earlier used to attribute the same act to Waidla. The majority insist that the misimpression thus conveyed to Sakarias's jury may have influenced its penalty decision. I disagree.

At the outset, I discern no bad faith in Ipsen's conduct. Our referee was never asked to make such a finding, and he did not do so. In my view, there is no basis for a bad faith determination. Ipsen adhered to the well-established rule against the knowing presentation of *false* evidence. Moreover, he presumably discharged his obligation to *give the defense* any otherwise unavailable evidence he possessed that materially undermined the prosecution's case against Sakarias. Nor was there any secret, at the time of Sakarias's trial, about Ipsen's case against Waidla. Because Sakarias's trial followed Waidla's, this information was by then a matter of public record.

Under such circumstances, the People would not generally be required to *introduce*, in their own case, evidence *helpful to the defense*. Instead, the prosecution could properly rely on the defense to expose the gaps and weaknesses in its proof. I see no reason why a different rule should apply in Sakarias's case simply because the omitted evidence was earlier presented against Waidla.

Further, I believe Ipsen demonstrated no bad faith by theorizing, in each defendant's trial, that the antemortem hatchet chop was inflicted by that defendant. I have two reasons for this conclusion. First, the law governing inconsistent prosecutorial arguments is complex and unsettled; indeed, a case presenting such issues is currently under review by the United States Supreme Court. (*Stumpf v. Mitchell* (6th Cir. 2004) *367 F.3d 594* (*Stumpf*), cert. granted *sub nom. Mitchell v. Stumpf* (2005) ___ U.S. ___ *[160 L. Ed. 2d 610, 125 S. Ct. 824].*) Because appellate judges significantly disagree about what a prosecutor may and may not do in this regard, there seems little basis to conclude that Ipsen's strategy constituted bad faith. Second, the evidence of who delivered the antemortem chopping blow is hardly as clear as the majority suggest. Our referee found that Ipsen himself was sincerely uncertain which of the two murderers had committed this particular act. Under these circumstances, I cannot find bad faith in Ipsen's efforts to make a plausible case against each petitioner.

* * *

Here, Ipsen did not use inconsistent theories to obtain capital murder judgments against two defendants, where only one could be guilty or death-eligible. There is no doubt that Sakarias and Waidla together committed the first degree murder of Viivi Piirisild with special circumstances, and that both men were enthusiastic participants in the gruesome attack. The only dispute in this case relates to a particular *detail* which a jury *could* consider in deciding whether death was the appropriate penalty for each killer. Under these circumstances, and given the uncertain state of the law, I cannot find in Ipsen's conduct an act of bad faith amounting to a constitutional violation.

. . . Ipsen was not an eyewitness to Viivi's murder. Neither Waidla nor Sakarias confessed to delivering the disputed blow. Evidence on that point was entirely circumstantial. In my view, it was not so clear as to preclude Ipsen from reserving personal judgment—as he did—and presenting the plausible case against each man.

As the majority notes, the case against Waidla is as follows: When the attack began in the Piirisilds' living room, Sakarias was using a knife, while Waidla was using the blunt edge of the hatchet to bludgeon the victim. At some point, she was moved from the living room to the bedroom. There is evidence she was already dead by that time, and the two hatchet chops to which Sakarias admitted were, he said, inflicted in the bedroom.

Hence, the earlier, antemortem chopping blow must have been inflicted in the living room, and by Waidla.

This is a plausible scenario, but a substantial case could be made against Sakarias as well. After all, neither Sakarias nor Waidla ever attributed *any* hatchet chops to Waidla. On the other hand, Sakarias conceded that he did use the hatchet to deliver such blows. Indeed, Sakarias admitted inflicting *two of the three* hatchet chops disclosed by the evidence, all of which were in relatively close proximity on the victim's head. As Ipsen implied in Sakarias's trial, one could infer that Sakarias had simply understated by one the number of chops he delivered. Moreover, while most of the bloodstains and spatters were found in the living room, there were significant spatters in the bedroom as well. In one place in the bedroom, a detective testified at Sakarias's trial, there was enough blood "to actually start to trickle down the wall." This was some, if not conclusive, evidence that the victim bled in the bedroom, and was thus still alive.

The majority claim Waidla must have inflicted the antemortem wound because the medical examiner testified at Waidla's trial that an abrasion on Viivi's back was probably caused by dragging, and that the "nonhemorrhagic" nature of the abrasion suggested it was sustained postmortem. Thus, the majority infer, the abrasion must have occurred when the victim, already dead, was dragged to the bedroom. Because Sakarias admitted only two chop wounds in the bedroom, the majority reason he must have inflicted the two postmortem wounds, and none other.

But this analysis is hardly conclusive. Expert opinions are often subject to debate and interpretation. Moreover, even if we credit an inference that the victim was already dead when she was moved to the bedroom, that does not prove Sakarias wielded the hatchet only thereafter. We know this weapon was transferred from Waidla to Sakarias at some point, but we do not know exactly when. Given the uncertain evidence, I conclude that so long as Ipsen did not introduce false evidence, he acted in good faith by presenting alternative theories about this detail of the attack. Having satisfied his discovery obligations, Ipsen could properly rely, in each case, on the due diligence of the defense to expose weaknesses in the People's proof.

By concluding that Ipsen could only present the case they think is stronger, the majority intrude much too far into matters which, for good reason, have traditionally been left to prosecutorial discretion. I cannot join the majority's attempt to second-guess the prosecution's strategy in this way.

In any event, I do not accept the majority's conclusion that Sakarias suffered prejudice on the issue of penalty. The undisputed details of Sakarias's role in this brutal murder are aggravated in the extreme. Though the Piirisilds had bestowed many kindnesses on Sakarias and Waidla, the two men decided they had been slighted by their benefactors. Filled with hate and greed, Sakarias and Waidla hatched a plan to burglarize and rob the couple. But once in the Piirisild home, they did not simply take property and leave. Instead, they "started waiting for Viivi" with murderous intent.

As the majority recite, Sakarias personally used his knife to stab Viivi at least four times in the chest. Two of these wounds were potentially fatal. Sakarias ceased his attack with the knife only when its handle broke off. He also inflicted at least two chopping wounds to Viivi's head with the hatchet. His jury must have understood that, regardless of whether Viivi was then still alive, Sakarias administered these blows for the purpose of ensuring her death.

Far from horrified at their bloody work, the murderers stayed for a snack, and Sakarias calmly ate liverwurst from the Piirisilds' refrigerator. Later, he made clear to the police his only regret—that they had not killed Avo Piirisild as well.

Thus, the uncontroverted evidence demonstrates Sakarias's full, remorseless involvement in the murder plot, and details the many grievous blows and wounds he administered during the joint attack on the victim. Under these circumstances, it stretches credulity to suggest that the issue whether he inflicted a single additional blow—gruesome as it was—could alone have tipped the jury's penalty determination.

The majority note that Ipsen made Sakarias's responsibility for the antemortem hatchet chop a significant theme of his argument. But such references occurred, for the most part, at the guilt phase of Sakarias's trial, where they could have caused no prejudice. As the majority concede, Ipsen gave this subject only two brief references at the penalty phase. The bulk of Ipsen's penalty argument was devoted to rebutting the defense case in mitigation, including Sakarias's claims of extreme mental disorder. In my view, this further reduces any chance that the penalty outcome was affected.

* * *

I would discharge the order to show cause as to both Waidla and Sakarias.

* * *

CHAPTER 21

SENTENCING

B. SENTENCING PROCEDURES

1. BURDEN OF PROOF

Page 1629, add prior to McMillan v. Pennsylvania (Two New Main Cases)

Blakely v. Washington

Supreme Court of the United States.
542 U.S. 296, 124 S.Ct. 2531 (2004).

* * *

■ JUSTICE SCALIA delivered the opinion of the Court.

Petitioner Ralph Howard Blakely, Jr., pleaded guilty to the kidnaping of his estranged wife. The facts admitted in his plea, standing alone, supported a maximum sentence of 53 months. Pursuant to state law, the court imposed an "exceptional" sentence of 90 months after making a judicial determination that he had acted with "deliberate cruelty." We consider whether this violated petitioner's *Sixth Amendment* right to trial by jury.

Petitioner married his wife Yolanda in 1973. He was evidently a difficult man to live with, having been diagnosed at various times with psychological and personality disorders including paranoid schizophrenia. His wife ultimately filed for divorce. In 1998, he abducted her from their orchard home in Grant County, Washington, binding her with duct tape and forcing her at knifepoint into a wooden box in the bed of his pickup truck. In the process, he implored her to dismiss the divorce suit and related trust proceedings.

When the couple's 13–year-old son Ralphy returned home from school, petitioner ordered him to follow in another car, threatening to harm Yolanda with a shotgun if he did not do so. Ralphy escaped and sought help when they stopped at a gas station, but petitioner continued on with Yolanda to a friend's house in Montana. He was finally arrested after the friend called the police.

* * *

The case then proceeded to sentencing. In Washington, second-degree kidnaping is a class B felony § 9A.40.030(3). State law provides that "no person convicted of a [class B] felony shall be punished by confinement ... exceeding ... a term of ten years." *§ 9A.20.021(1)(b)*. Other provisions of state law, however, further limit the range of sentences a judge may impose. *Washington's Sentencing Reform Act* specifies, for petitioner's offense of second-degree kidnaping with a firearm, a "standard range" of 49 to 53 months. . . . A judge may impose a sentence above the standard range if he finds "substantial and compelling reasons justifying an exceptional sentence." *The Act* lists aggravating factors that justify such a departure, which it recites to be illustrative rather than exhaustive. Nevertheless, "[a] reason offered to justify an exceptional sentence can be considered only if it takes into account factors other than those which are used in computing the standard range sentence for the offense." *State v. Gore, 143 Wn. 2d 288, 315–316, 21 P. 3d 262, 277 (2001).* When a judge imposes an exceptional sentence, he must set forth findings of fact and conclusions of law supporting it. A reviewing court will reverse the sentence if it finds that "under a clearly erroneous standard there is insufficient evidence in the record to support the reasons for imposing an exceptional sentence." *Gore, supra, at 315, 21 P. 3d, at 277.*

Pursuant to the plea agreement, the State recommended a sentence within the standard range of 49 to 53 months. After hearing Yolanda's description of the kidnaping, however, the judge rejected the State's recommendation and imposed an exceptional sentence of 90 months—37 months beyond the standard maximum. He justified the sentence on the ground that petitioner had acted with "deliberate cruelty," a statutorily enumerated ground for departure in domestic-violence cases.

Faced with an unexpected increase of more than three years in his sentence, petitioner objected. The judge accordingly conducted a 3–day bench hearing featuring testimony from petitioner, Yolanda, Ralphy, a police officer, and medical experts. After the hearing, he issued 32 findings of fact, concluding:

> "The defendant's motivation to commit kidnapping was complex, contributed to by his mental condition and personality disorders, the pressures of the divorce litigation, the impending trust litigation trial and anger over his troubled interpersonal relationships with his spouse and children. While he misguidedly intended to forcefully reunite his family, his attempt to do so was subservient to his desire to terminate lawsuits and modify title ownerships to his benefit.

"The defendant's methods were more homogeneous than his motive. He used stealth and surprise, and took advantage of the victim's isolation. He immediately employed physical violence, restrained the victim with tape, and threatened her with injury and death to herself and others. He immediately coerced the victim into providing information by the threatening application of a knife. He violated a subsisting restraining order." App. 48–49.

The judge adhered to his initial determination of deliberate cruelty.

Petitioner appealed, arguing that this sentencing procedure deprived him of his federal constitutional right to have a jury determine beyond a reasonable doubt all facts legally essential to his sentence. The State Court of Appeals affirmed. . . . The Washington Supreme Court denied discretionary review. We granted certiorari.

II

This case requires us to apply the rule we expressed in *Apprendi v. New Jersey, 530 U.S. 466, 490, 147 L. Ed. 2d 435, 120 S. Ct. 2348 (2000)*: "Other than the fact of a prior conviction, any fact that increases the penalty for a crime beyond the prescribed statutory maximum must be submitted to a jury, and proved beyond a reasonable doubt." This rule reflects two longstanding tenets of common-law criminal jurisprudence: that the "truth of every accusation" against a defendant "should afterwards be confirmed by the unanimous suffrage of twelve of his equals and neighbours," 4 W. Blackstone, Commentaries on the Laws of England 343 (1769)....

Apprendi involved a New Jersey hate-crime statute that authorized a 20–year sentence, despite the usual 10–year maximum, if the judge found the crime to have been committed " 'with a purpose to intimidate ... because of race, color, gender, handicap, religion, sexual orientation or ethnicity.' " In *Ring v. Arizona, 536 U.S. 584, 592–593, 153 L. Ed. 2d 556, 122 S. Ct. 2428* (2002), we applied *Apprendi* to an Arizona law that authorized the death penalty if the judge found one of ten aggravating factors. In each case, we concluded that the defendant's constitutional rights had been violated because the judge had imposed a sentence greater than the maximum he could have imposed under state law without the challenged factual finding....

... The State contends that there was no *Apprendi* violation because the relevant "statutory maximum" is not 53 months, but the 10–year maximum for class B felonies. It observes that no exceptional sentence may exceed that limit. Our precedents make clear, however, that the "statutory maximum" for *Apprendi* purposes is the maximum sentence a judge may impose *solely on the basis of the facts reflected in the jury verdict or admitted by the defendant.* See *Ring, supra, at 602, 153 L. Ed. 2d 556, 122 S. Ct. 2428* (" 'the maximum he would receive if punished according to the facts reflected in the jury verdict alone' ") (quoting *Apprendi, supra, at 483.*) In other words, the relevant "statutory maximum" is not the maximum sentence a judge may impose after finding additional facts, but the maximum he may impose *without* any additional findings. When a judge inflicts punishment that the jury's verdict alone does not allow, the jury has not found all the facts "which the law makes essential to the punishment," 1 J. Bishop, Criminal Procedure, (2d Ed 1872), § 87, at 55, and the judge exceeds his proper authority.

The judge in this case could not have imposed the exceptional 90–month sentence solely on the basis of the facts admitted in the guilty plea. Those facts alone were insufficient because, as the Washington Supreme Court has explained, "[a] reason offered to justify an exceptional sentence can be considered only if it takes into account factors other than those which are used in computing the standard range sentence for the offense," *Gore, 143 Wash. 2d, at 315–316, 21 P. 3d, at 277*, which in this case included the elements of second-degree kidnaping and the use of a firearm. Had the judge imposed the 90–month sentence solely on the basis of the plea, he would have been reversed. The "maximum sentence" is no more 10 years here than it was 20 years in *Apprendi* (because that is what the judge could have imposed upon finding a hate crime) or death in *Ring* (because that is what the judge could have imposed upon finding an aggravator).

The State defends the sentence by drawing an analogy to those we upheld in *McMillan v. Pennsylvania, 477 U.S. 79, 91 L. Ed. 2d 67, 106 S. Ct. 2411 (1986)*, and *Williams v. New York, 337 U.S. 241, 93 L. Ed. 1337, 69 S. Ct. 1079 (1949)*. Neither case is on point. *McMillan* involved a sentencing scheme that imposed a statutory *minimum* if a judge found a particular fact. *477 U.S., at 81, 91 L. Ed. 2d 67, 106 S. Ct. 2411*. We specifically noted that the statute "does not authorize a sentence in excess of that otherwise allowed for [the underlying] offense." *Williams* involved an indeterminate-sentencing regime that allowed a judge (but did not compel him) to rely on facts outside the trial record in determining whether to sentence a defendant to death. The judge could have "sentenced [the defendant] to death giving no reason at all." *Id., at 252, 93 L. Ed. 1337, 69 S. Ct. 1079*. Thus, neither case involved a sentence greater than what state law authorized on the basis of the verdict alone.

* * *

Because the State's sentencing procedure did not comply with the *Sixth Amendment*, petitioner's sentence is invalid.

III

Our commitment to *Apprendi* in this context reflects not just respect for longstanding precedent, but the need to give intelligible content to the right of jury trial. That right is no mere procedural formality, but a fundamental reservation of power in our constitutional structure. Just as suffrage ensures the people's ultimate control in the legislative and executive branches, jury trial is meant to ensure their control in the judiciary. See Letter XV by the Federal Farmer (Jan. 18, 1788), reprinted in 2 The Complete Anti–Federalist 315, 320 (H. Storing ed. 1981) (describing the jury as "securing to the people at large, their just and rightful controul in the judicial department"); John Adams, Diary Entry (Feb. 12, 1771), reprinted in 2 Works of John Adams 252, 253 (C. Adams ed. 1850) ("The common people, should have as complete a control . . . in every judgment of a court of judicature" as in the legislature); Letter from Thomas Jefferson to the Abbe Arnoux (July 19, 1789), reprinted in 15 Papers of Thomas Jefferson 282, 283 (J. Boyd ed. 1958) ("Were I called upon to decide whether the people had best be omitted in the Legislative or Judiciary department, I would say it is better to leave them out of the Legislative"); *Jones v. United States, 526 U.S. 227, 244–248, 143 L. Ed. 2d 311, 119 S. Ct. 1215 (1999)*. *Apprendi* carries out this design by ensuring that the judge's authority to sentence derives wholly from the jury's verdict. Without that restriction, the jury would not exercise the control that the Framers intended.

Those who would reject *Apprendi* are resigned to one of two alternatives. The first is that the jury need only find whatever facts the legislature chooses to label elements of the crime, and that those it labels sentencing factors—no matter how much they may increase the punishment—may be found by the judge. This would mean, for example, that a judge could sentence a man for committing murder even if the jury convicted him only of illegally possessing the firearm used to commit it—or of making an illegal lane change while fleeing the death scene. Not even *Apprendi*'s critics would advocate this absurd result. Cf. *530 U.S., at 552–553, 147 L. Ed. 2d 435, 120 S. Ct. 2348* (O'CONNOR, J., dissenting). The jury could not function as circuitbreaker in the State's machinery of justice if it were relegated to making a determination that the defendant at some point did something wrong, a mere preliminary to a judicial inquisition into the facts of the crime the State *actually* seeks to punish.

The second alternative is that legislatures may establish legally essential sentencing factors *within limits*—limits crossed when, perhaps, the sentencing factor is a "tail which wags the dog of the substantive offense." *McMillan, 477 U.S., at 88, 91 L. Ed. 2d 67, 106 S. Ct. 2411.* What this means in operation is that the law must not go *too far*—it must not exceed the judicial estimation of the proper role of the judge.

The subjectivity of this standard is obvious. Petitioner argued below that second-degree kidnaping with deliberate cruelty was essentially the same as first-degree kidnaping, the very charge he had avoided by pleading to a lesser offense. The court conceded this might be so but held it irrelevant. Petitioner's 90–month sentence exceeded the 53–month standard maximum by almost 70%; the Washington Supreme Court in other cases has upheld exceptional sentences 15 times the standard maximum. See *State v. Oxborrow, 106 Wn. 2d 525, 528, 533, 723 P.2d 1123, 1125, 1128 (1986)* (15–year exceptional sentence; 1–year standard maximum sentence); *State v. Branch, 129 Wn. 2d 635, 650, 919 P.2d 1228, 1235 (1996)* (4–year exceptional sentence; 3–month standard maximum sentence). Did the court go *too far* in any of these cases? There is no answer that legal analysis can provide. With *too far* as the yardstick, it is always possible to disagree with such judgments and never to refute them.

Another example of conversion from separate crime to sentence enhancement that JUSTICE O'CONNOR evidently does not consider going "too far" is the obstruction-of-justice enhancement, see *post*, at 6–7. Why perjury during trial should be grounds for a judicial sentence enhancement on the underlying offense, rather than an entirely separate offense to be found by a jury beyond a reasonable doubt (as it has been for centuries, see 4 W. Blackstone, Commentaries on the Laws of England 136–138 (1769)), is unclear.

Whether the *Sixth Amendment* incorporates this manipulable standard rather than *Apprendi*'s bright-line rule depends on the plausibility of the claim that the Framers would have left definition of the scope of jury power up to judges' intuitive sense of how far is *too far*. We think that claim not plausible at all, because the very reason the Framers put a jury-trial guarantee in the Constitution is that they were unwilling to trust government to mark out the role of the jury.

IV

... This case is not about whether determinate sentencing is constitutional, only about how it can be implemented in a way that respects the

Sixth Amendment. Several policies prompted Washington's adoption of determinate sentencing, including proportionality to the gravity of the offense and parity among defendants. See *Wash. Rev. Code Ann. § 9.94A.010* (2000). Nothing we have said impugns those salutary objectives.

Justice O'Connor argues that, because determinate sentencing schemes involving judicial factfinding entail less judicial discretion than indeterminate schemes, the constitutionality of the latter implies the constitutionality of the former. This argument is flawed on a number of levels. First, the *Sixth Amendment* by its terms is not a limitation on judicial power, but a reservation of jury power. It limits judicial power only to the extent that the claimed judicial power infringes on the province of the jury. Indeterminate sentencing does not do so. It increases judicial discretion, to be sure, but not at the expense of the jury's traditional function of finding the facts essential to lawful imposition of the penalty. Of course indeterminate schemes involve judicial factfinding, in that a judge (like a parole board) may implicitly rule on those facts he deems important to the exercise of his sentencing discretion. But the facts do not pertain to whether the defendant has a legal *right* to a lesser sentence—and that makes all the difference insofar as judicial impingement upon the traditional role of the jury is concerned. In a system that says the judge may punish burglary with 10 to 40 years, every burglar knows he is risking 40 years in jail. In a system that punishes burglary with a 10–year sentence, with another 30 added for use of a gun, the burglar who enters a home unarmed is *entitled* to no more than a 10–year sentence—and by reason of the *Sixth Amendment* the facts bearing upon that entitlement must be found by a jury.

But even assuming that restraint of judicial power unrelated to the jury's role is a *Sixth Amendment* objective, it is far from clear that *Apprendi* disserves that goal. Determinate judicial-factfinding schemes entail less judicial power than indeterminate schemes, but more judicial power than determinate *jury*-factfinding schemes. Whether *Apprendi* increases judicial power overall depends on what States with determinate judicial-factfinding schemes would do, given the choice between the two alternatives. Justice O'Connor simply assumes that the net effect will favor judges, but she has no empirical basis for that prediction. Indeed, what evidence we have points exactly the other way: When the Kansas Supreme Court found *Apprendi* infirmities in that State's determinate-sentencing regime in *State v. Gould, 271 Kan. 394, 404–414, 23 P. 3d 801, 809–814 (2001),* the legislature responded not by reestablishing indeterminate sentencing but by applying *Apprendi*'s requirements to its current regime. See *Kan. Stat. Ann. § 21–4718* (2003 Cum. Supp.). . . . The result was less, not more, judicial power.

Justice Breyer argues that *Apprendi* works to the detriment of criminal defendants who plead guilty by depriving them of the opportunity to argue sentencing factors to a judge. But nothing prevents a defendant from waiving his *Apprendi* rights. When a defendant pleads guilty, the State is free to seek judicial sentence enhancements so long as the defendant either stipulates to the relevant facts or consents to judicial factfinding. If appropriate waivers are procured, States may continue to offer judicial factfinding as a matter of course to all defendants who plead guilty. Even a defendant who stands trial may consent to judicial factfinding as to sentence enhancements, which may well be in his interest if relevant evidence would prejudice him at trial. We do not understand how *Apprendi* can possibly work to the detriment of those who are free, if they think its costs outweigh its benefits, to render it inapplicable.

Nor do we see any merit to JUSTICE BREYER'S contention that *Apprendi* is unfair to criminal defendants because, if States respond by enacting "17–element robbery crimes," prosecutors will have more elements with which to bargain.... Bargaining already exists with regard to sentencing factors because defendants can either stipulate or contest the facts that make them applicable. If there is any difference between bargaining over sentencing factors and bargaining over elements, the latter probably favors the defendant. Every new element that a prosecutor can threaten to charge is also an element that a defendant can threaten to contest at trial and make the prosecutor prove beyond a reasonable doubt. Moreover, given the sprawling scope of most criminal codes, and the power to affect sentences by making (even nonbinding) sentencing recommendations, there is already no shortage of *in terrorem* tools at prosecutors' disposal.... Any evaluation of *Apprendi*'s "fairness" to criminal defendants must compare it with the regime it replaced, in which a defendant, with no warning in either his indictment or plea, would routinely see his maximum potential sentence balloon from as little as five years to as much as life imprisonment, see *21 U.S.C. § § 841(b)(1)(A), (D),*[2] based not on facts proved to his peers beyond a reasonable doubt, but on facts extracted after trial from a report compiled by a probation officer who the judge thinks more likely got it right than got it wrong. We can conceive of no measure of fairness that would find more fault in the utterly speculative bargaining effects JUSTICE BREYER identifies than in the regime he champions. Suffice it to say that, if such a measure exists, it is not the one the Framers left us with.

* * *

JUSTICE BREYER also claims that *Apprendi* will attenuate the connection between "real criminal conduct and real punishment" by encouraging plea bargaining and by restricting alternatives to adversarial factfinding. The short answer to the former point (even assuming the questionable premise that *Apprendi* does encourage plea bargaining), is that the *Sixth Amendment* was not written for the benefit of those who choose to forgo its protection. It guarantees the *right* to jury trial. It does not guarantee that a particular number of jury trials will actually take place. That more defendants elect to waive that right (because, for example, government at the

---

2. To be sure, JUSTICE BREYER and the other dissenters would forbid those increases of sentence that violate the constitutional principle that tail shall not wag dog. The source of this principle is entirely unclear. Its precise effect, if precise effect it has, is presumably to require that the ratio of sentencing-factor add-on to basic criminal sentence be no greater than the ratio of caudal vertebrae to body in the breed of canine with the longest tail. Or perhaps no greater than the average such ratio for all breeds. Or perhaps the median. Regrettably, *Apprendi* has prevented full development of this line of jurisprudence.

moment is not particularly oppressive) does not prove that a constitutional provision guaranteeing *availability* of that option is disserved.

JUSTICE BREYER'S more general argument—that *Apprendi* undermines alternatives to adversarial factfinding—is not so much a criticism of *Apprendi* as an assault on jury trial generally. His esteem for "non-adversarial" truth-seeking processes, supports just as well an argument against either. Our Constitution and the common-law traditions it entrenches, however, do not admit the contention that facts are better discovered by judicial inquisition than by adversarial testing before a jury. See 3 Blackstone, Commentaries, at 373–374, 379–381. JUSTICE BREYER may be convinced of the equity of the regime he favors, but his views are not the ones we are bound to uphold.

Ultimately, our decision cannot turn on whether or to what degree trial by jury impairs the efficiency or fairness of criminal justice. One can certainly argue that both these values would be better served by leaving justice entirely in the hands of professionals; many nations of the world, particularly those following civil-law traditions, take just that course. There is not one shred of doubt, however, about the Framers' paradigm for criminal justice: not the civil-law ideal of administrative perfection, but the common-law ideal of limited state power accomplished by strict division of authority between judge and jury. As *Apprendi* held, every defendant has the *right* to insist that the prosecutor prove to a jury all facts legally essential to the punishment. Under the dissenters' alternative, he has no such right. That should be the end of the matter.

* * *

Petitioner was sentenced to prison for more than three years beyond what the law allowed for the crime to which he confessed, on the basis of a disputed finding that he had acted with "deliberate cruelty." The Framers would not have thought it too much to demand that, before depriving a man of three more years of his liberty, the State should suffer the modest inconvenience of submitting its accusation to "the unanimous suffrage of twelve of his equals and neighbours," rather than a lone employee of the State.

The judgment of the Washington Court of Appeals is reversed, and the case is remanded for further proceedings not inconsistent with this opinion.

* * *

■ JUSTICE O'CONNOR, with whom JUSTICE BREYER joins, and with whom THE CHIEF JUSTICE and JUSTICE KENNEDY join as to all but Part IV–B, dissenting.

The legacy of today's opinion, whether intended or not, will be the consolidation of sentencing power in the State and Federal Judiciaries. The Court says to Congress and state legislatures: If you want to constrain the sentencing discretion of judges and bring some uniformity to sentencing, it will cost you—dearly. Congress and States, faced with the burdens imposed by the extension of *Apprendi* to the present context, will either trim or eliminate altogether their sentencing guidelines schemes and, with them, 20 years of sentencing reform. It is thus of little moment that the majority does not expressly declare guidelines schemes unconstitutional, for, as residents of "*Apprendi*-land" are fond of saying, "the relevant inquiry is one not of form, but of effect." *Apprendi v. New Jersey, (2000)*. The "effect" of today's decision will be greater judicial discretion and less uniformity in sentencing. Because I find it implausible that the Framers would have considered such a result to be required by the *Due Process Clause* or the *Sixth Amendment*, and because the practical consequences of today's decision may be disastrous, I respectfully dissent.

I

One need look no further than the history leading up to and following the enactment of Washington's guidelines scheme to appreciate the damage that today's decision will cause. Prior to 1981, Washington, like most other States and the Federal Government, employed an indeterminate sentencing scheme. Washington's criminal code separated all felonies into three broad categories: "class A," carrying a sentence of 20 years to life; "class B," carrying a sentence of 0 to 10 years; and "class C," carrying a sentence of 0 to 5 years. Sentencing judges, in conjunction with parole boards, had virtually unfettered discretion to sentence defendants to prison terms falling anywhere within the statutory range, including probation—*i.e.*, no jail sentence at all....

This system of unguided discretion inevitably resulted in severe disparities in sentences received and served by defendants committing the same offense and having similar criminal histories.... Indeed, rather than reflect legally relevant criteria, these disparities too often were correlated with constitutionally suspect variables such as race. See also Breyer, The Federal Sentencing Guidelines and Key Compromises Upon Which They Rest, *17 Hofstra L. Rev. 1, 5 (1988)* (elimination of racial disparity one reason behind Congress' creation of the Federal Sentencing Commission).

To counteract these trends, the state legislature passed the *Sentencing Reform Act of 1981* .... The Act neither increased any of the statutory sentencing ranges for the three types of felonies (though it did eliminate the statutory mandatory minimum for class A felonies), nor reclassified any substantive offenses. It merely placed meaningful constraints on discretion to sentence offenders within the statutory ranges, and eliminated parole. There is thus no evidence that the legislature was attempting to manipulate the statutory elements of criminal offenses or to circumvent the procedural protections of the *Bill of Rights*. Rather, lawmakers were trying to bring some much-needed uniformity, transparency, and accountability to an otherwise " 'labyrinthine' sentencing and corrections system that 'lacked any principle except unguided discretion.' " (quoting F. Zimring, Making the Punishment Fit the Crime: A Consumers' Guide to Sentencing Reform, Occasional Paper No. 12, p. 6 (1977)).

Far from disregarding principles of due process and the jury trial right, as the majority today suggests, Washington's reform has served them. Before passage of the Act, a defendant charged with second degree kidnaping, like petitioner, had no idea whether he would receive a 10–year sentence or probation. The ultimate sentencing determination could turn as much on the idiosyncrasies of a particular judge as on the specifics of the defendant's crime or background. A defendant did not know what facts, if any, about his offense or his history would be considered relevant by the sentencing judge or by the parole board. After passage of the Act, a defendant charged with second degree kidnaping knows what his presumptive sentence will be; he has a good idea of the types of factors that a sentencing judge can and will consider when deciding whether to sentence him outside that range; he is guaranteed meaningful appellate review to protect against an arbitrary sentence. . . . Criminal defendants still face the same statutory maximum sentences, but they now at least know, much more than before, the real consequences of their actions.

Washington's move to a system of guided discretion has served equal protection principles as well. Over the past 20 years, there has been a substantial reduction in racial disparity in sentencing across the State. . . .

The majority does not, because it cannot, disagree that determinate sentencing schemes, like Washington's, serve important constitutional values. Thus, the majority says: "this case is not about whether determinate sentencing is constitutional, only about how it can be implemented in a way that respects the *Sixth Amendment*." But extension of *Apprendi* to the present context will impose significant costs on a legislature's determination that a particular fact, not historically an element, warrants a higher sentence. While not a constitutional prohibition on guidelines schemes, the majority's decision today exacts a substantial constitutional tax.

The costs are substantial and real. Under the majority's approach, any fact that increases the upper bound on a judge's sentencing discretion is an element of the offense. Thus, facts that historically have been taken into account by sentencing judges to assess a sentence within a broad range—such as drug quantity, role in the offense, risk of bodily harm—all must now be charged in an indictment and submitted to a jury, *In re Winship, 397 U.S. 358, 25 L. Ed. 2d 368, 90 S. Ct. 1068 (1970)*, simply because it is the legislature, rather than the judge, that constrains the extent to which such facts may be used to impose a sentence within a pre-existing statutory range.

While that alone is enough to threaten the continued use of sentencing guidelines schemes, there are additional costs. For example, a legislature might rightly think that some factors bearing on sentencing, such as prior bad acts or criminal history, should not be considered in a jury's determination of a defendant's guilt—such "character evidence" has traditionally been off limits during the guilt phase of criminal proceedings because of its tendency to inflame the passions of the jury. See, *e.g., Fed. Rule Evid. 404*; 1 E. Imwinkelried, P. Giannelli, F. Gilligan, & F. Leaderer, Courtroom Criminal Evidence 285 (3d ed. 1998). If a legislature desires uniform consideration of such factors at sentencing, but does not want them to impact a jury's initial determination of guilt, the State may have to bear the additional expense of a separate, full-blown jury trial during the penalty phase proceeding.

Some facts that bear on sentencing either will not be discovered, or are not discoverable, prior to trial. For instance, a legislature might desire that defendants who act in an obstructive manner during trial or post-trial proceedings receive a greater sentence than defendants who do not. See, *e.g.*, United States Sentencing Commission, Guidelines Manual, § 3C1.1 (Nov. 2003) (hereinafter USSG) (2–point increase in offense level for obstruction of justice). In such cases, the violation arises too late for the State to provide notice to the defendant or to argue the facts to the jury. A State wanting to make such facts relevant at sentencing must now either vest sufficient discretion in the judge to account for them *or* bring a separate criminal prosecution for obstruction of justice or perjury. And, the latter option is available only to the extent that a defendant's obstructive behavior is so severe as to constitute an already-existing separate offense, unless the legislature is willing to undertake the unlikely expense of criminalizing relatively minor obstructive behavior.

Likewise, not all facts that historically have been relevant to sentencing always will be known prior to trial. For instance, trial or sentencing proceedings of a drug distribution defendant might reveal that he sold primarily to children. Under the majority's approach, a State wishing such a revelation to result in a higher sentence within a pre-existing statutory range either must vest judges with sufficient discretion to account for it (and trust that they exercise that discretion) *or* bring a separate criminal prosecution. Indeed, the latter choice might not be available—a separate prosecution, if it is for an aggravated offense, likely would be barred altogether by the *Double Jeopardy Clause. Blockburger v. United States, 284 U.S. 299, 76 L. Ed. 306, 52 S. Ct. 180 (1932)* (cannot prosecute for separate offense unless the two offenses both have at least one element that the other does not).

The majority may be correct that States and the Federal Government will be willing to bear some of these costs. But simple economics dictate that they will not, and cannot, bear them all. To the extent that they do not, there will be an inevitable increase in judicial discretion with all of its attendant failings.

Washington's Sentencing Reform Act did not alter the statutory maximum sentence to which petitioner was exposed.

Petitioner was informed in the charging document, his plea agreement, and during his plea hearing that he faced a potential statutory maximum of 10 years in prison. The guidelines served due process by providing notice to petitioner of the consequences of his acts; they vindicated his jury trial right by informing him of the stakes of risking trial; they served equal protection by ensuring petitioner that invidious characteristics such as race would not impact his sentence.

Given these observations, it is difficult for me to discern what principle besides doctrinaire formalism actually motivates today's decision. The majority chides the *Apprendi* dissenters for preferring a nuanced interpretation of the *Due Process Clause and Sixth Amendment* jury trial guarantee that would generally defer to legislative labels while acknowledging the existence of constitutional constraints—what the majority calls the "the law must not go too far" approach. If indeed the choice is between adopting a balanced case-by-case approach that takes into consideration the values underlying the *Bill of Rights*, as well as the history of a particular sentencing reform law, and adopting a rigid rule that destroys everything in its path, I will choose the former. . . .

But even were one to accept formalism as a principle worth vindicating for its own sake, it would not explain *Apprendi*'s, or today's, result. A rule of deferring to legislative labels has no less formal pedigree. It would be more consistent with our decisions leading up to *Apprendi*, see *Almendarez-Torres v. United States, 523 U.S. 224, 140 L. Ed. 2d 350, 118 S. Ct. 1219 (1998)* (fact of prior conviction not an element of aggravated recidivist offense); *United States v. Watts, 519 U.S. 148, 136 L. Ed. 2d 554, 117 S. Ct. 633 (1997) (per curiam)* (acquittal of offense no bar to consideration of underlying conduct for purposes of guidelines enhancement); *Witte v. United States, 515 U.S. 389, 132 L. Ed. 2d 351, 115 S. Ct. 2199 (1995)* (facts increasing mandatory minimum sentence are not necessarily elements); and it would vest primary authority for defining crimes in the political branches, where it belongs. It also would be easier to administer than the majority's rule, inasmuch as courts would not be forced to look behind statutes and regulations to determine whether a particular fact does or does not increase the penalty to which a defendant was exposed.

The majority is correct that rigid adherence to such an approach *could conceivably* produce absurd results, but, as today's decision demonstrates, rigid adherence to the majority's approach *does and will continue* to produce results that disserve the very principles the majority purports to vindicate. The pre-*Apprendi* rule of deference to the legislature retains a built-in political check to prevent lawmakers from shifting the prosecution for crimes to the penalty phase proceedings of lesser included and easier-to-prove offenses—*e.g.*, the majority's hypothesized prosecution of murder in the guise of a traffic offense sentencing proceeding. There is no similar check, however, on application of the majority's " 'any fact that increases the upper bound of judicial discretion' " by courts.

* * *

IV

A

The consequences of today's decision will be as far reaching as they are disturbing. Washington's sentencing system is by no means unique. Numerous other States have enacted guidelines systems, as has the Federal Government. See, *e.g.*, *Alaska Stat. § 12.55.155 (2003); Ark. Code Ann. § 16–90–804 (Supp. 2003); Fla. Stat. § 921.0016 (2003); Kan. Stat. Ann. § 21–4701 et seq. (2003); Mich. Comp. Laws Ann. § 769.34* (West Supp. 2004); *Minn. Stat. § 244.10 (2002); N. C. Gen. Stat. § 15A–1340.16* (Lexis 2003); Ore. Admin. Rule § 213–008–0001 (2003); 204 Pa. Code § 303 *et seq.* (2004), reproduced following *42 Pa. Cons. Stat. Ann. § 9721* (Purden Supp. 2004); *18 U.S.C. § 3553; 28 U.S.C. § 991 et seq.* Today's decision casts constitutional doubt over them all and, in so doing, threatens an untold number of criminal judgments. Every sentence imposed under such guidelines in cases currently pending on direct appeal is in jeopardy. And, despite the fact that we hold in *Schriro v. Summerlin, post*, p. ___, that *Ring* (and *a fortiori Apprendi*) does not apply retroactively on habeas review, all criminal sentences imposed under the federal and state guidelines since *Apprendi* was decided in 2000 arguably remain open to collateral attack. . . .

The practical consequences for trial courts, starting today, will be equally unsettling: How are courts to mete out guidelines sentences? Do courts apply the guidelines as to mitigating factors, but not as to aggravating factors? Do they jettison the guidelines altogether? The Court ignores the havoc it is about to wreak on trial courts across the country.

* * *

What I have feared most has now come to pass: Over 20 years of sentencing reform are all but lost, and tens of thousands of criminal judgments are in jeopardy. *Apprendi, 530 U.S., at 549–559, 147 L. Ed. 2d 435, 120 S. Ct. 2348* (O'CONNOR, J., dissenting); *Ring, 536 U.S., at 619–621, 153 L. Ed. 2d 556, 122 S. Ct. 2428* (O'CONNOR, J., dissenting). I respectfully dissent.

■ JUSTICE KENNEDY, with whom JUSTICE BREYER joins, dissenting.

The majority opinion does considerable damage to our laws and to the administration of the criminal justice system for all the reasons well stated in JUSTICE O'CONNOR'S dissent, plus one more: The Court, in my respectful submission, disregards the fundamental principle under our constitutional system that different branches of government "converse with each other on matters of vital common interest." *Mistretta v. United States, 488 U.S. 361, 408, 102 L. Ed. 2d 714, 109 S. Ct. 647 (1989).* As the Court in *Mistretta* explained, the Constitution establishes a system of government that pre-supposes, not just " 'autonomy' " and " 'separateness,' " but also " 'inter-dependence' " and " 'reciprocity.' " *Id., at 381, 102 L. Ed. 2d 714, 109 S. Ct. 647* (quoting *Youngstown Sheet & Tube Co. v. Sawyer, 343 U.S. 579, 635, 96 L. Ed. 1153, 72 S. Ct. 863, 62 Ohio Law Abs. 417 (1952)* (Jackson, J., concurring)). Constant, constructive discourse between our courts and our legislatures is an integral and admirable part of the constitutional design. Case-by-case judicial determinations often yield intelligible patterns that can be refined by legislatures and codified into statutes or rules as general standards. As these legislative enactments are followed by incremental judicial interpretation, the legislatures may respond again, and the cycle repeats. This recurring dialogue, an essential source for the elaboration and the evolution of the law, is basic constitutional theory in action.

Sentencing guidelines are a prime example of this collaborative process. Dissatisfied with the wide disparity in sentencing, participants in the criminal justice system, including judges, pressed for legislative reforms. In response, legislators drew from these participants' shared experiences and enacted measures to correct the problems, which, as JUSTICE O'CONNOR explains, could sometimes rise to the level of a constitutional injury. As *Mistretta* recognized, this interchange among different actors in the constitutional scheme is consistent with the Constitution's structural protections.

To be sure, this case concerns the work of a state legislature, and not of Congress. If anything, however, this distinction counsels even greater judicial caution. Unlike *Mistretta*, the case here implicates not just the collective wisdom of legislators on the other side of the continuing dialogue over fair sentencing, but also the interest of the States to serve as laboratories for innovation and experiment. See *New State Ice Co. v. Liebmann, 285 U.S. 262, 311, 76 L. Ed. 747, 52 S. Ct. 371 (1932)* (Brandeis,

J., dissenting). With no apparent sense of irony that the effect of today's decision is the destruction of a sentencing scheme devised by democratically elected legislators, the majority shuts down alternative, nonjudicial, sources of ideas and experience. It does so under a faintly disguised distrust of judges and their purported usurpation of the jury's function in criminal trials. It tells not only trial judges who have spent years studying the problem but also legislators who have devoted valuable time and resources "calling upon the accumulated wisdom and experience of the Judicial Branch ... on a matter uniquely within the ken of judges," *Mistretta, supra, at 412, 102 L. Ed. 2d 714, 109 S. Ct. 647*, that their efforts and judgments were all for naught. Numerous States that have enacted sentencing guidelines similar to the one in Washington State are now commanded to scrap everything and start over.

* * *

■ Justice Breyer, with whom Justice O'Connor joins, dissenting.

The Court makes clear that it means what it said in *Apprendi v. New Jersey, 530 U.S. 466, 147 L. Ed. 2d 435, 120 S. Ct. 2348 (2000)*. In its view, the *Sixth Amendment* says that " 'any fact that increases the penalty for a crime beyond the prescribed statutory maximum must be submitted to a jury.' " *Ante*, at 5 (quoting *Apprendi, supra, at 490, 147 L. Ed. 2d 435, 120 S. Ct. 2348*). " 'Prescribed statutory maximum' " means the penalty that the relevant statute authorizes "solely on the basis of the facts reflected in the jury verdict." *Ante*, at 7 (emphasis deleted). Thus, a jury must find, not only the facts that make up the crime of which the offender is charged, but also all (punishment-increasing) facts about the *way* in which the offender carried out that crime.

It is not difficult to understand the impulse that produced this holding. Imagine a classic example—a statute (or mandatory sentencing guideline) that provides a 10–year sentence for ordinary bank robbery, but a 15–year sentence for bank robbery committed with a gun. One might ask why it should matter for jury trial purposes whether the statute (or guideline) labels the gun's presence (a) a *sentencing fact* about the way in which the offender carried out the *lesser* crime of ordinary bank robbery, or (b) a factual *element* of the *greater* crime of bank robbery with a gun? If the *Sixth Amendment* requires a jury finding about the gun in the latter circumstance, why should it not also require a jury to find the same fact in the former circumstance? The two sets of circumstances are functionally identical. In both instances, identical punishment follows from identical factual findings (related to, *e.g.*, a bank, a taking, a thing-of-value, force or threat of force, and a gun). The only difference between the two circumstances concerns a legislative (or Sentencing Commission) decision about which *label* ("sentencing fact" or "element of a greater crime") to affix to one of the facts, namely, the presence of the gun, that will lead to the greater sentence. Given the identity of circumstances apart from the label, the jury's traditional factfinding role, and the law's insistence upon treating like cases alike, why should the legislature's labeling choice make an important *Sixth Amendment* difference?

The Court in *Apprendi,* and now here, concludes that it should not make a difference. The *Sixth Amendment's* jury trial guarantee applies similarly to both. I agree with the majority's analysis, but not with its conclusion. That is to say, I agree that, classically speaking, the difference between a traditional sentencing factor and an element of a greater offense often comes down to a legislative choice about which label to affix. But I cannot jump from there to the conclusion that the *Sixth Amendment* always requires identical treatment of the two scenarios. That jump is fraught with consequences that threaten the fairness of our traditional criminal justice system; it distorts historical sentencing or criminal trial practices; and it upsets settled law on which legislatures have relied in designing punishment systems.

* * *

The majority ignores the adverse consequences inherent in its conclusion. As a result of the majority's rule, sentencing must now take one of three forms, each of which risks either impracticality, unfairness, or harm to the jury trial right the majority purports to strengthen. This circumstance shows that the majority's *Sixth Amendment* interpretation cannot be right.

A

A first option for legislators is to create a simple, pure or nearly pure "charge offense" or "determinate" sentencing system. See Breyer, The Federal Sentencing Guidelines and the Key Compromises upon Which They Rest, *17 Hofstra L. Rev. 1, 8–9 (1988).* In such a system, an indictment would charge a few facts which, taken together, constitute a crime, such as robbery. Robbery would carry a single sentence, say, five years' imprisonment. And every person convicted of robbery would receive that sentence— just as, centuries ago, everyone convicted of almost any serious crime was sentenced to death. See, *e.g.,* Lillquist, The Puzzling Return of Jury Sentencing: Misgivings About *Apprendi, 82 N. C. L. Rev. 621, 630 (2004).*

Such a system assures uniformity, but at intolerable costs. First, simple determinate sentencing systems impose identical punishments on people who committed their crimes in very different ways. When dramatically different conduct ends up being punished the same way, an injustice has taken place. Simple determinate sentencing has the virtue of treating like cases alike, but it simultaneously fails to treat different cases differently. Some commentators have leveled this charge at sentencing guideline systems themselves. See, *e.g.,* Schulhofer, Assessing the Federal Sentencing Process: The Problem Is Uniformity, Not Disparity, *29 Am. Crim. L. Rev. 833, 847 (1992)* (arguing that the "most important problem under the [Federal] Guidelines system is not too much disparity, but rather excessive uniformity" and arguing for adjustments, including elimination of mandatory minimums, to make the Guidelines system more responsive to relevant differences). The charge is doubly applicable to simple "pure charge" systems that permit no departures from the prescribed sentences, even in extraordinary cases.

Second, in a world of statutorily fixed mandatory sentences for many crimes, determinate sentencing gives tremendous power to prosecutors to manipulate sentences through their choice of charges. Prosecutors can simply charge, or threaten to charge, defendants with crimes bearing higher mandatory sentences. Defendants, knowing that they will not have a chance to argue for a lower sentence in front of a judge, may plead to charges that they might otherwise contest. Considering that most criminal cases do not go to trial and resolution by plea bargaining is the norm, the rule of *Apprendi*, to the extent it results in a return to determinate sentencing, threatens serious unfairness. See Bibas, Judicial Fact–Finding and Sentence Enhancements in a World of Guilty Pleas, *110 Yale L. J. 1097, 1100–1101 (2001)* (explaining that the rule of *Apprendi* hurts defendants by depriving them of sentencing hearings, "the only hearings they were likely to have"; forcing defendants to surrender sentencing issues like drug quantity when they agree to the plea; and transferring power to prosecutors).

B

A second option for legislators is to return to a system of indeterminate sentencing. . . . Under indeterminate systems, the length of the sentence is entirely or almost entirely within the discretion of the judge or of the parole board, which typically has broad power to decide when to release a prisoner.

When such systems were in vogue, they were criticized, and rightly so, for producing unfair disparities, including race-based disparities, in the punishment of similarly situated defendants. The length of time a person spent in prison appeared to depend on "what the judge ate for breakfast" on the day of sentencing, on which judge you got, or on other factors that should not have made a difference to the length of the sentence. . . . And under such a system, the judge could vary the sentence greatly based upon his findings about how the defendant had committed the crime—findings that might not have been made by a "preponderance of the evidence," much less "beyond a reasonable doubt." . . .

Returning to such a system would . . . do little to "ensure [the] control" of what the majority calls "the peopl[e,]" *i.e.*, the jury, "in the judiciary," since "the people" would only decide the defendant's guilt, a finding with no effect on the duration of the sentence. While "the judge's authority to sentence" would formally derive from the jury's verdict, the jury would exercise little or no control over the sentence itself. It is difficult to see how such an outcome protects the structural safeguards the majority claims to be defending.

C

A third option is that which the Court seems to believe legislators will in fact take. That is the option of retaining structured schemes that attempt to punish similar conduct similarly and different conduct differently, but modifying them to conform to *Apprendi*'s dictates. Judges would be able to depart *downward* from presumptive sentences upon finding that mitigating factors were present, but would not be able to depart *upward* unless the prosecutor charged the aggravating fact to a jury and proved it beyond a reasonable doubt. The majority argues, based on the single example of Kansas, that most legislatures will enact amendments along these lines in the face of the oncoming *Apprendi* train. It is therefore worth exploring how this option could work in practice, as well as the assumptions on which it depends.

1

This option can be implemented in one of two ways. The first way would be for legislatures to subdivide each crime into a list of complex crimes, each of which would be defined to include commonly found sentencing factors such as drug quantity, type of victim, presence of violence, degree of injury, use of gun, and so on. A legislature, for example, might enact a robbery statute, modeled on robbery sentencing guidelines, that increases punishment depending upon (1) the nature of the institution robbed, (2) the (a) presence of, (b) brandishing of, (c) other use of, a firearm, (3) making of a death threat, (4) presence of (a) ordinary, (b) serious, (c) permanent or life threatening, bodily injury, (5) abduction, (6) physical restraint, (7) taking of a firearm, (8) taking of drugs, (9) value of property loss, etc. Cf. United States Sentencing Commission, Guidelines Manual § 2B3.1 (Nov. 2003) (hereinafter USSG).

This possibility is, of course, merely a highly calibrated form of the "pure charge" system discussed in Part I–A, *supra*. And it suffers from some of the same defects. The prosecutor, through control of the precise charge, controls the punishment, thereby marching the sentencing system directly away from, not toward, one important guideline goal: rough uniformity of punishment for those who engage in roughly the same *real* criminal conduct. The artificial (and consequently unfair) nature of the resulting sentence is aggravated by the fact that prosecutors must charge all relevant facts about the way the crime was committed before a presentence investigation examines the criminal conduct, perhaps before the trial itself, *i.e.,* before many of the facts relevant to punishment are known.

This "complex charge offense" system also prejudices defendants who seek trial, for it can put them in the untenable position of contesting material aggravating facts in the guilt phases of their trials. Consider a defendant who is charged, not with mere possession of cocaine, but with the specific offense of possession of more than 500 grams of cocaine. Or consider a defendant charged, not with murder, but with the new crime of murder using a machete. Or consider a defendant whom the prosecution wants to claim was a "supervisor," rather than an ordinary gang member. How can a Constitution that guarantees due process put these defendants, as a matter of course, in the position of arguing, "I did not sell drugs, and if I did, I did not sell more than 500 grams" or, "I did not kill him, and if I did, I did not use a machete," or "I did not engage in gang activity, and certainly not as a supervisor" to a single jury? The system can tolerate this kind of problem up to a point (consider the defendant who wants to argue innocence, and, in the alternative, second-degree, not first-degree, murder). But a rereading of the many distinctions made in a typical robbery guideline, suggests that an effort to incorporate any real set of guidelines in a complex statute would reach well beyond that point.

The majority announces that there really is no problem here because "States may continue to offer judicial factfinding as a matter of course to all defendants who plead guilty" and defendants may "stipulate to the relevant facts or consent to judicial factfinding." The problem, of course, concerns defendants who do not want to plead guilty to those elements that, until recently, were commonly thought of as sentencing factors. As to those defendants, the fairness problem arises because States may very well decide that they will *not* permit defendants to carve subsets of facts out of the new, *Apprendi*-required 17–element robbery crime, seeking a judicial determination as to some of those facts and a jury determination as to others. Instead, States may simply require defendants to plead guilty to all 17 elements or proceed with a (likely prejudicial) trial on all 17 elements.

The majority does not deny that States may make this choice; it simply fails to understand *why* any State would want to exercise it. The answer is, as I shall explain in a moment, that the alternative may prove too expensive and unwieldy for States to provide. States that offer defendants the option of judicial factfinding as to some facts (*i.e.,* sentencing facts), say, because of fairness concerns, will also have to offer the defendant a second sentencing jury—just as Kansas has done. I therefore turn to that alternative.

2

The second way to make sentencing guidelines *Apprendi*-compliant would be to require at least two juries for each defendant whenever aggravating facts are present: one jury to determine guilt of the crime charged, and an additional jury to try the disputed facts that, if found, would aggravate the sentence. Our experience with bifurcated trials in the capital punishment context suggests that requiring them for run-of-the-mill sentences would be costly, both in money and in judicial time and resources. Cf. Kozinski & Gallagher, Death: The Ultimate Run–On Sentence, *46 Case W. Res. L. Rev. 1, 13–15,* and n. 64 (1995) (estimating the costs of each capital case at around $1 million more than each noncapital case); Tabak, How Empirical Studies Can Affect Positively the Politics of the Death Penalty, *83 Cornell L. Rev. 1431, 1439–1440 (1998)* (attributing the greater cost of death penalty cases in part to bifurcated proceedings). In the context of noncapital crimes, the potential need for a second indictment alleging aggravating facts, the likely need for formal evidentiary rules to prevent prejudice, and the increased difficulty of obtaining relevant sentencing information, all will mean greater complexity, added cost, and further delay. Indeed, cost and delay could lead legislatures to revert to the complex charge offense system described in Part I–C–1, *supra.*

The majority refers to an *amicus curiae* brief filed by the Kansas Appellate Defender Office, which suggests that a two-jury system has proved workable in Kansas. And that may be so. But in all likelihood, any such workability reflects an uncomfortable fact, a fact at which the majority hints, *ante,* at 14, but whose constitutional implications it does not seem to grasp. The uncomfortable fact that could make the system seem workable—even desirable in the minds of some, including defense attorneys—is called "plea bargaining." See Bibas, *110 Yale L. J., at 1150*, and n. 330 (reporting that in 1996, fewer than 4% of adjudicated state felony defendants have jury trials, 5% have bench trials, and 91% plead guilty). See also *ante,* at 14 (making clear that plea bargaining applies). The Court can announce that the Constitution requires at least two jury trials for each criminal defendant—one for guilt, another for sentencing—but only because it knows full well that more than 90% of defendants will not go to trial even once, much less insist on two or more trials.

What will be the consequences of the Court's holding for the 90% of defendants who do not go to trial? The truthful answer is that we do not know. Some defendants may receive bargaining advantages if the increased cost of the "double jury trial" guarantee makes prosecutors more willing to cede certain sentencing issues to the defense. Other defendants may be hurt if a "single-jury-decides-all" approach makes them more reluctant to risk a trial—perhaps because they want to argue that they did not know what was in the cocaine bag, that it was a small amount regardless, that they were unaware a confederate had a gun, etc. See Bibas, *110 Yale L. J., at 1100* ("Because for many defendants going to trial is not a desirable option, they are left without any real hearings at all"); *id., at 1151* ("The trial right does little good when most defendants do not go to trial").

At the least, the greater expense attached to trials and their greater complexity, taken together in the context of an overworked criminal justice system, will likely mean, other things being equal, fewer trials and a greater reliance upon plea bargaining—a system in which punishment is set not by judges or juries but by advocates acting under bargaining constraints. At the same time, the greater power of the prosecutor to control the punishment through the charge would likely weaken the relation between real conduct and real punishment as well. See, *e.g.,* Schulhofer, *29 Am. Crim. L. Rev., at 845* (estimating that evasion of the proper sentence under the Federal Guidelines may now occur in 20%–35% of all guilty plea cases). Even if the Court's holding does not further embed plea-bargaining practices (as I fear it will), its success depends upon the existence of present practice. I do not understand how the *Sixth Amendment* could *require* a sentencing system that will work in practice only if no more than a handful of defendants exercise their right to a jury trial.

The majority's only response is to state that "bargaining over elements . . . probably favors the defendant," adding that many criminal defense lawyers favor its position. But the basic problem is not one of "fairness" to defendants or, for that matter, "fairness" to prosecutors. Rather, it concerns the greater fairness of a sentencing system that a more uniform correspondence between real criminal conduct and real punishment helps to create. At a minimum, a two-jury system, by preventing a judge from taking account of an aggravating fact without the prosecutor's acquiescence, would undercut, if not nullify, legislative efforts to ensure through guidelines that punishments reflect a convicted offender's real criminal conduct, rather than that portion of the offender's conduct that a prosecutor decides to charge and prove.

Efforts to tie real punishment to real conduct are not new. They are embodied in well-established pre-guidelines sentencing practices—practices under which a judge, looking at a presentence report, would seek to tailor the sentence in significant part to fit the criminal conduct in which the offender actually engaged. For more than a century, questions of *punishment* (not those of guilt or innocence) have reflected determinations made, not only by juries, but also by judges, probation officers, and executive parole boards. Such truth-seeking determinations have rested upon both adversarial and non-adversarial processes. The Court's holding undermines efforts to reform these processes, for it means that legislatures cannot *both* permit judges to base sentencing upon real conduct *and* seek, through guidelines, to make the results more uniform.

In these and other ways, the two-jury system would work a radical change in pre-existing criminal law. It is not surprising that this Court has never previously suggested that the Constitution—outside the unique context of the death penalty—might require bifurcated jury-based sentencing. And it is the impediment the Court's holding poses to legislative efforts to achieve that greater systematic fairness that casts doubt on its constitutional validity.

D

Is there a fourth option? Perhaps. Congress and state legislatures might, for example, rewrite their criminal codes, attaching astronomically high sentences to each crime, followed by long lists of mitigating facts, which, for the most part, would consist of the absence of aggravating facts.... But political impediments to legislative action make such rewrites difficult to achieve; and it is difficult to see why the *Sixth Amendment* would require legislatures to undertake them.

It may also prove possible to find combinations of, or variations upon, my first three options. But I am unaware of any variation that does not involve (a) the shift of power to the prosecutor (weakening the connection between real conduct and real punishment) inherent in any charge offense system, (b) the lack of uniformity inherent in any system of pure judicial discretion, or (c) the complexity, expense, and increased reliance on plea bargains involved in a "two-jury" system. The simple fact is that the design of any fair sentencing system must involve efforts to make practical compromises among competing goals. The majority's reading of the *Sixth Amendment* makes the effort to find those compromises—already difficult—virtually impossible.

II

* * *

Given history's silence on the question of laws that structure a judge's discretion within the range provided by the legislatively labeled maximum term, it is not surprising that our modern, pre-*Apprendi* cases made clear that legislatures could, within broad limits, distinguish between "sentencing facts" and "elements of crimes." See *McMillan, 477 U.S., at 85–88, 91 L. Ed. 2d 67, 106 S. Ct. 2411.* By their choice of label, legislatures could indicate whether a judge or a jury must make the relevant factual determination. History does not preclude legislatures from making this decision. And, as I argued in Part I, *supra,* allowing legislatures to structure sentencing in this way has the dual effect of enhancing and giving meaning to the *Sixth Amendment's* jury trial right as to core crimes, while affording additional due process to defendants in the form of sentencing hearings before judges—hearings the majority's rule will eliminate for many.

Is there a risk of unfairness involved in permitting Congress to make this labeling decision? Of course. As we have recognized, the "tail" of the sentencing fact might "wag the dog of the substantive offense." *McMillan, supra, at 88, 91 L. Ed. 2d 67, 106 S. Ct. 2411.* Congress might permit a judge to sentence an individual for murder though convicted only of making an illegal lane change. See *ante,* at 10 (majority opinion). But that is the kind of problem that the *Due Process Clause* is well suited to cure. *McMillan* foresaw the possibility that judges would have to use their own judgment in dealing with such a problem; but that is what judges are there for. And, as Part I, *supra,* makes clear, the alternatives are worse—not only practically, but, although the majority refuses to admit it, constitutionally as well.

Historic practice . . . does not compel the result the majority reaches. And constitutional concerns counsel the opposite.

III

The majority also overlooks important institutional considerations. Congress and the States relied upon what they believed was their constitutional power to decide, within broad limits, whether to make a particular fact (a) a sentencing factor or (b) an element in a greater crime. They relied upon *McMillan* as guaranteeing the constitutional validity of that proposition. They created sentencing reform, an effort to change the criminal justice system so that it reflects systematically not simply upon guilt or innocence but also upon what should be done about this now-guilty offender. Those efforts have spanned a generation. They have led to state sentencing guidelines and the Federal Sentencing Guideline system.... These systems are imperfect and they yield far from perfect results, but I cannot believe the Constitution forbids the state legislatures and Congress to adopt such systems and to try to improve them over time. Nor can I believe that the Constitution hamstrings legislatures in the way that JUSTICE O'CONNOR and I have discussed.

IV

Now, let us return to the question I posed at the outset. Why does the *Sixth Amendment* permit a jury trial right (in respect to a particular fact) to depend upon a legislative labeling decision, namely, the legislative decision to label the fact a *sentencing fact,* instead of an *element of the crime?* The answer is that the fairness and effectiveness of a sentencing system, and the related fairness and effectiveness of the criminal justice system itself, depends upon the legislature's possessing the constitutional authority (within due process limits) to make that labeling decision. To restrict radically the legislature's power in this respect, as the majority interprets the *Sixth Amendment* to do, prevents the legislature from seeking sentencing systems that are consistent with, and indeed may help to advance, the Constitution's greater fairness goals.

To say this is not simply to express concerns about fairness to defendants. It is also to express concerns about the serious practical (or impractical) changes that the Court's decision seems likely to impose upon the criminal process; about the tendency of the Court's decision to embed further plea bargaining processes that lack transparency and too often mean nonuniform, sometimes arbitrary, sentencing practices; about the obstacles the Court's decision poses to legislative efforts to bring about greater uniformity between real criminal conduct and real punishment; and ultimately about the limitations that the Court imposes upon legislatures' ability to make democratic legislative decisions. Whatever the faults of guidelines systems—and there are many—they are more likely to find their cure in legislation emerging from the experience of, and discussion among, all elements of the criminal justice community, than in a virtually unchangeable constitutional decision of this Court.

V

Taken together these three sets of considerations, concerning consequences, concerning history, concerning institutional reliance, leave me where I was in *Apprendi, i.e.,* convinced that the Court is wrong. Until now, I would have thought the Court might have limited *Apprendi* so that its underlying principle would not undo sentencing reform efforts. Today's case dispels that illusion. At a minimum, the case sets aside numerous state efforts in that direction. Perhaps the Court will distinguish the Federal Sentencing Guidelines, but I am uncertain how. As a result of today's decision, federal prosecutors, like state prosecutors, must decide what to do next, how to handle tomorrow's case.

Consider some of the matters that federal prosecutors must know about, or guess about, when they prosecute their next case: (1) Does today's decision apply in full force to the Federal Sentencing Guidelines? (2) If so, must the initial indictment contain all sentencing factors, charged as "elements" of the crime? (3) What, then, are the evidentiary rules? Can the prosecution continue to use, say presentence reports, with their conclusions reflecting layers of hearsay? Cf. *Crawford v. Washington, 541 U.S. 36, ___, ___-___, 158 L. Ed. 2d 177, 124 S. Ct. 1354 (2004) (slip op., at 27, 32–33)* (clarifying the *Sixth Amendment's* requirement of confrontation with respect to testimonial hearsay). Are the numerous cases of this Court holding that a sentencing judge may consider virtually any reliable information still good law when juries, not judges, are required to determine the matter? See, *e.g., United States v. Watts, 519 U.S. 148, 153–157, 136 L. Ed. 2d 554, 117 S. Ct. 633 (1997) (per curiam)* (evidence of conduct of which the defendant has been acquitted may be considered at sentencing). Cf. *Witte v. United States, 515 U.S. 389, 399–401, 132 L. Ed. 2d 351, 115 S. Ct. 2199 (1995)* (evidence of uncharged criminal conduct used in determining sentence). (4) How are juries to deal with highly complex or open-ended Sentencing Guidelines obviously written for application by an experienced trial judge? See, *e.g.,* USSG § 3B1.1 (requiring a greater sentence when the defendant was a leader of a criminal activity that involved four or more

participants or was *"otherwise extensive"* (emphasis added)); § § 3D1.1–
3D1.2 (highly complex "multiple count" rules); § 1B1.3 (relevant conduct
rules).

Ordinarily, this Court simply waits for cases to arise in which it can
answer such questions. But this case affects tens of thousands of criminal
prosecutions, including federal prosecutions. Federal prosecutors will proceed with those prosecutions subject to the risk that all defendants in those
cases will have to be sentenced, perhaps tried, anew. Given this consequence and the need for certainty, I would not proceed further piecemeal;
rather, I would call for further argument on the ramifications of the
concerns I have raised. But that is not the Court's view.

For the reasons given, I dissent.

United States v. Booker

Supreme Court of the United States.
___ U.S. ___, 125 S.Ct. 738 (2005).

* * *

■ JUSTICE STEVENS delivered the opinion of the Court in part.

JUSTICE SCALIA, JUSTICE SOUTER, JUSTICE THOMAS, and JUSTICE GINSBURG join
this opinion.

The question presented in each of these cases is whether an application
of the Federal Sentencing Guidelines violated the *Sixth Amendment*. In
each case, the courts below held that binding rules set forth in the
Guidelines limited the severity of the sentence that the judge could lawfully
impose on the defendant based on the facts found by the jury at his trial. In
both cases the courts rejected, on the basis of our decision in *Blakely v.
Washington,* the Government's recommended application of the Sentencing
Guidelines because the proposed sentences were based on additional facts
that the sentencing judge found by a preponderance of the evidence. We
hold that both courts correctly concluded that the *Sixth Amendment* as
construed in *Blakely* does apply to the Sentencing Guidelines. In a separate
opinion authored by Justice Breyer, the Court concludes that in light of
this holding, two provisions of the *Sentencing Reform Act of 1984* (SRA)
that have the effect of making the Guidelines mandatory must be invalidated in order to allow the statute to operate in a manner consistent with
congressional intent.

I

Respondent Booker was charged with possession with intent to distribute at least 50 grams of cocaine base (crack). Having heard evidence that
he had 92.5 grams in his duffel bag, the jury found him guilty of violating
21 U.S.C. § 841(a)(1) [21 USCS § 841(a)(1)]. That statute prescribes a
minimum sentence of 10 years in prison and a maximum sentence of life
for that offense. *§ 841(b)(1)(A)(iii).*

Based upon Booker's criminal history and the quantity of drugs found
by the jury, the Sentencing Guidelines required the District Court Judge to

select a "base" sentence of not less than 210 nor more than 262 months in prison. The judge, however, held a post-trial sentencing proceeding and concluded by a preponderance of the evidence that Booker had possessed an additional 566 grams of crack and that he was guilty of obstructing justice. Those findings mandated that the judge select a sentence between 360 months and life imprisonment; the judge imposed a sentence at the low end of the range. Thus, instead of the sentence of 21 years and 10 months that the judge could have imposed on the basis of the facts proved to the jury beyond a reasonable doubt, Booker received a 30–year sentence.

Over the dissent of Judge Easterbrook, the Court of Appeals for the Seventh Circuit held that this application of the Sentencing Guidelines conflicted with our holding in *Apprendi v. New Jersey, (2000)*, that "[o]ther than the fact of a prior conviction, any fact that increases the penalty for a crime beyond the prescribed statutory maximum must be submitted to a jury, and proved beyond a reasonable doubt." The majority relied on our holding in *Blakely v. Washington, (2004)*, that "the 'statutory maximum' for *Apprendi* purposes is the maximum sentence a judge may impose *solely on the basis of the facts reflected in the jury verdict or admitted by the defendant.*" The court held that the sentence violated the *Sixth Amendment*, and remanded with instructions to the District Court either to sentence respondent within the sentencing range supported by the jury's findings or to hold a separate sentencing hearing before a jury.

Respondent Fanfan was charged with conspiracy to distribute and to possess with intent to distribute at least 500 grams of cocaine in violation of *21 USC § § 846, 841(a)(1)*, and *841(b)(1)(B)(ii) [21 USCS § § 846, 841(a)(1)*, and 841(b)(1)(B)(ii)]. He was convicted by the jury after it answered "Yes" to the question "Was the amount of cocaine 500 or more grams?" Under the Guidelines, without additional findings of fact, the maximum sentence authorized by the jury verdict was imprisonment for 78 months.

A few days after our decision in *Blakely*, the trial judge conducted a sentencing hearing at which he found additional facts that, under the Guidelines, would have authorized a sentence in the 188–to–235 month range. Specifically, he found that respondent Fanfan was responsible for 2.5 kilograms of cocaine powder, and 261.6 grams of crack. He also concluded that respondent had been an organizer, leader, manager, or supervisor in the criminal activity. Both findings were made by a preponderance of the evidence. Under the Guidelines, these additional findings would have required an enhanced sentence of 15 or 16 years instead of the 5 or 6 years authorized by the jury verdict alone. Relying not only on the majority opinion in *Blakely*, but also on the categorical statements in the dissenting opinions and in the Solicitor General's brief in *Blakely*, the judge concluded that he could not follow the particular provisions of the Sentencing Guidelines "which involve drug quantity and role enhancement." Expressly refusing to make "any blanket decision about the federal guidelines," he followed the provisions of the Guidelines that did not implicate the *Sixth Amendment* by imposing a sentence on respondent "based solely upon the guilty verdict in this case." *Ibid.*

* * *

In ... petitions, the Government asks us to determine whether our *Apprendi* line of cases applies to the Sentencing Guidelines, and if so, what portions of the Guidelines remain in effect.

The questions presented are:

"1. Whether the *Sixth Amendment* is violated by the imposition of an enhanced sentence under the United States Sentencing Guidelines based on the sentencing judge's determination of a fact (other than a prior conviction) that was not found by the jury or admitted by the defendant.

"2. If the answer to the first question is 'yes,' the following question is presented: whether, in a case in which the Guidelines would require the court to find a sentence-enhancing fact, the Sentencing Guidelines as a whole would be inapplicable, as a matter of severability analysis, such that the sentencing court must exercise its discretion to sentence the defendant within the maximum and minimum set by statute for the offense of conviction." Pet. for Cert. (I).

In this opinion, we explain why we agree with the lower courts' answer to the first question. In a separate opinion for the Court, Justice Breyer explains the Court's answer to the second question.

II

* * *

In Blakely v. Washington, 542 U.S. 296, 124 S.Ct. 2531 (2004), we dealt with a determinate sentencing scheme similar to the Federal Sentencing Guidelines.

* * *

As the dissenting opinions in *Blakely* recognized, there is no distinction of constitutional significance between the Federal Sentencing Guidelines and the Washington procedures at issue in that case.... This conclusion rests on the premise, common to both systems, that the relevant sentencing rules are mandatory and impose binding requirements on all sentencing judges.

If the Guidelines as currently written could be read as merely advisory provisions that recommended, rather than required, the selection of particular sentences in response to differing sets of facts, their use would not implicate the *Sixth Amendment*. We have never doubted the authority of a judge to exercise broad discretion in imposing a sentence within a statutory range. See *Apprendi*; *Williams v. New York, (1949)*. Indeed, everyone agrees that the constitutional issues presented by these cases would have been avoided entirely if Congress had omitted from the SRA the provisions that make the Guidelines binding on district judges; it is that circumstance that makes the Court's answer to the second question presented possible. For when a trial judge exercises his discretion to select a specific sentence within a defined range, the defendant has no right to a jury determination of the facts that the judge deems relevant.

The Guidelines as written, however, are not advisory; they are mandatory and binding on all judges. While subsection (a) of § 3553 of the sentencing statute lists the Sentencing Guidelines as one factor to be considered in imposing a sentence, subsection (b) directs that the court "*shall* impose a sentence of the kind, and within the range" established by the Guidelines, subject to departures in specific, limited cases. Because they are binding on judges, we have consistently held that the Guidelines have the force and effect of laws. See, e.g., Mistretta v. United States.

The availability of a departure in specified circumstances does not avoid the constitutional issue, just as it did not in *Blakely* itself. The Guidelines permit departures from the prescribed sentencing range in cases in which the judge "finds that there exists an aggravating or mitigating circumstance of a kind, or to a degree, not adequately taken into consideration by the Sentencing Commission in formulating the guidelines that should result in a sentence different from that described." ... Importantly, however, departures are not available in every case, and in fact are unavailable in most. In most cases, as a matter of law, the Commission will have adequately taken all relevant factors into account, and no departure will be legally permissible. In those instances, the judge is bound to impose a sentence within the Guidelines range.

* * *

Booker's is a run-of-the-mill drug case, and does not present any factors that were inadequately considered by the Commission. The sentencing judge would therefore have been reversed had he not imposed a sentence within the level 32 Guidelines range.

Booker's actual sentence, however, was 360 months, almost 10 years longer than the Guidelines range supported by the jury verdict alone. To reach this sentence, the judge found facts beyond those found by the jury: namely, that Booker possessed 566 grams of crack in addition to the 92.5 grams in his duffel bag. The jury never heard any evidence of the additional drug quantity, and the judge found it true by a preponderance of the evidence. Thus, just as in *Blakely*, "the jury's verdict alone does not authorize the sentence. The judge acquires that authority only upon finding some additional fact." There is no relevant distinction between the sentence imposed pursuant to the Washington statutes in *Blakely* and the sentences imposed pursuant to the Federal Sentencing Guidelines in these cases.

* * *

It is quite true that once determinate sentencing had fallen from favor, American judges commonly determined facts justifying a choice of a heavier sentence on account of the manner in which particular defendants acted. In 1986, however, our own cases first recognized a new trend in the legislative regulation of sentencing when we considered the significance of facts selected by legislatures that not only authorized, or even mandated, heavier sentences than would otherwise have been imposed, but increased the range of sentences possible for the underlying crime. See *McMillan v. Pennsylvania, (1986)*. Provisions for such enhancements of the permissible sentencing range reflected growing and wholly justified legislative concern about the proliferation and variety of drug crimes and their frequent identification with firearms offences.

The effect of the increasing emphasis on facts that enhanced sentencing ranges, however, was to increase the judge's power and diminish that of the jury. It became the judge, not the jury, that determined the upper limits of sentencing, and the facts determined were not required to be raised before trial or proved by more than a preponderance.

As the enhancements became greater, the jury's finding of the underlying crime became less significant. And the enhancements became very serious indeed.... Respondent Booker (from 262 months to a life sentence); respondent Fanfan (from 78 to 235 months); *United States v. Rodriguez, 73 F.3d 161, 162–163 (CA7 1996)* (Posner, C. J., dissenting from denial of rehearing en banc) (from approximately 54 months to a life sentence); *United States v. Hammoud, 381 F.3d 316, 361–362 (CA4 2004)* (en banc) (Motz, J., dissenting) (actual sentence increased from 57 months to 155 years).

... The new sentencing practice forced the Court to address the question how the right of jury trial could be preserved, in a meaningful way guaranteeing that the jury would still stand between the individual and the power of the government under the new sentencing regime. And it is the new circumstances, not a tradition or practice that the new circumstances have superseded, that have led us to the answer ... and developed in *Apprendi* and subsequent cases culminating with this one. It is an answer not motivated by *Sixth Amendment* formalism, but by the need to preserve *Sixth Amendment* substance.

* * *

IV

... We recognize, as we did in *Apprendi* ... and *Blakely*, that in some cases jury fact finding may impair the most expedient and efficient sentencing of defendants. But the interest in fairness and reliability protected by the right to a jury trial—a common-law right that defendants enjoyed for centuries and that is now enshrined in the *Sixth Amendment*—has always outweighed the interest in concluding trials swiftly.

* * *

Accordingly, we reaffirm our holding in *Apprendi:* Any fact (other than a prior conviction) which is necessary to support a sentence exceeding the maximum authorized by the facts established by a plea of guilty or a jury verdict must be admitted by the defendant or proved to a jury beyond a reasonable doubt.

■ JUSTICE BREYER delivered the opinion of the Court in part.*

* * *

We here turn to the second question presented, a question that concerns the remedy. We must decide whether or to what extent, "as a matter of severability analysis," the Guidelines "as a whole" are "inappli-

---

* The Chief Justice, Justice O'Connor, Justice Kennedy, and Justice Ginsburg join this opinion.

cable ... such that the sentencing court must exercise its discretion to sentence the defendant within the maximum and minimum set by statute for the offense of conviction.''

We answer the question of remedy by finding the provision of the federal sentencing statute that makes the Guidelines mandatory, incompatible with today's constitutional holding. We conclude that this provision must be severed and excised, as must one other statutory section, which depends upon the Guidelines' mandatory nature. So modified, the Federal Sentencing Act, makes the Guidelines effectively advisory. It requires a sentencing court to consider Guidelines ranges, but it permits the court to tailor the sentence in light of other statutory concerns as well.

I

We answer the remedial question by looking to legislative intent. We seek to determine what "Congress would have intended" in light of the Court's constitutional holding....

One approach ... would retain the Sentencing Act (and the Guidelines) as written, but would engraft onto the existing system today's *Sixth Amendment* "jury trial" requirement. The addition would change the Guidelines by preventing the sentencing court from increasing a sentence on the basis of a fact that the jury did not find (or that the offender did not admit).

The other approach, which we now adopt, would ... make the Guidelines system advisory while maintaining a strong connection between the sentence imposed and the offender's real conduct—a connection important to the increased uniformity of sentencing that Congress intended its Guidelines system to achieve.

Both approaches would significantly alter the system that Congress designed. But today's constitutional holding means that it is no longer possible to maintain the judicial factfinding that Congress thought would underpin the mandatory Guidelines system that it sought to create and that Congress wrote into the Act. Hence we must decide whether we would deviate less radically from Congress' intended system (1) by superimposing the constitutional requirement announced today or (2) through elimination of some provisions of the statute.

To say this is not to create a new kind of severability analysis. Rather, it is to recognize that sometimes severability questions (questions as to how, or whether, Congress would intend a statute to apply) can arise when a legislatively unforeseen constitutional problem requires modification of a statutory provision as applied in a significant number of instances.

* * *

In today's context—a highly complex statute, interrelated provisions, and a constitutional requirement that creates fundamental change—we cannot assume that Congress, if faced with the statute's invalidity in key applications, would have preferred to apply the statute in as many other instances as possible. Neither can we determine likely congressional intent mechanically. We cannot simply approach the problem grammatically, say, by looking to see whether the constitutional requirement and the words of the Act are linguistically compatible.

Nor do simple numbers provide an answer. It is, of course, true that the numbers show that the constitutional jury trial requirement would lead to additional decisionmaking by juries in only a minority of cases. Prosecutors and defense attorneys would still resolve the lion's share of criminal matters through plea bargaining, and plea bargaining takes place without a jury. Many of the rest involve only simple issues calling for no upward Guidelines adjustment. And in at least some of the remainder, a judge may find adequate room to adjust a sentence within the single Guidelines range to which the jury verdict points, or within the overlap between that range and the next highest.

But the constitutional jury trial requirement would nonetheless affect every case. It would affect decisions about whether to go to trial. It would affect the content of plea negotiations. It would alter the judge's role in sentencing. Thus we must determine likely intent not by counting proceedings, but by evaluating the consequences of the Court's constitutional requirement in light of the Act's language, its history, and its basic purposes.

While reasonable minds can, and do, differ about the outcome, we conclude that the constitutional jury trial requirement is not compatible with the Act as written and that some severance and excision are necessary.... That is to say, in light of today's holding, we compare maintaining the Act as written with jury factfinding added (the dissenters' proposed remedy) to the total invalidation of the statute, and conclude that Congress would have preferred the latter. We then compare our own remedy to the total invalidation of the statute, and conclude that Congress would have preferred our remedy.

II

Several considerations convince us that, were the Court's constitutional requirement added onto the Sentencing Act as currently written, the requirement would so transform the scheme that Congress created that Congress likely would not have intended the Act as so modified to stand. First, the statute's text states that "[t]he court" when sentencing will consider "the nature and circumstances of the offense and the history and characteristics of the defendant." In context, the words "the court" mean "the judge without the jury," not "the judge working together with the jury." A further statutory provision, by removing typical "jury trial" evidentiary limitations, makes this clear. See § 3661 (ruling out any "limitation . . . on the information concerning the [offender's] background, character, and conduct" that the "court . . . may receive").

* * *

Second, Congress' basic statutory goal—a system that diminishes sentencing disparity—depends for its success upon judicial efforts to determine, and to base punishment upon, the *real conduct* that underlies the crime of conviction. That determination is particularly important in the federal system where crimes defined as, for example, "obstruct[ing], delay[ing], or affect[ing] commerce or the movement of any article or commodity in commerce, by … extortion," or, say, using the mail "for the purpose of executing" a "scheme or artifice to defraud," can encompass a vast range of very different kinds of underlying conduct. But it is also important even in respect to ordinary crimes, such as robbery, where an act that meets the statutory definition can be committed in a host of different ways. Judges have long looked to real conduct when sentencing. Federal judges have long relied upon a presentence report, prepared by a probation officer, for information (often unavailable until *after* the trial) relevant to the manner in which the convicted offender committed the crime of conviction.

* * *

To engraft the Court's constitutional requirement onto the sentencing statutes, however, would destroy the system. It would prevent a judge from relying upon a presentence report for factual information, relevant to sentencing, uncovered after the trial. In doing so, it would, even compared to pre-Guidelines sentencing, weaken the tie between a sentence and an offender's real conduct. It would thereby undermine the sentencing statute's basic aim of ensuring similar sentences for those who have committed similar crimes in similar ways.

Several examples help illustrate the point. Imagine Smith and Jones, each of whom violates the Hobbs Act in very different ways…. Smith threatens to injure a co-worker unless the co-worker advances him a few dollars from the interstate company's till; Jones, after similarly threatening the co-worker, causes far more harm by seeking far more money, by making certain that the co-worker's family is aware of the threat, by arranging for deliveries of dead animals to the co-worker's home to show he is serious, and so forth. The offenders' behavior is very different; the known harmful consequences of their actions are different; their punishments both before, and after, the Guidelines would have been different. But, under the dissenters' approach, unless prosecutors decide to charge more than the elements of the crime, the judge would have to impose similar punishments.

Now imagine two former felons, Johnson and Jackson, each of whom engages in identical criminal behavior: threatening a bank teller with a gun, securing $50,000, and injuring an innocent bystander while fleeing the bank. Suppose prosecutors charge Johnson with one crime (say, illegal gun possession), and Jackson with another (say, bank robbery). Before the Guidelines, a single judge faced with such similar real conduct would have been able (within statutory limits) to impose similar sentences upon the two similar offenders despite the different charges brought against them. The Guidelines themselves would ordinarily have required judges to sentence the two offenders similarly. But under the dissenters' system, in these circumstances the offenders likely would receive different punishments.

Consider, too, a complex mail fraud conspiracy where a prosecutor may well be uncertain of the amount of harm and of the role each indicted individual played until after conviction—when the offenders may turn over financial records, when it becomes easier to determine who were the leaders and who the followers, when victim interviews are seen to be worth the time. In such a case the relation between the sentence and what actually occurred is likely to be considerably more distant under a system with a jury trial requirement patched onto it than it was even prior to the Sentencing Act, when judges routinely used information obtained after the verdict to decide upon a proper sentence.

This point is critically important. Congress' basic goal in passing the Sentencing Act was to move the sentencing system in the direction of increased uniformity. That uniformity does not consist simply of similar sentences for those convicted of violations of the same statute—a uniformity consistent with the dissenters' remedial approach. It consists, more importantly, of similar relationships between sentences and real conduct, relationships that Congress' sentencing statutes helped to advance and that Justice Stevens' approach would undermine. . . .

Third, the sentencing statutes, read to include the Court's *Sixth Amendment* requirement, would create a system far more complex than Congress could have intended. How would courts and counsel work with an indictment and a jury trial that involved not just whether a defendant robbed a bank but also how? Would the indictment have to allege, in addition to the elements of robbery, whether the defendant possessed a firearm, whether he brandished or discharged it, whether he threatened death, whether he caused bodily injury, whether any such injury was ordinary, serious, permanent or life threatening, whether he abducted or physically restrained anyone, whether any victim was unusually vulnerable, how much money was taken, and whether he was an organizer, leader, manager, or supervisor in a robbery gang? If so, how could a defendant mount a defense against some or all such specific claims should he also try simultaneously to maintain that the Government's evidence failed to place him at the scene of the crime? Would the indictment in a mail fraud case have to allege the number of victims, their vulnerability, and the amount taken from each? How could a judge expect a jury to work with the Guidelines' definitions of, say, "relevant conduct," which includes "all acts and omissions committed, aided, abetted, counseled, commanded, induced, procured, or willfully caused by the defendant; and [in the case of a conspiracy] all reasonably foreseeable acts and omissions of others in furtherance of the jointly undertaken criminal activity"? *How* would a jury measure "loss" in a securities fraud case—a matter so complex as to lead the Commission to instruct judges to make "only . . . a reasonable estimate"? How would the court take account, for punishment purposes, of a defendant's contemptuous behavior at trial—a matter that the Government could not have charged in the indictment?

Fourth, plea bargaining would not significantly diminish the consequences of the Court's constitutional holding for the operation of the Guidelines. Rather, plea bargaining would make matters worse. Congress enacted the sentencing statutes in major part to achieve greater uniformity in sentencing, *i.e.*, to increase the likelihood that offenders who engage in similar real conduct would receive similar sentences. The statutes reasonably assume that their efforts to move the trial-based sentencing process in the direction of greater sentencing uniformity would have a similar positive impact upon plea-bargained sentences, for plea bargaining takes place *in the shadow of* (*i.e.*, with an eye towards the hypothetical result of) a potential trial.

That, too, is why Congress, understanding the realities of plea bargaining, authorized the Commission to promulgate policy statements that would assist sentencing judges in determining whether to reject a plea agreement after reading about the defendant's real conduct in a presentence report (and giving the offender an opportunity to challenge the report). This system has not worked perfectly; judges have often simply accepted an agreed-upon account of the conduct at issue. But compared to pre-existing law, the statutes try to move the system in the right direction, *i.e.*, toward greater sentencing uniformity.

The Court's constitutional jury trial requirement, however, if patched onto the present Sentencing Act, would move the system backwards in respect both to tried and to plea-bargained cases. In respect to tried cases, it would effectively deprive the judge of the ability to use post-verdict-acquired real-conduct information; it would prohibit the judge from basing a sentence upon any conduct other than the conduct the prosecutor chose to charge; and it would put a defendant to a set of difficult strategic choices as to which prosecutorial claims he would contest. The sentence that would emerge in a case tried under such a system would likely reflect real conduct less completely, less accurately, and less often than did a pre-Guidelines, as well as a Guidelines, trial.

Because plea bargaining inevitably reflects estimates of what would happen at trial, plea bargaining too under such a system would move in the wrong direction. That is to say, in a sentencing system modified by the Court's constitutional requirement, plea bargaining would likely lead to sentences that gave greater weight, not to real conduct, but rather to the skill of counsel, the policies of the prosecutor, the caseload, and other factors that vary from place to place, defendant to defendant, and crime to crime. Compared to pre-Guidelines plea bargaining, plea bargaining of this kind would necessarily move federal sentencing in the direction of diminished, not increased, uniformity in sentencing. It would tend to defeat, not to further, Congress' basic statutory goal.

Such a system would have particularly troubling consequences with respect to prosecutorial power. Until now, sentencing factors have come before the judge in the presentence report. But in a sentencing system with the Court's constitutional requirement engrafted onto it, any factor that a prosecutor chose not to charge at the plea negotiation would be placed beyond the reach of the judge entirely. Prosecutors would thus exercise a power the Sentencing Act vested in judges: the power to decide, based on relevant information about the offense and the offender, which defendants merit heavier punishment.

In respondent Booker's case, for example, the jury heard evidence that the crime had involved 92.5 grams of crack cocaine, and convicted Booker of possessing more than 50 grams. But the judge, at sentencing, found that the crime had involved an additional 566 grams, for a total of 658.5 grams. A system that would require the jury, not the judge, to make the additional

"566 grams" finding is a system in which the prosecutor, not the judge, would control the sentence. That is because it is the prosecutor who would have to decide what drug amount to charge. He could choose to charge 658.5 grams, or 92.5, or less. It is the prosecutor who, through such a charging decision, would control the sentencing range. And it is different prosecutors who, in different cases—say, in two cases involving 566 grams—would potentially insist upon different punishments for similar defendants who engaged in similar criminal conduct involving similar amounts of unlawful drugs—say, by charging one of them with the full 566 grams, and the other with 10. As long as different prosecutors react differently, a system with a patched-on jury factfinding requirement would mean different sentences for otherwise similar conduct, whether in the context of trials or that of plea bargaining.

Fifth, Congress would not have enacted sentencing statutes that make it more difficult to adjust sentences *upward* than to adjust them *downward*. As several United States Senators have written in an *amicus* brief, "the Congress that enacted the 1984 Act did not conceive of—much less establish—a sentencing guidelines system in which sentencing judges were free to consider facts or circumstances not found by a jury or admitted in a plea agreement for the purpose of adjusting a base-offense level *down*, but not *up*, within the applicable guidelines range. Such a one-way lever would be grossly at odds with Congress's intent." Brief for Senator Orrin G. Hatch et al. as *Amici Curiae* 22. Yet that is the system that the dissenters' remedy would create....

For all these reasons, Congress, had it been faced with the constitutional jury trial requirement, likely would not have passed the same Sentencing Act. It likely would have found the requirement incompatible with the Act as written. Hence the Act cannot remain valid in its entirety. Severance and excision are necessary.

III

We now turn to the question of *which* portions of the sentencing statute we must sever and excise as inconsistent with the Court's constitutional requirement. Although, as we have explained, we believe that Congress would have preferred the total invalidation of the statute to the dissenters' remedial approach, we nevertheless do not believe that the entire statute must be invalidated. Most of the statute is perfectly valid.... And we must "refrain from invalidating more of the statute than is necessary." Indeed, we must retain those portions of the Act that are (1) constitutionally valid, (2) capable of "functioning independently," and (3) consistent with Congress' basic objectives in enacting the statute.

Application of these criteria indicates that we must sever and excise two specific statutory provisions: the provision that requires sentencing courts to impose a sentence within the applicable Guidelines range (in the absence of circumstances that justify a departure), and the provision that sets forth standards of review on appeal, including *de novo* review of departures from the applicable Guidelines range. With these two sections excised (and statutory cross-references to the two sections consequently invalidated), the remainder of the Act satisfies the Court's constitutional requirements.

As the Court today recognizes in its first opinion in these cases, [without] . . . the provision that makes "the relevant sentencing rules . . . mandatory and impose[s] binding requirements on all sentencing judges"— the statute falls outside the scope of *Apprendi*'s requirement. . . .

The remainder of the Act "function[s] independently." Without the "mandatory" provision, the Act nonetheless requires judges to take account of the Guidelines together with other sentencing goals. The Act nonetheless requires judges to consider the Guidelines "sentencing range established for . . . the applicable category of offense committed by the applicable category of defendant," the pertinent Sentencing Commission policy statements, the need to avoid unwarranted sentencing disparities, and the need to provide restitution to victims. And the Act nonetheless requires judges to impose sentences that reflect the seriousness of the offense, promote respect for the law, provide just punishment, afford adequate deterrence, protect the public, and effectively provide the defendant with needed educational or vocational training and medical care.

Moreover, . . . the Act continues to provide for appeals from sentencing decisions irrespective of whether the trial judge sentences within or outside the Guidelines range in the exercise of his discretionary power under. We concede that the excision of [mandatory sentences] requires the excision of a different, appeals-related section, which sets forth standards of review on appeal. . . .

[This] excision . . . does not pose a critical problem for the handling of appeals. That is because, as we have previously held, a statute that does not *explicitly* set forth a standard of review may nonetheless do so *implicitly*. . . . And in this instance those factors, in addition to the past two decades of appellate practice in cases involving departures, imply a practical standard of review already familiar to appellate courts: review for "unreasonable[ness]."

* * *

[W]e [do not] share the dissenters' doubts about the practicality of a "reasonableness" standard of review. "Reasonableness" standards are not foreign to sentencing law. The Act has long required their use in important sentencing circumstances—both on review of departures, and on review of sentences imposed where there was no applicable Guideline. Together, these cases account for about 16.7% of sentencing appeals. See United States Sentencing Commission, 2002 Sourcebook of Federal Sentencing Statistics 107 n 1, 111 (at least 711 of 5,018 sentencing appeals involved departures), 108 (at least 126 of 5,018 sentencing appeals involved the imposition of a term of imprisonment after the revocation of supervised release). That is why we think it fair (and not, in Justice Scalia's words, a "gross exaggeratio[n]," to assume judicial familiarity with a "reasonableness" standard. And that is why we believe that appellate judges will prove capable of facing with greater equanimity than would Justice Scalia what he calls the "daunting prospect," of applying such a standard across the board).

Neither do we share Justice Scalia's belief that use of a reasonableness standard "will produce a discordant symphony" leading to "excessive sentencing disparities," and "wreak havoc" on the judicial system. The Sentencing Commission will continue to collect and study appellate court decisionmaking. It will continue to modify its Guidelines in light of what it learns, thereby encouraging what it finds to be better sentencing practices. It will thereby promote uniformity in the sentencing process.

Regardless, in this context, we must view fears of a "discordant symphony," "excessive disparities," and "havoc" (if they are not themselves "gross exaggerations") with a comparative eye. We cannot and do not claim that use of a "reasonableness" standard will provide the uniformity that Congress originally sought to secure. Nor do we doubt that Congress wrote the language of the appellate provisions to correspond with the mandatory system it intended to create.... But, as by now should be clear, that mandatory system is no longer an open choice. And the remedial question we must ask here is, which alternative adheres more closely to Congress' original objective: (1) retention of sentencing appeals, or (2) invalidation of the entire Act, including its appellate provisions? The former, by providing appellate review, would tend to iron out sentencing differences; the latter would not. Hence we believe Congress would have preferred the former to the latter—even if the former means that some provisions will apply differently from the way Congress had originally expected. But, as we have said, we believe that Congress would have preferred even the latter to the system the dissenters recommend, a system that has its own problems of practicality.

* * *

The system remaining after excision, while lacking the mandatory features that Congress enacted, retains other features that help to further ... [Congressional] objectives.

As we have said, the Sentencing Commission remains in place, writing Guidelines, collecting information about actual district court sentencing decisions, undertaking research, and revising the Guidelines accordingly. The district courts, while not bound to apply the Guidelines, must consult those Guidelines and take them into account when sentencing.... The courts of appeals review sentencing decisions for unreasonableness. These features of the remaining system, while not the system Congress enacted, nonetheless continue to move sentencing in Congress' preferred direction, helping to avoid excessive sentencing disparities while maintaining flexibility sufficient to individualize sentences where necessary. We can find no feature of the remaining system that tends to hinder, rather than to further, these basic objectives. Under these circumstances, why would Congress not have preferred excision of the "mandatory" provision to a system that engrafts today's constitutional requirement onto the unchanged pre-existing statute—a system that, in terms of Congress' basic objectives, is counterproductive?

* * *

Ours, of course, is not the last word: The ball now lies in Congress' court. The National Legislature is equipped to devise and install, long-term, the sentencing system, compatible with the Constitution, that Congress judges best for the federal system of justice.

* * *

In respondent Booker's case, the District Court applied the Guidelines as written and imposed a sentence higher than the maximum authorized solely by the jury's verdict. The Court of Appeals held *Blakely* applicable to the Guidelines, concluded that Booker's sentence violated the *Sixth Amendment*, vacated the judgment of the District Court, and remanded for resentencing. We affirm the judgment of the Court of Appeals and remand the case. On remand, the District Court should impose a sentence in accordance with today's opinions, and, if the sentence comes before the Court of Appeals for review, the Court of Appeals should apply the review standards set forth in this opinion.

* * *

In respondent Fanfan's case, the District Court held *Blakely* applicable to the Guidelines. It then imposed a sentence that was authorized by the jury's verdict—a sentence lower than the sentence authorized by the Guidelines as written. Thus, Fanfan's sentence does not violate the *Sixth Amendment*. Nonetheless, the Government (and the defendant should he so choose) may seek resentencing under the system set forth in today's opinions. Hence we vacate the judgment of the District Court and remand the case for further proceedings consistent with this opinion.

* * *

■ JUSTICE STEVENS, with whom JUSTICE SOUTER joins, and with whom JUSTICE SCALIA joins except for Part III and footnote 17, dissenting in part. [Omitted]

* * *

■ JUSTICE SCALIA, dissenting in part. [Omitted]

* * *

I respectfully dissent.

■ JUSTICE THOMAS, dissenting in part. [Omitted]

* * *

■ JUSTICE BREYER, with whom THE CHIEF JUSTICE, JUSTICE O'CONNOR, and JUSTICE KENNEDY join, dissenting in part. [Omitted]

* * *

CHAPTER 23

APPELLATE AND OTHER POST-TRIAL REMEDIES FEDERAL HABEAS CORPUS

D. FEDERAL PRISONERS

Add as section D to page 1679:

In *Hamdi v. Rumsfeld*, 542 U.S. 507, 124 S.Ct. 2633 (2004) the Court upheld the right of the federal government to detain enemy combatants. However, the Court held that such a detainee would retain the right of habeas corpuse 28 U.S.C. § 2241.

The statute governing habeas corpus allowed aliens detained in Guantanamo Bay Naval Base in Cuba, a territory over which the United States government exercised plenary and exclusive jurisdiction to pursue petitions for writs of habeas corpus. The statute conferred jurisdiction over these cases in United States courts. *Rasul v. Bush*, 542 U.S. 466, 124 S.Ct. 2686 (2004).

†